SRI LANKAN CRISIS

Anatomy of Ethnicity, Peace and Security

SRI LANKAN CRISIS

Anatomy of Ethnicity, Peace and Security

M S Kulandaswamy

AUTHORSPRESS

First Published 2000
by Authorspress

E-35/103, Jawahar Park (Shree Ganesh Complex),
Laxmi Nagar, Delhi-110 092
e-mail: authorspress@yahoo.com

Typeset in NewCenturySchlbk by Chitra Computers

Sri Lankan Crisis: Anatomy of Ethnicity, Peace and Security
ISBN 81-7273-033-0

Printed in India at Tarun Offset, Delhi.

Preface

The ethnic conflict in Sri Lanka has serious implications for India owing to the presence of Tamil multitudes in Tamil Nadu who sympathise with their brethren in Sri Lanka. India's perception of threat to its security in the Indian Ocean region is largely governed by political and military developments in Sri Lanka.

To trace back the Indian interests in Sri Lanka, the issue of expatriate Tamils had assumed importance for India even in pre-independence period. These Tamils of Indian origin who were employed in the tea and rubber plantation under the British colonial rule, have distinct socio-economic problems different from those of the Sri Lankan Tamils. The Indian Tamil political leadership has not been involved in the mainstream of Tamil politics in Sri Lanka and it does not support the cause of Tamil separatism. Hence, it has entered into some sort of alliance with the successive governments in order to secure the interests of the Indian Tamils. In this context, the issue of status and citizenship rights of Indian Tamils which arose in the post-independence period, was taken up by India who amicably settled the issue with the Sri Lankan government in later years.

Regarding the Sri Lankan Tamils who had raised the call for a separate state, as early as 1976, the Indian government had remained aloof from such political development in Sri Lanka. Subsequently, with growing discrimination against Tamils and serious ethnic riots in 1983, India voiced its concern for the safety and security of the Tamils in Sri Lanka. So, when the riots broke out between the Tamil and Sinhalese communities in July, 1983, India found itself in a delicate situation. It felt that it had some moral responsibility in the safety and security of the Tamils in Sri Lanka. Moreover, in ensuring their safety, India had to impress interfering in the island's internal affairs.

With the fall of Elephant Pass it was clear that the LTTE would go for the jungular. Equipped with captured artillery and equipment purchased clandestinely from outside, the LTTE is in a position to match the army's firepower. Now the war over Jaffna has become a do-or-die battle not just for the 25,000 troops stationed in the Peninsula but also for the Sri Lankan Government. To boost the sagging morale of the army, the President has decided to suspend all developmental work and focus on defence. Even if Jaffna Peninsula falls to the LTTE, the war is far from over. If LTTE Supremo Prabhakaran declares Eelam it would be a pyrrhic cry. For unless his forces capture the Eastern province where Tamils constitute on 30 per cent of the population, it will prove a major obstacle in winning over the local population. Taking Jaffna will give Prabhakaran tremendous bargaining power when he sits for peace talks which are certain to resume after the battle is over. Talks for devolution of power—which the President Kumaratunga had initiated by suggesting that the North and East provinces get more autonomy and possibly making Sri Lanka a federal state rather than a unitary one—had broken down.

India has stepped into the diplomatic void and offered to mediate with "all the parties" concerned if they are agreeable. It is certain to be a tortuous process but something that is absolutely necessary. But with the scent of victory still fresh, the Tigers may find it difficult to give up speaking with guns.

Author

Contents

1

Introduction

The geopolitical configuration of Sri Lanka in the South Asian region holds the key to its broader security environment. So, it is pertinent to examine its relationship with India which occupies a significant position in the regional set-up.

In the South Asian region, the regional security environment is largely governed by the pre-eminent position of India. So, India enjoys an asymmetrical relationship with its neighbours in terms of ethnic, religious and socio-cultural ties which have a strong impact on their mutual relations. In the post-independence period, India has pursued a cordial policy in matters of bilateral relations with its smaller neighbours. Hence, it maintained good relations with Bhutan and Nepal by entering into the treaties and agreements in view of China's emergence in the region. But at the southern end, it had shown some sort of acquiescence towards the continued British presence in Sri Lanka.

In the context of the Indo-Lankan relations, the strategic dimension continues to be an independent variable. From colonial times, naval strategists have emphasised Sri Lanka's importance in the defence calculations of India. For the British, Sri Lanka had been integral to the defence of India as it served as a vital link in their sea communications eastwards. India after its independence, continued to adhere to the principle of strategic importance of Sri Lanka on the lines of the British theory in the sub-continent. This is evident from the writings in the early years of independence and even the years immediately preceding them. Hence, most Indian writers, politicians and strategists had sought to emphasise the strategic unity of India and Sri Lanka and argued for a closer union between the two countries.

From India's security point of view, Sri Lanka has been of serious strategic importance in the Indian Ocean region. But over the years, India's approach to the problem of security in the Indian Ocean has been, by and large, in "conformity with both the traditions of anti-colonial struggle and the country's own enlightened self-interest."

However, in the wake of British withdrawal from the east of Suez, the United States forwarded the 'power vacuum' theory to establish herself firmly in the Indian Ocean for its strategic interest. India rejected this idea of power vacuum in the Indian Ocean region and sought the cooperation of all the new Asian countries "to meet the challenges that come with a measure of self-respect, dignity, self-reliance without looking to Washington or Moscow." In response, Sri Lanka forwarded a proposal to declare Indian Ocean as a 'Zone of Peace' (IOZOP) in the United Nations after the issue was discussed in Cairo and Lusaka Conferences of Non-aligned states. So, India has viewed the military presence of major powers in the South Asian region as a threat to the regional security which itself is India's main concern. In this context, India's view of substantial strategic unity encompassing its neighbours impinge upon the bilateral and regional relations in the South Asian region. Hence, locational factor has always been more important in determining the nature of the Indo-Lankan relationship than disparities in their size and population. Moreover, Sri Lanka shares some commonalties with India in matters of history, language, ethnicity, and culture. So for all purposes, India's concept of 'strategic unity' of South Asia has been emphasised with Sri Lanka as an organic part in its defence calculations. Nevertheless, being separated from India by a narrow stretch of water, Sri Lanka "is close enough to be influenced by India but unlike the other small states in the region which are geographically linked to India by a land mass, she is distant enough to maintain her own identity." Such a perception has resulted in an ambivalent attitude of Sri Lanka towards India with a kind of love-hate relationship.

Under Nehru, India pursued a policy of enlightened self-interest without any antagonism towards its small neighbours. But it had its own geopolitical sensitivities to the developments in Sri Lanka. On the part of Sri Lanka, just after independence, the problem of defining its citizenship had assumed serious external dimensions with the status of plantation workers of Indian origin. Hence, the Sri Lankan Prime Minister, Mr. D.S. Senanayake, entered into a lengthy correspondence with Prime Minister Nehru of India in order to find a solution to the admission of Indians to Sri Lankan citizenship. But there was no agreement between them. In the process, this question of citizenship for persons of Indian origin in Sri Lanka—many of whom had become stateless in the fifties and sixties—became a thorny issue in Indo-Lanka relations.

However, when S.W.R.D. Bandaranaike came to power in 1956, the Sri Lankan perception of Indian threat appeared to have faded away. Gradually, under Mr. and Mrs. Bandaranaike's rule in Sri Lanka, the Indo-Lankan relations were very friendly and cordial. During this phase, India extended her defence parameters concomitant to the growth of her military-industrial potential, especially in the 1970's, and Sri Lanka could realise the Indian strategic perspective. So, the Bandaranaike period of 1956-65 and 1970-77, interspersed as it was between the regime of Dudley Senanayake (1965-70), provided a striking contrast to the earlier phase of Indo-Lanka relations. This was partly because the Bandaranaikes were personally close to the Nehru family and shared India's anti-colonial non-alignment ideology. Thus, as a sign of mutual peace and understanding, Mr. S.W.R.D. Bandaranaike demonstrated his faith in India by getting the British vacate their bases at Trincomalee and Katunayake in 1957. However, the defence agreement was not abrogated. Later on, this consensus approach to Sri Lanka's defence and security was best expressed by Felix. R. Bankaranaike at a time when he was not only Finance Minister and Deputy Minister of External

Affairs, but also Chief Advisor and the most influential person in Mrs. Bandaranaike's first administration. Regarding the defence agreements with the British Commonwealth, he said:

> But we cannot depend only on military agreement with the Commonwealth. That is our position. In other words, we do not think that the question of abandoning military agreements or otherwise comes into play in this business. As far as we are concerned, the agreements that are there will remain and our friendship with nations will be built independently. We shall seek to keep on friendly terms with all countries.

In the meantime, one of the factors which had aroused the fear psychosis about India was the demographic threat of swamping of the island nation by the swelling number of Indians in Sri Lanka. This fear seemed real enough in the fifties and early sixties when the incidence of illicit immigration from South India to Sri Lanka compounded the problems caused by the unresolved status of about a million plantation workers of Indian origin in the island. However, Mrs. Sirimavo Bandaranaike, during her first administration in 1964, laid the basis for the resolution of this problem by signing with the then Prime Minister of India Lal Bahadur Shastri, a citizenship agreement (Shastri-Sirimavo Pact) which sought to eradicate the "statelessness" of these plantation Tamils by providing for the grant of Sri Lankan citizenship to some of them and repatriation to India of others. This agreement was extended by another one signed by Bandaranaike with Prime Minister Indira Gandhi during her second administration in 1974. Subsequently, it was amplified by the citizenship legislation passed by the J. R. Jayewardene government in 1986 and 1988.

It was during Mrs. Bandaranaike's period of office that the maritime boundaries separating the two countries were demarcated and the question of a small island of Kachchai Thivu was resolved. The island was placed on the Sri Lankan side of the maritime boundary. Hence, the resolution of the maritime boundary problem was also a triumph of diplomacy in Indo-Lankan relations. But later, with the UNP coming to power under J.R. Jayewardene in 1977, there was a total shift in Sri Lanka's foreign policy priorities. Since the new policy was pro-American in its stand with overtones of anti-Indianism, so, the Trincomalee Tank farm tender was given to the western consortium of three nations overlooking the Indian Oil Corporation's own tender for the tank farm.

Apart from these new trends in Sri Lanka's foreign policy and their security implication for India, the precipitation of the ethnic crisis in July 1983 was a turning point which showed Sri Lanka's disregard to India's sentiments. India had since assumed some role in the matters concerning the Tamils in the island. Moreover, it had stakes in the peaceful solution of the Tamil problem as is evident from the later developments when Indian involvement was crucial in Sri Lanka.

In this context, the two main problems inhibiting the relations between India and Sri Lanka can be identified and taken up in the study of their conflictual perception of security. The first problem arises out of India's concern about the security of the subcontinent, and its fear that the presence in Sri Lanka of countries unfriendly to India would be a threat to peace and security in the region. For this reason, it has viewed the external power's military involvement in Sri Lanka as a threat to its own security. The second problem crops up due to the spillover effect of the Sri Lankan ethnic conflict in India and the consequent Indian role in the domestic problem of Sri Lanka.

As both the issues are interrelated, it needs a serious examination to study the ethnic conflict from these perspectives. Hence, for a better understanding of the mutual security interests, it is pertinent to study the military involvement of external powers in Sri Lanka as a background to the study of Indo-Lanka relations in greater details.

In the aftermath of July 1983 violence, there was a massive spurt in Tamil militancy. The Tamil guerillas in their separatist struggle launched serious attacks on security forces and others who had opposed them. But the Sri Lankan government lacked proper military apparatus to meet the growing insurgency in the country. Hence, President Jayawardene requested for military assistance from both Britain and the United States. The United States, though it had improved relations with Sri Lanka, responded unfavourably as it disliked to trouble India. In the meantime, India became concerned with rumours that Sri Lanka had asked for military assistance from the United States, the United Kingdom, Pakistan and Bangladesh in the wake of the 1983 riots.

Moreover, in the existing pattern of regional ties in South Asia, India became extremely sensitive to the possibility of the US role in Sri Lanka's ethnic crisis and subsequent military presence in the region. It could understand the subtleties of American policy which accorded greater priorities to Sri Lanka and its maritime facilities. This was quite understandable in view of the greater need for American facilities in the India Ocean for its increased naval presence, and to develop Sri Lankan and other similar alternatives as back-up options in the event of the denial of Subic Buy in the Philippines to the US Navy at some further date. On the other hand, in consideration of the Indian defence perimeter which included Sri Lanka for all strategic concerns, the natural harbour of Trincomalee was vital to the security interests of India.

In this context, the importance of Sri Lanka had been emphasised by a naval strategist in the following words: "Sri Lanka is as important to India as Eire is to the United Kingdom or Taiwan to China....As long as Sri Lanka is friendly or neutral, India has nothing to worry about but if there be any danger of the island falling under the domination of a power hostile to India, India cannot tolerate such a situation endangering her territorial integrity."

Thus, India became extremely sensitive to the possibility of a US role in the South Asian Region, particularly to an overt or covert arrangement with Sri Lanka, providing for the use by the American Navy of the strategic harbour at Trincomalee. Such a scenario was highly dangerous for India as it posed a grave threat to its security.

So, following the July 1983 disturbances in Sri Lanka, there emerged a new strategic thinking in India which emphasised the strategic unity of South Asia and India's predominant role in defence and regional security. It came to a shape when Mrs. Indira Gandhi enunciated this idea which became known as the "Indira Doctrine". According to this doctrine, India had no intention of intervening in domestic conflicts of a South Asian country and at the same time, it strongly opposed intervention by any country in the internal affairs of another. Moreover, it warned that it would not tolerate any external intervention in a conflict situation in any South Asian country if the intervention had any implicit or explicit anti-Indian implications. This meant that no South Asian government should seek external military assistance with an anti-Indian bias from any other country. Further, it provided that if a South Asian country genuinely needed external help to deal with a serious internal conflict situation or a threat to its government, it should seek help from the neighbouring countries including India. But the exclusion of India from such a contingency would be considered as an anti-Indian move. This doctrine was reflected for a long time in the foreign policy making of India, which sought for the consolidation of its regional security interests.

In this context, the military presence of external powers in Sri Lanka had a serious impact on the Indo-Lankan relations. First, the British involvement was manifest with the Sri Lankan government employing a private British security firm named Keeny Meeny Services (KMS) having ex-Special Air Services (SAS) personnel, "to train intelligence gathering units and a paramilitary police counter-insurgency group." The British government had taken a lenient view of this issue involving its own national. But gradually, the issue became complicated with British pilots flying helicopters and aircrafts in attack upon Tamil areas. Some other British mercenaries were also involved in leading the ground attacks against the guerrillas. Regarding the direct military involvement, official denials were issued by the British government. But Western news reports confirmed that two Britons and one South African were manning helicopter gunships which regularly bombed targets in Tamil areas.

Concerning the American involvement in the strategic and military build-up of Sri Lanka, there was a succession of US dignitaries who visited Sri Lanka and supported all American help. These included US Defence Secretary, Caper Weinberger, who had an unscheduled stopover in Colombo in August 1983 for talks with President Jayewardene. This was followed by a four-day visit by General Vernon Walters, President Reagan's Ambassador-at-large, who assisted the Sir Lankan government in the drafting of the agreement with Israel for military help. As a result, the Israeli-interest section was set up under the auspices of the US Embassy in Colombo on 24 May 1984. Though there were conflicting reports about the number of Israeli experts, yet it was admitted that Israeli military advisers were involved in the training of the Sri Lankan armed forces in counter-insurgency and internal security. In this process, the US had an indirect military involvement through the Israeli presence in Sri Lanka. It was obvious from the statement of Foreign Minister, A.C.S. Hameed, in June 1984 that "We looked into the terrorist problem and set out to find the best foreign service available to us. Finally, we decided on the Israelis and asked the Americans to help us arrange it."

In the meantime, the US was closely monitoring the developments in Sri Lanka. It was prepared to give considerable military aid to Sri Lanka for a deal over the naval base of Trincomalee which could be used for its own advantage. So, a congressional mission led by Senator Joseph Addabo, Chairman of the Defence Appropriation Committee, visited Sri Lanka and told the press that the "upgrading of Sri Lanka's navy and training of its personnel would be two of the first American concern."

However, for Sri Lanka, the US tilt in the foreign policy had lucrative returns in terms of increased American aid including American advisers for rural development, an agricultural experimental station near Trincomalee, and the help of the peace corps volunteers to teach English. In exchange, Sri Lanka had to grant certain facilities and concessions to the US in the nature of Trincomalee Tank

Farm deal which was given to a Singapore-based US company after rejecting the Indian tender. But later, the contract was revoked when India produced conclusive evidence that one of the firms involved in the contract was a bogus one. Nevertheless, the very modalities of the tender operation in 1983 buttressed the Indian impression that Sri Lanka was getting increasingly enmeshed in the US strategic initiatives in the Indian Ocean.

Moreover, the Voice of America (VOA) agreement which Sri Lanka had signed as early as in 1951 with the USA was extended in 1983 with significant changes. Under the earlier agreement, Sri Lanka had the right to scrutinise all material for broadcast by the VOA. This clause was dropped in the 1983 agreement. Besides, the expanded facilities of the VOA were such as to make it one of the most powerful transmission stations in Asia. It was also believed that these facilities could serve intelligence purpose for the US ship in the Indian Ocean region.

Hence, the growing American involvement in Sri Lanka caused serious concern for India who strongly opposed to "any big power gaining hegemony over Sri Lanka, which is situated near its underbelly as it were." In this matter, the visit of Richard Murphy, an Assistant Secretary of State, who headed the South Asia and Near East sections in the US State Development, was an important political development. According to some news reports, Murphy presided over a conference of US ambassadors of the states of the Indian subcontinent in Colombo, which mainly discussed about India's increasingly dominant role in South Asia and the means to counter it.

Apart from its American connection, the Ja[illegible]
regime also received help from China and [illegible]
China maintained that the ethnic con[illegible]
an internal affair of that country [illegible]
arms to Sri Lanka since [illegible]
involvement, Sri Lanka r[illegible]
after the July 1983 vi[illegible]
exchange of officials [illegible]
1985, an estimat[illegible]

officers and others ranks completed their courses in counter-insurgency, artillery and basic training in Pakistan. Pakistan was also reportedly training Sri Lankan homeguards and air force and naval personnel. It was also supplying a large amount of heavy and medium artillery to Sri Lanka for its fight against the Tamil separatists. Though the American involvement caused serious security concern to India, Pakistan's role in Sri Lanka was seen as a challenge to India's pre-eminence in the region. Hence, reacting to the reports of arms supply to Sri Lanka by Pakistan, the then Prime Minister Mrs. Gandhi stated in December 1983 that while every country had a right to arm itself, it should not be "used against its own people or against us." The Indian government also expressed its reservations regarding the role of foreign agencies like the Israeli Mossad and the British SAS in Sri Lanka. Moreover, the American involvement was deplored by India, as External Affairs Minister, Mr. Khurshid Alam Khan, stated in Parliament, "We do not like that the VOA transmitter be put in Sri Lanka. We do not want this type of intrusion."

So, all in all, the external powers involvement in Sri Lanka caused serious concern to India in its security perspective which viewed "Sri Lanka as part of its sphere of influence". Earlier, India had followed a relatively restrained approach to the Sri Lankan politics till 1983. But subsequently, with the exacerbation of the ethnic conflict and involvement of foreign powers, India sought to play a constructive role in the affairs of Sri Lanka.

In 1989, Sri Lanka faced a triple crisis of the sort that few, if any other, nations have faced and survived: a threat
...wer posed by the JVP; twin secessionist threats—
...LTTE and the other, the implicit threat of
...us model, posed by the North Eastern
...in the latter part of its period of
...t least an erosion of the
...te in the form of the
...in the north and the
...elped constitute an
...of a regime that
...e as before (the

Accord itself was evidence of that) over significant sections of the people who had demonstrated that they were not willing to live as before, and an establishment which was so badly split that the anti-systemic forces were able to surge forward. The mainstream opposition was at various levels infiltrated and implicated in some way or another with the JVP. Even on the very date of the handing over of nominations for the Presidential elections the chief opposition candidate came forward as head of an alliance which consisted of among other parties, the Student Front of the JVP.

The establishment's response was one of massive retaliation. It had been said at times by some in the establishment that a 1965 Jakarta solution was the answer which was exactly what the JVP had in mind. They wanted to polarise the situation, to depict the regime as a puppet of India—in addition to being undemocratic and dictatorial. By de-legitimising the regime and narrowing its support base, they would have been able to absorb whatever casualties were inflicted upon them, and eventually overthrow the system. Premadasa stepped in and provided the buffer-cum-shock absorber. He provided the profile of a reformist—a very genuine profile—one that gave the system a certain amount of flexibility. Bradman Weerakoon in his book *The Making of Premadasa* has pointed out that Premadasa had a different trajectory to that of the average and even the above-average establishment politician. His founding of the Sucharitha Movement and his stint in the Sri Lankan version of the Labour Party gave him a different quality, a different sensibility. It was such a man who interposed himself between the anti-systemic forces and the democratic system.

He succeeded in grasping the nettle. The insurgency was thriving on the de-legitimisation of the democratic system that took place at the hands of the predecessor regime, in the first place through the referendum of 1982, and in the second place as a result of the India-Lanka Accord. These two acts had discredited and de-legitimised the system, and made it appear as undemocratic, and perhaps more importantly, incapable of defending national sovereignty, thus realising the fondest dream of any insurgent movement to be able to fight an enemy that appeared both unpatriotic and dependent upon a foreign power, specially one generally perceived as a traditional foe. Premadasa took the risk, the gamble of unilaterally asking the IPKF to leave. Once it became obvious from the official responses of Rajiv Gandhi that the Indian troops would not leave even after the lapse of the 29 July deadline, it was the JVP's slogan of a "Patriotic war" to get rid of the IPKF that would have gained legitimacy in the eyes of the masses.

This was dangerous since the JVP had made the formation of a so-called patriotic front, a necessary task in the preparation for the 'patriotic war'. This situation was also particularly dangerous for the democratic system since the rapid growth of insurgency enhanced the probability of a military take over, supported by the UNP's ultra right-wing old guard. It also posed a severe threat to the other anti-UNP parties as well, since neither the so-called patriotic front that the JVP was trying to establish nor the 'patriotic' war it was attempting to wage, would have ever been under the leadership of these democratic oppositional forces. Both the 'patriotic war' and the 'patriotic front' were nothing but stepping stones in the JVP's attempt to overthrow the regime and seize State power.

Another crucial aspect of the scenario at the time was the rift in the ranks of the ruling party. The JVP tried to step up its violence with the express intention of doing one of two things. The first was to make President Premadasa a virtual prisoner of the Joint Operations Command and the UNP's old guard. By thus circumscribing his autonomy they hoped to efface the element of change and underscore the contrasting elements continuity in the pre-and post-Presidential election situations.

The other option was to create a situation in which all factions of the UNP's old guard would have converged in a coup attempt of a chaste President Premadasa. Such a displacement to the right within the regime would have resulted in the setting up of an ultra right wing civilian-military junta, which would have been so de-legitimised, and would have had so narrow a base of support, that toppling it, albeit after a very bloody interregnum, would have been very easy indeed for the JVP.

In 1989, the JVP stood at the confluence of four currents of dissent generated by the following causes: socio-economic grievances, accumulated over eleven years due to the polarisation generated by the 'open economy' of the UNP; the political practice of the UNP which fashioned a semi-authoritarian political system and resorted sporadically to state-terrorism—the ethic terrorism of the Liberation Tigers of Tamil Eelam (LTTE)—and third and fourth were legitimate factors. The JVP used these, but chauvinism was the determining factor.

For all their bragging, the regime was hard put to tackle the JVP challenge, primarily because all the instrumentalities for repression, the 'repressive state apparatuses' were as suffused with populist chauvinism as were the 'ideological state apparatuses'. Given the consciousness of the intermediate strata, the class composition of these apparatuses may eventually go against the class interests they are supposed to subserve? There was an undercurrent of 'ideological osmosis' like the July 1983 riots. Since the middle echelons of the military were not so much pro-UNP as pro-SLEP, they would have remained neutral in such an event and even the pro-UNP officers would have been hard put to fire at mutinous soldiers.

Hitherto the JVP had been unable to win over the working class. But this class was, and is, linked by many connecting threads to the rural petite bourgeois milieu from which the JVP springs. It is also heavily influence by the Sinhala print media such as the *Divaina*, whose feature writers plugged a clearly pro-JVP line. It would be foolish therefore to assume that the working class inoculated against the appeal of the JVP. Indeed the JVP mixed 'patriotic' and 'nationalist' with class appeals in much the same way as A. E. Goonesinha, the founder leader of the Labour Party, did in a similar period of economic crisis (the 1930's).

JVP-sponsored labour unrest would not have taken the form of traditional trade union-based agitation, but rather of a series, and then a wave of wild-cat strikes from below backed up by economic sabotage and urban terrorism along the lines of Italy's Red Brigades. This would have been exceedingly difficult to curb and would have had the twin effects of damaging the economy and causing a deterioration in the security environment in the Colombo metropolitan area.

The killing of 18 superintendents of tea estates, for example, posed a severe threat to the tea economy. If this had been stepped up and supplemented by economic sabotage at the factories, the JVP would have been able to knock the bottom out of the country's economy.

That which was true of the tea economy was true of the economy as a whole. Any economy is embedded in an invisible matrix, and cannot function without a certain minimal climate of confidence. The killing of middle managers and civil administrators, which the JVP had commenced, would eventually have caused the economy to cease to function, to be paralysed to atrophy, at first at the periphery but creeping in on the capital itself. Shortages and scarcities might have caused the middle classes to shift away form the government with many persons belonging to this class reverting to supporting the UNP's old guard.

There is a strong ethic bonding between the Sinhala army and police units in the north-east and the Sinhala settlers there. If the Tamil groups and the IPKF attempted to coerce these Sinhala civilians, especially in the Trincomalee area, fire-fights may have broken out with the Sinhala military. JVP sympathisers in the latter and LTTE sympathisers in the former would have quite deliberately striven to provoke such a situation—which was fairly easily done. Sinhala military men in other parts of the island would have questioned the logic of fighting their own boys (the JVP) if Sinhala soldiers were killed by the IPKF or pro-Indian Tamil groups. The JVP's propaganda would have gained great credibility in their eyes. If JVP attacks had taken place against the IPKF, it is very unlikely that Sri Lankan army personnel would have taken on the former in defence of the latter.

As a cumulative result of all these, the Sri Lankan military may have fissured along the lines of pro-UNP old guard (former national security faction), Pro-SLEP-MEP elements, and pro-JVP ones. The pro-SLEP might itself have shortsightedly attempted to fish in troubled waters, hoping to be installed in office by a coup. There may have been, therefore, two parallel or contending coup projects—the 1962 type ultra right one and the 1966 Sinhala-Buddhist populist version. The 1962 coup was an elitist, right wing, largely Christian, conspiracy led by senior officers. The 1966 coup plot was more populist, led by junior and middle ranking officers who were exclusively Sinhala-Buddhist and motivated by majoritarian sentiments.

In any event the Sri Lankan military stood in danger of being fissured like the Filipino army in the last days of Marcos; or split outright like the Lebanese army or subject to a mutiny and chain of coups and counter-coups like the Bangladeshi military in 1975, resulting in an ultraright wing civilian-military junta which the JVP would have found very easy to topple due to its narrow social base, or disintegrating in the face of unremitting mass pressure and agitation as did the Russian military in 1917 and the Iranian in 1979; or giving rise to a radical left putsch form within its own ranks as happened in Ethiopia in 1974 and Portugal in 1975; or generating a nationalist populist coup of which examples are legion throughout the Third World from Nasser to Juan Velasco Alvarado of Peru.

All these would have added up to classic 'revolutionary crisis' of the sort sketched out more than once by Lenin. When the JVP made its final bid for power, the beleaguered regime is likely to have sought Indian military support. Though it may have agonised over the decision, India would have seen no option but to intervene in order to prevent what it would have seen as a 'mini-Cuba' on its southern doorstep. Given the JVP's ideology of chauvinism, Delhi would also have perceived a threat to the lives of Tamils living in the south and in the plantations. This then would have been the final rung of the 'escalation ladder. Such an Indian intervention in the south would have been Rohana Wijeweera's wildest dream come true, because he would have been able to play a combination of Dutugemunu, Kirthi Wijayaabahu, Sandino and Ho Chi Minh.

Perhaps he could not have won because nobody would have supplied him Stinger missiles. Nor does Sri Lanka have a land order with safe havens just across it and which facilitates transport of weapons. However, neither could the Indians have won. They would have been devoid of any significant local support and would have been fighting in a heavily populated and hostile environment with plenty of natural cover and built-up areas. It is not only the JVP that the Indians would have faced but also, very probably, a large number of dissident units of the Sri Lankan military, heavily armed, with plenty of combat experience in recent years, led by patriotic younger officers and fighting in guerrilla formation (probably with JP cadres playing the role of political commissars). The battle for Colombo may have made the battle of Jaffna look like a walk through Disneyland for the Indian soldier. An Indian naval blockade, together with the indiscriminate use of its power and heavy weaponry, would have caused devastation and famine among the Lankan people.

All Sri Lankan Sinhalese school children grow up reading romantic nationalist fiction based on the Mahavamsa. With at least a 50,000-strong foreign army on the country's soil—one from a big neighbour perceived of as historic foe and in league with the traditional foe, the Tamils—absolutely nothing could have prevented the JVP from having a vast recruitment base. Whatever military measures were taken, however many insurgents were killed or captured, the IPKF presence would have more than compensated as a growth factor for these losses. It is also possible that Pakistan and China would have been so unhappy at the Indian involvement, that they would have supplied the insurgent forces with sophisticated weaponry.

How was this to be prevented? How could Sri Lanka have pulled out of this downward spiral which was turning into a nosedive and would have culminated in a destructive crash? The key to the solution was the withdrawal of the IPKF, as Premadasa correctly understood. Sending off the IPKF, was the lesser of two evils because it was clear the

Tamil separatist terrorist provided less fuel for the flames of the JVP insurgency than the presence of the IPKF. The empirical evidence of this was the relative strength of the JVP during the hightide of Eelam terrorism (1985 to 1987) and the post-Accord/IPKF phase (1987 to 1989). The presence and the role of the IPKF which certainly had some initial utility and become counter-productive in its political effects and consequences in the south. The reactivation of large-scale ethnic terrorism in the aftermath of the sending back of the IPKF was therefore for more dangerous than that posed by its prolonged presence. From a narrow military point of view, the Sri Lankan armed forces might then have had to fight two wars instead of one. However, the removal of the IPKF was calculated to deprive the JVP of its most attractive and powerful appeal, thus causing the southern insurgency to decline. Thus at worst the Sri Lankan army would have had to fight one-and-a-half wars.

Sending back the IPKF was a calculated risk, but one worth taking. It was an unavoidable trade off. This does not mean that a peace-keeping force was not necessary. The Tamil people had a legitimate fear concerning their fate at the hands of the Sri Lankan army and the IPKF. What stood between the Tamil people and the Sinhala army was the IPKF, not the LTTE, because the LTTE could not prevent the Sinhala army from taking Vadamarachchi. (The Sri Lankan Army was three days, march away from Jaffna when the airdrop took place.) Furthermore, what stood between the Sinhala civilians in the east and the LTTE was also the IPKF. With the LTTE contained by the IPKF, they could no longer engage in killing 300 people in two days as they did in October 1987. Hence a third force, a buffer, was necessary. It could not be a Sinhala force.

Since India and Sri Lanka are both respected members of the NAM, an NAPKF was the best option. This would have also excluded those states that helped militarise the Sri Lankan state during the ethnic war. This proposal had the following advantages: India would have found it difficult to object since that would have called into question its commitment to the Non-Aligned Movement. This proposal would also have neutralised Indian sensitivity to Western powers intruding into its sphere of influence, on its southern flank, and the JVP's main slogan would have been neutralised. They would have also found it exceedingly difficult to whip up hostility against Yugoslavian, Indonesian and Zimbabwean troops. That section of the Tamil people which wanted the IPKF removed would also have been won over. Given the high intensity crisis and the availability of alternatives (such as those set out above), it was erroneous to argue, as did the EPRLF and Delhi, that Colombo should wait for the CVF (Citizens Volunteer Force), the Tamil police and the Tamil battalions of the Sri Lankan army to be set up to complete the withdrawal of the IPKF.

The Tamil national question was indeed central to the political situation in the country and to the strategic perspectives of the Sri Lankan left, until the powerful recrudescence of the JVP. Just as the Nazi attack on the Soviet Union in 1941 changed the character of the Second World War, the armed attacks by the JVP on the left in the aftermath of the PPC of 1986, the killing of Daya Pathirana by JVP assassins in December 1986 and the onslaught on the main Tamil Left organisation, the EPRLF, by the LTTE in the same month, mark the transition to a qualitatively different conjuncture in which the Tamil national question no longer remained the key link. The Indo-Lanka Accord signalled a fundamental change in the character of the Tamil national question in that it put an end, for the time being, to the old ethnic war and to the military pressure on the Tamil nation by the Sinhala state. In the post-Accord period, the central question of the political situation in the country was the threat posed by the JVP to the state and civil society as a whole.

SRI LANKAN TAMILS

Ethnic identity is not an essentialist force lying latent within every society, waiting to erupt into violent secessionism. There is no ethnic group inherently prone to separatism or secession: whether it moves in that direction is in large part dependent on the degree of centralisation and majoritarianism that accompanies the nation-building effort and on the degree to which diverse cultures within a national space are accorded autonomy and recognition.

Sri Lankan Tamils regard their nationalism as the story of a people driven from moderation and desired accommodation to secessionism because of Sinhalese chauvinism. In contrast, Dravidian nationalism began as a potentially secessionist movement in the 1970s but became accommodationist once it realised the political dispensation of independent India that offered it an opportunity to come to power at the state level and accorded it a degree of autonomy on questions of language and culture. The degree of such autonomy was never to be sure enough to fully satisfy Dravidian aspirations, yet it proved sufficient to deflect that movement from secessionism.

The tendency in mainstream scholarship that sees Dravidian and Sri Lankan Tamil nationalisms as being intimately related to and energising each other is more a reflection of the anxieties of nation building in post-colonial societies and of the strongly ingrained suspicion of movements that seek to loosen the tight embrace of majoritarian nationalism, rather than of any persuasive historical evidence as such. This hermeneutics of suspicion *vis-a-vis* ethnicity is buttressed by electoral and geopolitical calculations, in both countries, that encourage an opportunistic twining of the two Tamil nationalisms.

Both this suspicion of ethnicity and the twining of the two Tamil nationalisms are powerfully supported by an international relations discourse that avers that the ideal nation-state is a homogenised, uniform, and sovereign space in which sectarian loyalties, especially those that may cross national boundaries, have no place.

The process of linking of the Sri Lankan Tamil movement to external forces such as the Dravidian movement was a critical step in both diminishing and exaggerating it as far as Sri Lankan society was concerned. It diminished Sri Lankan Tamil nationalism by: (a) portraying it as externally inspired and therefore traitorous; (b) indicating a primordial sentiment among the Tamils, thus minimising Sinhalese responsibility for Tamil grievances; and (c) denying Sri Lankan Tamils cultural originality and autonomy by seeing them as derivative appendages of a larger cultural and intellectual formation in Tamil Nadu.

It simultaneously exaggerated Tamil nationalism in that the threat posed by the eleven million Sri Lankan Tamils could now be alloyed with the fifty-five million Tamils of Tamil Nadu, justifying a violent and intransigent response by the state. Mainstream scholarship in India and Sri Lanka thus winds up, first combining and then essentialising Tamil ethnicity in the two societies.

In ancient and medieval Tamil kingdoms, literature, poetry, martial castes and militarist culture, they seek the origins of Tamil discourses of self-determination, methods of armed struggle, the LTTE's cyanide culture, and other aspects of their movement. Imputing unchanging characteristics and continuity to the Tamil across centuries marked by dramatic transformations is a violently reductive and essentialising argument that Edward said describes as orientalism.

In the contemporary context, the argument suffers from two more failings: first, it misunderstands the uniquely modern transnational and global forces that inform the tactics and strategy of a guerrilla outfit like the LTTE. And second, the imputing of such unchanging essence to the Tamils denies any sense of politics as an open-ended, agentive process in which a negotiation with not an effacement of difference is possible.

To understand the tactics, strategy, and ideology of a late-modern guerrilla group such as the LTTE, one may be better served by authors who locate terrorism in a quintessentially modernist and disenchanted secular frame, than by authors who discern enduring Tamil martial traditions or some inherent penchant for self-immolation and suicide going back centuries. The depiction of an essentialist Tamil identity in both societies emerges and gains currency because of its utility in a discursive framework that unites scholarship with the Indian and Sri Lankan states in the suspicion of ethnicity.

TAMIL NATIONALISM

The Sri Lankan Tamils see theirs as a reluctant transition from a politics of desired accommodation to violent secessionism. In their view, this transition has occurred on account of the majority's view of Sri Lanka as primarily the abode of Sinhala Buddhists, with other communities playing, at best, a supporting role. This majoritarian vision has been translated into reality in the decades since independence by the steady political, economic, and socio-cultural marginalisation of the Tamils.

During the British colonial regime, Sri Lankan Tamils came to occupy a large share of civil service positions and acquired a considerable degree of economic clout. Whatever the origins of such disproportionate success in the colonial period, the decades since independence have seen a sharp swing in the opposite direction in terms of both economic and political power. At independence Sri Lanka was a polity dominated by an isolated cosmopolitan, English-educated, Westernised Sinhalese-Tamil bourgeoisie who provided the underpinning for the island's stable set-up. Prior to independence, the British set up the Soulbury Commission on the Constitution to assess the question of ethnic ratios in the new Parliament. The leader of the All Ceylon Tamil Congress (ACTC), G. G. Ponnambalam, argued for an equal division of power, with the country as a whole being divided into a hundred territorial units, fifty of which would be earmarked as general and fifty for the various minorities together.

To argue for equal representation for minorities in a context where nearly three-quarters of the country was Sinhala-Buddhist seems audacious in retrospect. Yet such was the climate of the times that not only was this possibility entertained seriously, but at one point, with the support of the Sinhalese political elite, a compromise that awarded fifty-seven units to the Sinhalese and forty-three to all the minorities was actually offered. Clearly, ethnicity had not yet overpowered alternative forms of identity at this time.

More importantly, the fifty-fifty episode reflects a political culture still centred in the anglicised and

Westernised elites. In retrospect, the Tamils' sticking to their guns on fifty-fifty and not grabbing the offer of fifty-seven to forty-three made by the Soulbury Commission was seen as a tactical error on their part. This error was reflected in the first elections to the new Parliament when the Sinhalese captured 67 per cent of the seats, a share that would increase and stay around 80 per cent in later decades. Once acquiring political power became a matter of numbers, party competition in mass elections on the basis of universal adult suffrage, with no special provisions for minority or communal representation forces, were set in motion that would make the genteel politics of Colombo's Cinnamon Garden elites forever obsolete. The temptation to rally three-quarters of the population under the rubric of Sinhala-Buddhist identity by the invention of enmity against Tamils was impossible to resist.

Sri Lankan politics entered a phase in which the mobilisation of Sinhala ethnic identity around the triad of the race, the land, the faith became the norm. The two main political parties, the United National Party (UNP) and the Sri Lanka Freedom Party (SLFP), were thereafter locked in a battle for the allegiance of the majority, and the appeal to ethnic chauvinism became a staple of everyday politics. Almost upon independence, the UNP regime disenfranchised nine hundred thousand estate Tamils through legislations passed in 1948 and 1949.

In fact, the preceding two decades had witnessed the steady erosion of their voting rights, an erosion that Sri Lankan Tamils supported every bit as much as the Sinhalese and the British did. The disenfranchisement of the estate Tamils was one of the reasons for a split in Ponnambalam's ACTC, which had acquiesced with UNP's actions in exchange for a ministerial portfolio for Ponnambalam. This exchange, as opposed by a faction within the party and their exit, led to the emergence of the Ilangi Tamil Arasu Kadchi (the Federal Party).

The Federal Party began to voice its disquiet on a number of matters, including the changing demographic balance between the Tamils and the Sinhalese in regions that the former regarded as their traditional homelands largely on account of state-sponsored settlement of Sinhalese there through irrigation schemes. The issue of the traditional homelands of Tamils perfectly showcases the tensions underlying post-colonial nationalism and the ways in which modernity is translated into the vernacular in that space.

For Tamils, increasingly aware of their status as a precarious minority, the aforementioned demographic changes would be akin to a colonisation of their areas of habitation. The areas of large Sri Lanka Tamil majorities have been contracting over the years, leaving by 1981 only Jaffna and Mullaitivu in the far north and Batticaloa in the east as districts of large Tamil numerical preponderance.

Sri Lanka Tamils in 1911 formed a majority of the populations of all districts in the northern and eastern provinces. Since this is no longer the case, the territories of the Tamil homeland may be thought of as shrinking. From the Tamil perspective, both their claim to an antiquity in Sri Lanka equal to that of the Sinhalese and their ultimate bargaining chip in the event of a complete breakdown of relations with the majority community rested on preserving their majority in areas they considered traditional homelands.

During the 1950s, the Federal Party was articulating the demand for a separate Tamil majority region with a high degree of provincial autonomy in a federal rather than a unitary order. On the issue of what exactly the Federal Party desired at this stage, there is an interesting difference of opinion that, once again, pertains to the unique forms in which modernity enters and is domesticated in post-colonial space.

The Federal Party was ambiguous about its position on secessionism even at this early stage, and in giving their speeches in Tamil, the leaders of the party were openly secessionist. In contrast, when they spoke in English in Parliament, for example, they stayed clear of such secessionist talk. This difference left their real position on regional autonomy dangerously ambiguous.

The Tamil minority was being held to a standard that the majority community would itself fail resoundingly. Even urbane and articulate exponents of the English language, such as Jayewardene, routinely used the terms Sri Lankan and Sinhala interchangeably. The tendency to equate Sri Lankan with Sinhala was even more pronounced when such leaders spoke in Sinhalese.

Entry of modern nationalism into the post-colonial realm has to face a discomfiting question: Is it possible that in countries such as Sri Lanka and India a liberal-democratic idea of the nation, with equal and individual rights for all citizens, had a very limited ambit and that for most people the nation evoked more particularistic affiliations?

The Tamils see the 1950s and 1960s as a period of repeated betrayals by the Sinhalese political leadership. In the movement toward secession, June 1956 came to be regarded as a critical turning point. In that month, Parliament under the new Prime Minister, Solomon Bandaranaike of the SLFP, passed the Official Language Act declaring Sinhala to be the sole language of administration. Tamil non-violent protest and satyagraha were met with violence from the Sinhalese, many of whom felt the act did not go far enough in ensuring Sinhala domination over Tamils in official discourse.

As a response to Sinhala Only Act, the Federal Party upped its demands: from self-governing districts based on a Swiss cantonal model to a model that would eventually weld the Tamil-speaking areas of the north and east into larger, provincial or regional units. However, even such limited demands for regional autonomy consistently ran against a newly self-aware majority that regarded such demands as the entering wedge of the break-up of Sri Lanka and as occasions for a violent response. In an effort to take some of the sting out of the Sinhala Only Act, on July 26, 1957, the Prime Minister, who was evidently more moderate than the rank-and-file supporters of the SLFP, signed an agreement with the leader of the Federal Party, Chelvanayagam. This agreement, which came to be known as the Bandaranaike-Chelvanayagam Pact (or the B-C Pact), marked the next critical milestone of the Tamils of Sri Lanka.

The B-C Pact tried to accomplish four things:

1) It gave Tamil official status for administration in the northern and eastern provinces;
2) It implicitly recognised the principle that some portions of Sri Lanka constituted a traditional habitat or homeland of the Tamils by its proposal to set limits on the settling of Sinhalese peasants in newly irrigated areas of the north and east so that the existing Tamil majorities stayed intact;
3) It promised to re-examine the question of the disenfranchisement of the estate Tamils that had occurred in 1948-49;
4) In discussions of autonomy, it implicitly escalated the territorial unit from that of districts to that of regions or provinces.

By mid-1958, the pact lay in shambles, however. From the Tamil perspective, Bandaranaike reneged on his promises as he was unable to resist the wave of Sinhalese opposition to the pact. Save for the milquetoast passage of an amendment to the Sinhala Only Act of 1956 that resurrected a clause on reasonable use of the Tamil language, it seemed a complete betrayal to the Tamils.

Moreover, Federal Party members, who launched a non-violent movement for the implementation of the pact, were attacked, and in May of 1958 the country exploded in communal riots that made the violence of 1956 look insignificant. The Prime Minister had been completely outflanked by Jayewardene and UNP supporters, who embarked on a march to Kandy to register their opposition to the pact, as well as by extremists within the SLFP and the Buddhist clergy. Bandaranaike had supposedly given away one-third of the land and two-thirds of the coastline to one-tenth of the population.

The elections in 1960 saw the SLFP acquire a sizable majority in Parliament, allowing them to ignore promises made to the Federal Party before the elections. In March 1965, just prior to the next round of general elections, Chelvanayagam entered into another pact, this time with Dudley Senanayake, the UNP leader. As it turned out, for the UNP to form the government and for Senanayake to become Prime Minister, they needed the support of the Federal Party. Although this need was leveraged by the Federal Party into a promise that the Senanayake-Chelvanayagam Pact would meet a different fate from the B-C pact, events transpired otherwise.

Although the Tamil-proposed district councils saw their autonomy sharply curtailed by direct central government oversight, the pact implicitly recognised the northern and eastern provinces as Tamil-speaking areas. It moreover agreed in principle that Tamil-speaking people should be given preference in allotments made for new lands that came under irrigation.

The government ran into serious and violent opposition led by the SLFP during parliamentary sessions in early 1966 as it debated the Senanayake-Chelvanayagam Pact. The wheel now turned full circle with the SLFP in opposition, turning the heat on the UNP regime for violating the sanctity of Sinhala Only Act and for other envisaged amendments to implement the pact. By October 1966, the UNP had lost three by-elections to the SLFP, and by the middle of 1968, faced with a Sinhalese backlash to the proposed devolution in the District Councils Bill, Senanayake admitted defeat and unilaterally abrogated his pact with Chelvanayagam.

From the Tamil perspective, it was obvious that, individuals aside, the very structure of post-colonial politics in a unitary state militated against any solution to their problems. The Federal Party quit its participation in government. The tremendous victory of the SLFP in the Parliamentary elections of 1970 and the Prime Ministership of Mrs. Sirimao Bandaranaike pushed the Sinhala-Tamil divide to unbridgeable proportions. The SLFP quickly enacted into law what had become a reality for most Tamils: the Sinhalese regarded the island as exclusively theirs. Ceylon was renamed Sri Lanka, and by a fiat the new Parliament was deemed a Constituent Assembly for the task of writing for Sri Lanka a Constitution of its own to replace the colonial period's Soulbury Constitution in operation until then. Besides reinscribing Sinhala as the sole official language of the country, the Constitution of 1972 abolished sectioning of the previous document, which served as a protector of minority rights.

Section 6 of Chapter II of the new Constitution removed any ambiguity regarding the second-class citizenship of those who were not Buddhist: "The Republic of Sri Lanka shall give to Buddhism the foremost place and accordingly it shall be the duty of the State to protect and foster Buddhism while assuring to all religions the rights granted by Section 18 (i)(d)."

Further, the regime enacted a policy of standardisation of marks obtained by students in high school examinations, which resulted in Tamil students having to excel their Sinhalese counterparts by wide margins to gain access to much sought after degrees in medicine, engineering, and sciences. The disastrous results of standardisation begun in 1970 were compounded by another policy, enacted in 1973, by which admissions to universities were to be based on the population of the area or province. Thus, the "over-educated" northern province with an overwhelmingly Tamil population saw its share of admissions into science programmes drop from 27.5 per cent to seven per cent between 1969 and 1974.

By the mid-1970s, with the vast majority of high school graduates in the northern province seeing their access to university education choked off and unemployment at 43 per cent for Tamil youth, the socio-economic underpinnings of a militant guerrilla movement had been laid. In a protest against the decisions to arbitrarily declare Parliament a Constituent Assembly, Sinhala, the sole official language, and Buddhism the state religion, and against the revocation of sections that had provided minorities with some protection, Chelvanayagam resigned his parliamentary seat on October 2, 1972, to coincide with the birthday of Mahatma Gandhi. He then proclaimed his re-election to Parliament to be a referendum on whether Sri Lankan Tamils wished to live under the Constitution of 1972 or to secede. Put simply, if he won re-election, it would be interpreted as a definitive statement that Sri Lankan

Tamils wished to secede and form a separate nation. Despite attempts to delay the election on various pretences, when it was eventually held on February 6, 1975, Chelvanayagam won with the largest majority that his constituency, Kankesuntarai, had ever seen.

In May 1972, the various Tamil parties now coalesced under the Tamil United Front (TUF), which was renamed the Tamil United Liberation Front (TULF) in 1975 to indicate its explicitly secessionist aim. This aim was buttressed in the Vaddukoddai resolution of May 14, 1976, when the TULF called on the Tamils of Sri Lanka to throw themselves fully in the sacred fight for freedom and to flinch not till the goal of a sovereign socialist state of Tamil Eelam was reached.

The formation of the TULF marked the first time in nearly three decades that the various factions of the Sri Lankan Tamils stood united, as it combined the ACTC and the Federal Party. It also marked a period in which the Sri Lankan Tamils arrived at an understanding with the estate Tamils, though on most issues their interests were still divergent.

In 1977, the three leading Tamil figures of this moderate phase—Ponnambalam, Murugeysen Tiruchelvam, and Chelvanayagam—passed away. Over the next few years, faced with escalating Sinhala violence and a history of betrayals of and paltry rewards for moderate Tamil leaders, the Tamils would turn to a new brand of politicians: armed, militant rebel youth. The youth had witnessed first-hand what they considered to be the bankruptcy of moderate Tamil politics in preceding decades. With the exception of Chelvanayagam, their leaders seemed ready to sell the Tamil people down the river in exchange for petty ministerial perks in Sinhala-dominated regimes.

On the other hand, Sinhalese politicians, even the best of them, were incapable of making and politically delivering any concession to Tamil cultural, political, and economic autonomy. Faced with this narration of recent history, Tamil militant groups regarded moderation and compromise with the political establishment as options that had been tried repeatedly and had conclusively failed.

While the Sinhalese used Tamils as a whetstone for producing a sense of self-identity, the Tamils became conscious of themselves as an ethnic minority as a consequence of the process of majoritarian nation building. That is, the building of the nation along majoritarian lines served as the impetus for the emergence of ethno-nationalism.

DRAVIDIAN MOVEMENT

A close look at the Dravidian movement indicates that their secessionist tendencies, both historically and in recent years were grossly exaggerated, and their connections with Sri Lankan Tamils were nowhere near as intimate as Indian and Sri Lankan governments or mainstream scholarship would have it. A number of works have examined the rise of a form of Tamil nationalism from the late-nineteenth century onward.

The Justice Party (South Indian Liberal Federation) is notable for its coinage and use of the category non-Brahmin, in the genealogy of Dravidianism. The Justice Party was a party of the elite, in fact of the petty royalty that had been the mainstay of native support for the colonial regime. Formed in 1916, they were a product of the limited electoral franchise of the time, the growing enumeration of group identities, and the selective favours bestowed on such groups by the colonial regime. As the census and other classifying and data-gathering efforts of the Madras administration revealed, Brahmins were vastly over-represented in the educated sections of the populace and the civil service bureaucracy, as well as among professional elites. The Justice Party sought a redressal of Brahmin over-representation in favour of non-Brahmin castes by petitioning the colonial state.

The ostensibly progressive and radical aspect of justice's political programme—the anti-Brahmin or non-Brahmin ideology—did not expand into an anti-casteist critique of Tamil society or of the wider Sanskritic culture of the Brahmins. Instead, it preferred to restrict itself to the parameters of an intra-elite competition for spoils of colonial office. In that competition, the category non-Brahmin served the Justice Party in good stead, given the tremendous over-representation of Brahmins in middle-class professions in turn-of-century Madras. That non-Brahmin upper castes represented by justice were similarly over-represented compared to the vast majority of the populace of the Madras presidency was a matter left delicately alone.

The Justice Party made its first demand for secession in June 1940. The structure of political and economic opportunity that underwrote its rise in the earlier period had long passed. The electoral franchise had greatly expanded beyond the limited realm of the 1910s because of a series of concessions made by the British, culminating with the Government of India Act of 1935, allowing for self-government at the provincial level. Congress, by now a mass-based political party, had made tremendous inroads in the Madras presidency in the 1920s and 1930s and had come to power with huge majorities in the elections to the provincial government of the Madras Presidency in 1937, elections in which the Justice Party was routed. The rise of Periyar E. V. Ramaswami Naicker's Self-Respect Movement in the 1930s had outflanked the non-Brahmin platform of Justicites. Not only had Periyar's movement expanded anti-Brahminism into a much wider anti-casteist and rationalist ideology, it also brought into mass politics the castes and classes of people with whom Justicites did not associate.

It was in this context of being literally rendered irrelevant that the Justice Party, which had a history of collaboration with the colonial regime, made a last ditch effort to throw a spanner in the wheels of Congress and curry favour with the colonial regime by its demand for a separate and loyalist state of Dravidanad. At this time, Periyar united the Self-Respect Movement with justice and joined in the demand for Dravidanad. His own motivations for demanding Dravidanad were vastly different from that of justice and thus merit close attention.

Periyar had been elected President of the Justice Party in 1939, when he was in jail because of his actions during the anti-Hindi language agitations of the preceding year. He joined in the demand for a separate state not out of any programmatic attraction to the Justice Party's policies and platform, but rather as the culmination of a far-reaching social and ideological critique of mainstream Indian nationalism represented by the Congress. He had cut his political spurs in Congress in the mid-1910s but had left it because of principled objections to its consistent refusal to give prominence to issues of social reform, especially regarding caste, in its movement to unite the nation.

Especially in the Madras Presidency, Congress was dominated by Brahmins, most of whom, for all their democratic and equalitarian rhetoric, remained incurably bigoted and casteist in their personal, professional, and political lives. Their vision of independence for all Indians rang hollow, given their deeply ingrained notions on caste and their belief in the innate superiority of Brahmanic and Sanskritic culture over the rest of India. Based on a wide-ranging critique of Congress's hegemonic mainstream nationalism, one that relied heavily on a symbology of politics both North Indian and Sanskritic in its inspiration, Periyar left the Congress Party and started the Self-Respect Movement that dominated the Madras Presidency in the 1930s.

At its peak, the movement launched a determined assault against caste, Sanskritic culture, imposition of Hindi language, and North Indian domination of Indian society. Periyar's was an eclectic attack, occasionally inspired by rationalism, at other times by a version of socialism or communism, and at still others by an iconoclastic atheism. The high point of the Self-Respect Movement was reached during Congress rule over the Madras Presidency in 1937-39. At that time, Congress declared Hindi the national language, and Periyar's Self-Respecters led the fight against its imposition in Madras.

Periyar argued that peninsular India, especially Tamil society, had once been an egalitarian and progressive Dravidian civilisation in which caste was unknown. It was the North Indian, in the form of the Brahmin, who brought into the south the pernicious institutions of caste and many another objectionable practices characteristic of the north's

Sanskritic culture. Consequently, his anti-Hindi language agitation was part of a more thoroughgoing critique of northern Indian hegemony, Sanskritic culture, and their local representatives, the Brahmins. His argument for a separate Dravidanad had an underlying cosmology and a degree of societal support that were quite different from the narrowly instrumental calculations of the justice Party.

In June 1940, in Kanchipuram, the first Dravidanad Separation Conference was held. A map of the desired country revealed, to put it mildly, a rather expansive cartographic imagination. It included the entirety of peninsular India, all of the eastern coastline, and incredibly parts of Bengal. The striking aspect of this representation of desired space is that at no time did Periyar or the Justice Party ever consider including Jaffna or any portion of Tamil majority provinces in Sri Lanka, which were as little as twenty miles away, even as they included those who showed no affinity for the political cause of the Tamils: namely, other so-called Dravidian peoples of Karnataka, Kerala, and Andhra Pradesh as well as those even farther afield, such as in Bengal.

The Justice Party dissolved into the newly formed Dravida Kazhagam, in 1944. The DK espoused Periyar's ideology and was variously committed to anti-casteism, rationalism, anti-Brahminism, atheism, anti-North Indian hegemony, non-Sanskritic culture, socialism, and opposition to the Hindi language. All of these commitments were combined into an overarching ideology of Dravidianism that became the main rhetorical trope in Tamil politics for decades to come. At the point of its formation, the DK was both secessionist and loyalist. The next months would see the disappearance of the idea of secession and a similarly rapid distancing of the Dravidian movement from its loyalist lineage in the Justice Party and in Periyar himself. At the outset, many of the younger political leaders were concerned that the loyalist history of Justice Party would delegitimate the DK. In fact, one of the reasons for renaming the new organisation was to distance itself from this history.

By mid-1947, a faction within DK, led by C. N. Annadurai, was already arguing for a revision of the party line on Indian independence. A public split soon occurred with Periyar declaring August 15, 1947, independence day, to be a day of mourning, but Annadurai and others in DK celebrated it as a day of freedom and rejoicing. In October 1947, significantly, Annadurai and his followers boycotted the Dravida Kazhagam conference on the separation of Dravidanadu. Matters between Periyar and Annadurai came to a head, and on September 17, 1949, DK split into two parties, and the newly formed Dravida Munnetra Kazhagam (DMK), led by Annadurai, left the fold with more than 75 per cent of the total membership of DK.

DMK, especially after it gained power in Tamil Nadu in 1967, went about the task of revising its loyalist history with a vengeance. This revisionism was proof of the fact that the Dravidian movement was bereft of ideology from its very beginnings and little more than an opportunistic product of the factional politics of the early twentieth century. Such revisionism indicates the vacuous character of the Dravidian movement and the parties that emerged from it.

At one level, the progressive ideology and content of the anti-Brahmin movement are discounted as being no more than a product of factional rivalries among the elite classes of early twentieth-century Madras, and, at another, the later revisionism of DMK is moralistically critiqued for its eternally demagogic and spurious character.

In a surge of patriotism, DMK is supposed to have discovered the error of its ways and disavowed secession thereafter. An additional factor that supposedly spurred DMK to give up on Dravidanad was the passage of the Sixteenth Amendment to the Indian Constitution, which proscribed speech questioning the sovereignty and integrity of India, and required all candidates for political office to take an oath reaffirming the sovereignty of the nation.

DMK had given up on secession long before the Chinese invasion or the sixteenth Amendment to the Constitution; indeed, the very split of DMK from DK in 1949 arose from the desire to distance itself from the secessionist genealogy. Additionally, in a series of meetings between 1958 and 1960, the *de jure* status of the party on secession was discussed threadbare and by November 1960, there emerged a consensus that the Dravidanadu demand should be publicly abandoned.

The Dravidian nationalism lost its secessionist character even before the early 1960s on account of federal accommodation and the opportunities contained therein is buttressed by the events that followed soon after forgetting the lessons they ought to have learned from the earlier abortive attempt to impose Hindi on Tamil Nadu, the central government decided to give it another shot in the mid-1960s. Tamil Nadu was immediately wracked by violent anti-Hindi protests and a resurgence of both anti-North Indian sentiment and renewed talk of secession.

Rather than regard this resurgence as a sign of the ineradicable secessionism of the Tamil, we ought to frame it within a discussion of majoritarian nationalism and the rights of peripheral, minority cultures. Given the powerful linkages made in Tamil society between the imposition of the Hindi language and the issue of North Indian hegemony, Sanskritic culture versus local practice, caste and Brahmin domination, and Aryan versus Dravidian civilisation, the issue quickly went beyond language and spread to the emotive issue of majoritarianism versus the rights of peripheral minorities. Language became the metaphor for the relationship that ought to govern centre and state, and the violent anti-Hindi agitations in Tamil Nadu at this time are indicative of the fact that ethnonationalism is not an essentialist force so much as it is a response to forced unification on some principle of majoritarianism. The experiences of Tamil Nadu in the mid-1960s indicate further that subaltern feelings against majoritarian nationalism were effectively neutered by institutionalised politics and DMK.

Most works on Dravidianism suggest that the anti-Hindi agitations weren't so much led or abetted by DMK as they were instances of its leadership's efforts to check the violence and radicalism of the movement. The growing moderation of DMK was completed once it came to power in the state assembly elections of 1967. Since then, DMK has been loyal to the central government almost to a fault, which is also indicated by the changing pattern of electoral alignments in the state.

The Dravidian movement managed to attack and demolish caste privilege based on the Sanskritic authority of the Brahmin, even while it simultaneously strengthened the institution of caste itself in Tamil society and was co-opted by a society still obsessed by notions of ritual pollution and purity. The Dravidian movement has done little to ameliorate the worsening conditions of those at the lowest end of the caste ladder, while on the other hand, the fissure between Brahmin and non-Brahmin is being healed at the top under the aegis of Tamil nationalism.

From the early 1970s on, as any real threat of secession receded, the DMK and AIADMK's rhetorical espousing of the cause of Tamil peoples increased for two important reasons: first, both parties desired to distinguish themselves from their main political rival at the state level, namely, the Congress Party; and second, once the AIADMK emerged as a breakaway party of considerable following, the two Dravidian parties competed with each other to lay claims to Tamil heritage and distinctiveness with increasingly overblown rhetoric.

Ironically, the two Dravidian parties, self-anointed role as spokesmen for a worldwide Tamilakam, their sponsorship of gaudy pseudo-historical conferences that rewrote world history from a Tamil-centric perspective, their espousal of the causes of Tamil peoples everywhere, including Sri Lanka, are all better understood as reflecting this diminution of their actual secessionist threat, rather than as continuing their proclivity toward secession, as mainstream scholarship would aver.

The trajectory and development of the Dravidian movement in Tamil Nadu was opposite that of the Sri Lankan Tamils. In large part, the movement away from secession toward accommodation was enabled by the federal political dispensation of India, centralised and increasingly authoritarian though it was.

DIVERGENT NATIONALISMS

The putative linkage between the two Tamil movements in India and Sri Lanka was used to justify the Sinhalese state's annihilatory response to the issue of Tamil nationalism in Sri Lanka; and in the case of India, it was used as the perfect alibi to adopt an interventionist posture regarding Sri Lankan domestic affairs.

There is nothing objectionable about Tamils in India expressing concern about the treatment of Tamils in Sri Lanka. In fact, the multiple violences and discriminations visited upon Tamils by the Sri Lankan state since independence have merited condemnation on humanitarian grounds, and if such protests came from Tamil Nadu, well, so much the better for that state. It might be more worthwhile, however, to ponder over why the expression of concern by Tamil "here" about the welfare of a Tamil "there" produces acute suspicion and discomfort among state elites and many scholars in both India and Sri Lanka, and why such expressions of concern are immediately interpreted as evidence of the primordial and dangerously essentialist Tamil character underlying both movements.

One of the most noticeable aspects of the Dravidian movement was its material and ideological basis in anti-Brahminism. In contrast, Brahmins, who constituted less than one per cent of Sri Lankan Tamils, were nowhere near as important in Jaffna or Ceylon's Tamil community as their counterparts were in Tamil Nadu. The impact of colonial rule had led to a different political economy, one in which the Brahmin stayed predominantly within the religious fold, while the agricultural caste of the Vellalars came to dominate both the professional, educated classes and the agrarian sector.

The impact of Christianity was far greater in Tamil society in Sri Lanka, than in Tamil society in Tamil Nadu and the Vellalar variety of Hinduism was one that was considerably intermixed with Christianity, in a forceful rebuttal of the claim that Sri Lankan Tamil nationalism had close cultural and political ties to the Dravidian movement in Tamil Nadu.

Jaffna Tamil leaders of the early twentieth century did not typically dwell on their Dravidian roots. Many of them may have gone back and forth between Jaffna and South India, participating in political life in both places, but their two-way access was a result more of colonial ties between South India and Sri Lanka than of a common culture. Moreover, the early founders of separatist ideology were not Hindus at all, but good Jaffna Christians.

In Tamil Nadu, the attack against local Brahminism could be coupled with a powerful critique of Sanskritic culture and North Indian hegemony, which gave a powerful fillip to a regional or separatist ideology. None of these factors were germane to the Sri Lankan case. Beginning with non-Brahminism, the Dravidian movement at its apex expanded into a full-scale critique of caste.

The Dravidian movement was often long on anti-casteist rhetoric and short on improving the lives of those at the bottom, it is a fact that some of the most egregious and overt aspects of caste discrimination had largely disappeared from Tamil society in India by the 1960s. For example, the exclusion of lower castes from entering temples was one of the first things to go in Tamil Nadu, almost with independence itself. Yet, in Sri Lankan Tamil society, not only was the domination of the Vellalars overwhelming, but most such overtly exclusionary aspects remained intact.

Even as late as that, the renowned Vellalar Tamil nationalist leader, one time cabinet Minister, and professor of mathematics, C. Suntheralingam, found it politically feasible to lead a movement against temple entry for lower-caste Tamils in Sri Lanka. Indeed, after 1956, the pressure to present a united front against Sinhalese ought to have given great impetus to Tamils to cross such caste barriers, but this was not so. It was mainly the Marxists among Tamils who initiated such moves, and the Federal Party joined in this enterprise especially after 1956 but as the mainstream political party of the Tamil minority and dependent on *vellala* votes it was much more circumspect in dealing with these issues. It would be 1977 before a so-called lower-caste person would be elected from Sri Lankan Tamil society to Parliament, in the fifth general elections of independent Sri Lanka. In Tamil Nadu, not only had the Nadar leader K. Kamaraj served a stint as Tamil Nadu's Chief Minister, but he had also brokered the succession of two Prime Ministers and acquired the sobriquet 'kingmaker' by then.

The deferential, casteist, and conservative Tamil society of Jaffna must have regarded the anti-caste rhetoric and programme of the Self-Respect Movement and Dravidian ideology with some degree of alarm and certainly with considerable distaste. This reaction was further reflected in the superior and aloof attitude they adopted toward the estate Tamils of Indian origin, largely on account of the lower caste and class position these Tamils occupied, in their view.

To secure redress as a minority, Sri Lankan Tamil elites focused their attention on Colombo in the decades immediately before and after independence. There was little or nothing to be gained and much to be lost by making common cause with Tamils in Madras at this time. In an effort to assert their claims to the Sinhalese majority, it was logical for them to prove their antiquity in Sri Lanka and their distance from the Tamils of India.

Another source of Ceylon Tamil nationalism is the emphatic assertion of Sri Lanka as the legitimate and ancient home of the Tamils and of Tamil institutions. Nothing annoys the Tamils of Sri Lanka more than the argument, used by Sinhalese to placate Tamil opinion, that their culture and language are preserved adequately and are flourishing in South India and there was, therefore, no need to make a special provision in Sri Lanka. The Tamils react to this by emphasising their separateness from India, the longevity of the Tamil tradition in Sri Lanka, and by asserting, with dubious historical arguments, their contemporaneity with Sinhalese settlements in Sri Lanka.

During the critical turning points of Sri Lankan Tamil nationalism in the 1950s and 1960s, DMK politicians, who were then in the opposition in the state legislature and central Parliament, encouraged the Indian government to take an active stance and pressure the Sri Lankan regime to alter its policies toward the Tamils. They were even more outspoken in their comments on the betrayal of the estate Tamils in the legislation of 1948-49 and in the Sirimavo Shastri Pact of October 1964, which envisaged the repatriation of half a million estate Tamils to India within fifteen years.

The discourse of danger that regards every expression of ethnic solidarity as suspicious ought not to blind us to the fact that, on this occasion, the DMK was expressing humanitarian concerns that were eminently worthy of support. At the same time, it is important to recognise that the DMK concern for the welfare of the Sri Lankan Tamil or the estate Tamils rarely proceeded beyond rhetoric. Speeches in the Indian Parliament and in the State Legislative Assembly in Madras were directed at target audiences within the electorate of Tamil Nadu.

When it came to support for the cause of the Tamils in Sri Lanka, the story was depressingly familiar: the DMK found little reason in the 1950s and 1960s to do anything more than pay lip service to it. In the 1970s, the rewriting of the Constitution, standardisation, and the anti-Tamil riots of 1977 were occasions in which the DMK and AIADMK tried to outdo one another in party competition by vociferously espousing the cause of the Sri Lankan Tamils. Yet, it is easy to exaggerate the degree of such support: for all their speeches in Parliament and processions taken out by the opposition party, there is little evidence of any material or other form of overt, or even covert, support by the Dravidian parties for Sri Lankan Tamils.

Soon after independence, Sri Lankan Tamil leaders occasionally made references to the desirability of joining in a federation with India. Such references were, in fact, made not only by Tamil politicians in Sri Lanka, but by a number of parties and individuals at this time all across South Asia.

The nation-states created in 1947-48 had not yet begun to exercise a complete thrall over the imaginations of everyone in the region. But even at this time, leaders such as Chelvanayagam found their overtures to Tamil politicians across the straits unwelcome. In the 1970s, a series of significant events demonstrate the correctness of DMK regimes when it came to matters involving Indo-Lankan relations.

In 1973, when M. Karunanidhi of DMK was Chief Minister, a Sri Lankan Tamil militant, Kuttimani, was captured in Tamil Nadu. He was wanted by Colombo for attempting to smuggle dynamite into Sri Lanka. Kuttimani was arrested and deported to Sri Lanka to serve his prison term.

In November 1973, the same DMK regime arrested three Sri Lankan Tamils for violating the Indian Passport Act, and they too were handed over to the Sri Lankan government. It was around this time that the leader of the Sri Lankan Tamils, Chelvanayagam, visited Tamil Nadu and New Delhi in an effort to rouse support for the Tamil cause in Sri Lanka. Although he received a warm welcome in Madras, he did not get the expected response.

Despite the expression of sympathy it had been made clear to him by the DMK leaders, that the Federal Party's cause was an internal matter of Sri Lanka. Efforts by other Sri Lankan Tamil leaders in New Delhi proved similarly fruitless. Given the close friendship that existed at this time between the two Prime Ministers, Sirimavo Bandaranaike and Indira Gandhi, India's reluctance to enter this Sri Lankan domestic issue was perhaps not unexpected.

In 1977, when anti-Tamil riots of unprecedented severity rocked Sri Lanka, the response from Tamil Nadu was more vociferous, but still nowhere near as strong or outraged as befitting a party and a state supposedly sympathetic to the idea of Tamil pan-nationalism. The opposition DMK took out processions against the riots and organised a general strike in support of Tamils in Sri Lanka. In contrast, the Indian government led at this time by Morarji Desai of the Janata Party and the AIADMK regime in Tamil Nadu both expressed their concern regarding the safety of Indian nationals in Sri Lanka but stayed clear of commenting on the issue in any significant way.

During the Fifth International Tamil Research Conference held in Madurai, Tamil Nadu, the leader of the TULF, Appapillai Amirthalingam, spoke in the course of his address about the problems of Sri Lankan Tamils and the discrimination and violence of the Sinhalese.

The Chief Minister of Tamil Nadu, M. G. Ramachandran of AIADMK, responded that the Tamil conference was an inappropriate place to advocate the political ideologies of individuals or movements. He further noted that Tamil Nadu wished to retain a cordial relationship with neighbouring countries and governments. The timing of this event merits attention: January 1981 would be the last time the Chief Minister of Tamil Nadu needed to take such a diplomatically correct stance on Sri Lankan affairs for some time to come. Soon after, there would be a sharp change in policy on Sri Lanka and the Tamil question there at the level of the central government in New Delhi, producing in its wake a new set of opportunities and enunciative spaces for both the Tamil parties in Tamil Nadu and Jaffna, as well as for the central governments in Delhi and Colombo. It was in this dramatically altered context that the pogrom of July 1983 against the Sri Lankan Tamils would explode, inaugurating a different era in relations between the two Tamil ethnicities.

Tamil ethnicity was a common essentialist force underlying both Sri Lankan Tamil nationalism and Dravidianism. They arose from distinctly different social formations and moved along opposite political trajectories. Although the logic of electoral politics and competition often meant that the Dravidian parties tried to outdo the other in rhetorically espousing the causes of various Tamil diaspora, this rhetoric never translated into any form of material support for the Sri Lankan Tamil cause. The suspicion of ethnicity and the valorisation of a univocally sovereign model of the nation have together produced a tendency to essentialise Tamil there and here and to combine them into a primordial threat to the principle of the nation-state.

The year 1971 was an important step in the ongoing self- fashioning of India. First, it signified the emergence of

India as a country to be reckoned with as a regional power of significance. Second, it gave a tremendous fillip to incipient notions of India's historical destiny as the regional hegemony of South Asia and induced a strong aversion to the presence of any extra-regional interference therein. Third, it inaugurated the idea that India had a legitimate interest in the fate of so-called kindred ethnic minorities in neighbouring countries, on whose behalf it may intervene if circumstances so dictated. Finally, it set in motion for the central government of dealing both with neighbour countries and with states domestically.

The emergence of Bangladesh pushed certain sections among the Sri Lankan Tamils further along the road to Eelam and created expectations regarding the possible role that the central government in India might play in helping them achieve it. Later in 1977, the newly formed TULF came up with a Six-Point Demands list that echoed the six-point formula used by Mujibur Rahman and the Awami League in the months leading up to the secession of Bangladesh. These demands were: give the Tamil language official status; make Sri Lanka a secular state; decentralise administrative structures; write the fundamental rights of minorities into the Constitution; abolish the caste system; and give citizenship to all those who seek it.

2

Refugees from Sri Lanka

The Tamil Nadu government drew up a contingency plan towards the end of April to face a possible large-scale refugee influx from Sri Lanka, where the war had reached a critical phase. This is quite in tune with its declared policy since 1990 that "although we may not invite refugees, there is no alternative to receiving them and providing for them."

Even as the Liberation Tigers of Tamil Eelam captured Elephant Pass on April 22, signalling an intensified battle for the Jaffna Peninsula, the state government reportedly received intelligence information that some 3,000 Tamils were waiting on the shores of Sri Lanka to cross over to India. It geared itself to accommodate new arrivals at the Mandapam transit camp in Ramanathapuram district. The district administration arranged to repair existing shelters in the camp and construct new ones in the event of an influx. It was also planned to shift 1,200 of the about 8,000 refugees, who are now in the camp to camps in other districts. The families that were to be shifted were identified and intimated.

Surprisingly, the inflow was not as large as expected, at least up to May 18, three full weeks after the reported receipt of intelligence information. In fact, the arrivals appeared to be less than normal records indicate that usually the flow reaches its peak during the month of May. Up to May 18, only 114 refugees had arrived as against last May's figure of 762, according to the refugee arrival list provided by the Naval Detachment in Rameswaram. The government figure for May is still lower at 39 (up to May 18). Twenty-seven Tamils arrived at Arichamunai on the Dhanushkodi coast on May 5, and 12 joined them at the Mandapam camp on May 9. There was no refugee arrival after May 9, and the naval authorities described the period as a "refugee-free week". However, 72 refugees from a camp in Talaimannar arrived in Rameswaram on May 21. The less-than-normal flow of refugees is attributed to several factors. According to some observers, the Tamils may have been blocked at the exit points, with the Sri Lankan Army and the Navy intensifying their vigil in order to avert any possible LTTE intrusion. Further, LTTE or pro-LTTE elements themselves may have barred the Tamil's exit as the Tigers now need their presence in the island to fulfil their needs of manpower and blood. Yet another suggestion is linked to sudden changes in the situation at the diplomatic level with the LTTE's offer of temporary truce and indications about India's stand.

Another view attributes the trend to the stand taken by New Delhi and to a larger extent the Tamil Nadu government, in whose attitudes some observers see a sea change between 1990 and 2000. They recall that in 1990, when the conflict had worsened, the people of Tamil Nadu had sympathised with the suffering Sri Lankan Tamils and the state government, headed by Chief Minister M. Karunanidhi, rolled out the red carpet for the refugees, whose number crossed the onelakh mark. But political compulsions have now forced the state government to view the refugee issue in a different perspective altogether. Being a part of the National Democratic Alliance (NDA) dispensation at the centre, the ruling Dravida Munnetra Kazhagam (DMK) is virtually on the horns of the dilemma. Even as it is eager to outshine its more vociferous pro-Eelam allies, the Marumalarchi Dravida Munnetra Kazhagam (MDMK) and the Pattali Makkal Katchi (PMK), it cannot afford to ignore the cautious line taken by the national democratic Alliance (NDA) government and endorsed by several national parties, as also the changed perspective of a vast majority of people in Tamil Nadu on the "Eelam" demand and the Sri Lankan Tamil organisations, including the banned LTTE, in the wake of the assassination of Rajiv Gandhi in May 1991.

The DMK government has therefore to adopt a more cautious approach to the refugee problem. It has to make it clear that the Sri Lankan Tamils, who are genuinely affected, can be received and provided for, but that it would ensure a strict vigil against any possible entry of terrorist elements in the garb of refugees. Observers who blame the decline in the number of refugees on the central and state governments feel that the larger-than-normal naval presence near the island and the reported questioning of refugees by the Q-Branch police in an attempt to ascertain any links with terrorist organisations might have instilled fear in the minds of prospective refugees and the boatmen, both Sri Lankan and Indian, who usually handle their transit through less-than-legal means.

Agreeing that the vigil along the coast had been intensified, particularly after the killing of Rajiv Gandhi and the banning of the LTTE, the naval authorities and the police said that there was nothing unjustified about it. Lieutenant Commander C. Satish, Executive Officer, Naval Detachment, Rameswaram, said: "We are not at war with the LTTE. But our business is to stop any kind of infiltration by the LTTE or any other terrorist organisation, whose presence on the Indian soil will harm our security interests." The police asserted that it was well within their powers to screen refugees for weapons and possible terrorist links in the interests of national security. The naval authorities said that they could not ignore the view that a substantial number of arrivals this year could be members of terrorist organisations who are opposed to the LTTE and are seen as helping the Sri Lankan Army.

Joint surveillance exercises by the Navy and the Coast Guard and round-the-clock patrolling by naval vessels and helicopters are part of the contingency plans for the coast. The naval authorities set up a Forward Observation Post (FOP) at Arichamunai in April to monitor the movement of boats and ships. The FOP has started serving its objective, a naval official said. The post is manned by four marine commandos. Four watch-towers are proposed in order to check militant activities. The Coast Guard has been provided with facilities to watch the movement of aircraft.

Meanwhile, the Ramanathapuram district administration has cautioned the Indian fishermen against going beyond the permitted marine zone. In order to indicate the Indian border, a board has been erected at Ainthamthittu off Dhanushkodi. The administration and the police were ready to meet any eventuality. Besides regular search operations, surprise checks are made to detect any militants.

The state police have also stepped up security. Security around Mandapam and other refugee camps has been tightened, and entry by outsiders into these camps is prohibited. The police seeks to provide access control measures at the camps and plans are afoot to raise a compound wall around the transit camp.

Search operations are on inside the transit camp also in order to avert the intrusion of militants. Police sources said that 13 checkposts had been set up in Ramanathapuram district, each manned by police officers of the rank of Sub-inspector. Day and night foot patrolling and formation of village vigilance committees are other measures introduced in the district.

From 1902 until 1948, when Sri Lanka achieved independence, was ruled by Britain. From the mid-19th century and more frequently during the 19th century Sri Lanka faced a steady stream of immigrants, mainly from South India, linked to the British economic activity that prevailed at the time. In the 1830's British enterprises developed coffee plantations in the hill country of then Ceylon. Later towards the end of the 19th century rubber plantations were also opened in the midlands and the low country areas of the country. All this hectic economic activity necessitated an extensive and cheap labour force which Sri Lanka could not provide at that time. The most practical alternative was to obtain this requirement from nearby South India, which had a surfeit of cheap unskilled labour, ideally suited for the Sri Lankan plantations.

Several factors subscribed to this unprecedented migration. The principal advantage was proximity. Travel facilities were unrestricted, at least until Sri Lanka gained independence in 1948 and difficulties arose over the preponderance of South Indian Tamils in the majority of the estates. Almost the entire South Indian labour force was Hindu by religion and were part of the joint family system which prevails in several parts of India. These workers left behind part of their families in South India and they were often obliged to send regular remittances to their dependents back home and invariably a substantial part of their savings were repatriated. They even undertook journeys to visit their kith and kin periodically. The short journey involved also suited the British plantation managers as in the event of any depression in the industry some of the estate workers could be asked to return. Conversely, in the event of any economic distress in South India due to drought, crop failure or famine the scale of South Indian immigration would substantially increase.

Therefore, what emerged at the very inception of South Indian immigrations was that the Indian estate workers lived a life of isolation in separate estate communities, cut off from all contacts with the surrounding Sinhala villages and never participating in their political and social life.

It is also important to recognise that the estate workers from South India, who lived mainly in the plantation areas, were very different to the indigenous Tamil community of Sri Lanka who had left India many centuries ago and had become a vital part of the mainstream of Sri Lanka. The first controversy arose during this reform which was based on the recommendations of the Donoughmore Commission which had proposed that a semi-responsible form of government based on adult franchise be introduced in Sri Lanka and that all existing forms of separate communal representation be abolished. Sinhala leaders had difficulties with the franchise question as it was feared that the introduction of universal adult franchise would lead to the unrestricted enfranchisement of Indian residents in Sri Lanka.

The second critical development was the depression in the early 1930's which seriously affected the plantations and created problems of severe unemployment. Sinhala leaders were firmly convinced that this was mainly due to the practice of free immigration from South India and throughout the 1930's they began to exert sustained pressure in the State Council, as the Sri Lankan parliament was then known, for the curtailment of estate labour immigration. Of course the British planting interests and even British officials circles did not support the view that such restrictions were either desirable or possible.

Therefore, when independence was achieved by both countries, India in 1947 and Sri Lanka the following year in 1948, the stage was set for a major confrontation between the two countries over this contentious issue, often involving the Prime Ministers themselves.

It is interesting to take note of the series of meetings that took place between the two countries during this period to try to ease this problem. The first was the Indo-Ceylon Relations Exploratory Conference in November 1940 followed by the Indo-Ceylon Conference in September 1941. Then followed an important meeting at the Prime Ministerial level between Pandit Nehru and Prime Minister Senanayake in 1947. This was mainly concerned with two questions. Firstly, who among the 80,000 Indian residents in Sri Lanka should be considered eligible for Sri Lankan citizenship and, secondly, how they should be admitted to such citizenship and what criteria should be adopted.

The Ceylon Citizenship Act provided for two types of citizenship: by descent and by registration. The provisions relating to citizenship by descent applied mainly to indigenous Sri Lankans, and very few Indian residents could claim citizenship by registration with its rigid residence prerequisites.

On the other hand, the Indian and Pakistani Residents Act of 1949 laid down somewhat less restrictive conditions for the grant of citizenship to the Indian community. Basically an applicant for registration under this Act had to possess the special residential qualification of continued residence in Sri Lanka before January 1, 1946 of seven years for married persons, ten years for others, occasional absence from the Island for less than one year not being deemed a break in the continuity of residence. In addition, he was required to possess an "assured income of a reasonable amount" and prove that no disability rendered it impossible for him to comply with the laws of Sri Lanka. If married, his wife and dependent children should have been resident with him in Sri Lanka during the qualifying period of residence required by the Act. India's reaction to the Act was very adverse and Pandit Nehru in his correspondence with Prime Minister D. S. Senanayake in 1948 found the Citizenship Act unacceptable.

In fact the process of registration and investigation of applications became so slow and tedious that even by 1962 only 134,188 Indians had been granted citizenship under this Act. It was only in the 1950's that the aspect of "Statelessness" crept to this problem. From the very outset Sri Lanka's assumption, as enunciated at the highest levels, was that those Indians who had failed to qualify for Sri Lankan citizenship were unquestionably Indian nationals and the Indian government would regard them as such. The Government of India was clearly unwilling to accept this position. Although India had not passed a specific citizenship law until 1955 the Indian Constitution had made provision for acquisition of Indian nationality by overseas Indians under Article 5 of the Indian Constitution which stated categorically that only a person born in India, or one of whose parents was born in India or a person who had been ordinarily resident in India for over five years prior to the inauguration of the Indian Constitution would be regarded as an Indian citizen.

Under Article 8, persons of Indian origin, ordinarily resident outside India, would be regarded as Indian citizens only if they were registered as such after application to the Diplomatic Representative of India in the country where such persons resided.

However, behind the scene were some other serious reasons for these attitudes on the part of the two governments.

In Sri Lanka, apart from the question of unemployment, there were increasing demands, mainly by the members of the Kandan (hill country) community that the Indian workers were depriving them of their legitimate livelihood in the plantations. This was also frequently taken up in parliament. On the Indian side was the situation that the Indian estate workers mainly hailed from South India and, if repatriated, would eventually have to be resettled there. This was a problem which the centre in New Delhi could not unilaterally decide on without consulting the southern states, and centre-state relations in India have always been bedevilled by such problems. Another cogent reason, which in fact Pandit Nehru explained to Prime Minister SWRD Bandarnaike, was that there were over twelve million Indians overseas in countries such as Malaya, Burma and South Africa, and if India accepted the principle of repatriation, as advocated by Sri Lanka, the same concession would have to be extended to the Indian nationals in these countries.

In this climate of conflict and uncertainty the first realistic appraisal took place at the high level meeting on the Indo-Ceylon Agreement relating to persons of Indian origin in Ceylon attended by Prime Minister Sir John Kotelawala, Mr. Dudley Senanayake and Mr. SWRD Bandaranaike, Leader of the Opposition, among others which took place in New Delhi in 1954. For the first time at this meeting, illicit immigration between the two countries was taken up by the two Prime Ministers as part of this question. However, even this agreement lent itself to divergent interpretations. The Sri Lankan government continued to maintain that only two categories of Indian residents in Sri Lanka would emerge as a result of the agreement, nationals of Sri Lanka and nationals of India. The Indian government envisaged a third category of "Stateless persons" in addition to these two whose status would have to be further reviewed by the two governments. After further debate and disagreement between the two governments the Prime Minister of India, Mr. Lal Bahadur Shastri, and the Sri Lankan Prime Minister, Mrs. Sirimavo Bandaranaike, inspired by a mutual desire to explore every possibility of reaching an equitable compromise on this vexatious question of persons of Indian origin in Sri Lanka, finally held a historic meeting in New Delhi in October 1964. The agreement, concluded on October 30, 1964 between the Governments of India and Sri Lanka, provided that India would agree to accept, within a period of

15 years, as repatriates, 525,000 persons of Indian origin living in Sri Lanka with their natural increase, and that Sri Lanka would agree to grant citizenship to 300,000 persons with their natural increase. The objective of the agreements was to ensure that all stateless persons of Indian origin in Sri Lanka be enabled to become citizens of one country or the other.

The period of repatriation was phased over a seventeen-year period so that on the one hand, Sri Lanka would not be faced with a large exodus of plantation labour if the time frame was shorter, and on the other hand, India would not be faced with the problem of rehabilitating a large number of repatriates within a short period. Despite the sincere and intensive effort on the part of both governments to fulfil the terms of the agreement there was ultimately an excess in the number of applicants for Sri Lankan citizenship and a shortfall in the number who applied for Indian citizenship. Therefore in the final count, 94,000 persons were reckoned to be in this category, who would have to be deemed stateless. In a spirit of accommodation and in a desire to strengthen bilateral relations Sri Lanka generously accepted this additional commitment of 94,000 persons which meant that Sri Lanka's eventual intake was 469,000 persons. On the other hand, India gave an undertaking that it will grant Indian citizenship to all of the 506,000 persons who had applied for citizenship and repatriate them to India. This process is yet underway.

It may be of interest to briefly reflect on how these various changes affected the living conditions of these stateless persons of South Indian origin. As stated earlier, until the beginning of the 19th century, this category which consisted mainly of plantation workers did not encounter too many problems.

Mostly illiterate, they lead a life of comparative isolation in their rather frugal estate quarters, with the estates also providing minimum facilities for children's schooling, health care and other needs. However, they were content as their basic need of repatriating a part of their saving back to the rest of their families in South India and even periodic visits to their kith and kin were freely permitted. In later years, with increasing resistance and even some hostility to their continuing presence in the plantations by mainly the Kandyan Sinhala community which was status, undoubtedly made their lives less comfortable. This was the time when there was progressive 'Ceylonisation' not only of employment but also of trade and industry. This was officially described as a process "to ensure a higher percentage of participation by the nationals of the country in trade, commerce and industrial activities, as regards management, labour and finance."

However, by the 1960 and 1970's, when the Indo/Ceylon Agreements of 1964 and 1974 had more or less settled the 'Stateless' problem, the situation of the Indians in Sri Lanka, particularly of those who had since been conferred Sri Lankan citizenship, was completely normalised and they were treated not differently to those Sri Lankans who had acquired citizenship by descent.

A brief comment also on the political representation of the Indian community. The Ceylon Indian Congress (CIC) was founded way back in 1939 to protect the interests of the Indian estate workers in Sri Lanka.

Incidentally Pandit Nehru visited Sri Lanka in 1939 as a special emissary of the Indian National Congress and he was considered as one of the founders of the CIC. Perhaps due to the circumstances of its origin the CIC long retained marked signs of Indian influence.

The successful settlement of what might have been a continuing stateless problem between Sri Lanka and India was indeed a triumph for statesmanship at the highest level. After so many decades of difficult and often acrimonious debate over this question, an agreement was finally reached between the two governments at the highest level in a spirit of compromise that was indeed a good example of how the self-interests of two countries, large and small, were made secondary to the larger interests of maintaining and strengthening good relations between two neighbours who had, up to that time, not known any other political problem in the long history of their cordial relationship.

A careful perusal of the statute book of Sri Lanka reveals the total absence of provisions with regard to refugee protection. The laws governing immigration and emigration are silent on this subject.

Neither the Controller of the Immigration and Emigration (the Controller) nor any other official possesses guidelines or authority to determine refugee status, to provide protection to asylum applicants and refugees or to enforce the principle of non-refoulement. Only The Extradition Law No: 8 of 1977 marginally provides for this latter aspect by prohibiting the extradition of persons who may be persecuted on the basis of race, religion, nationality or political opinion. The final determination relating to non-extradition is to be made by the courts. Although Sri Lanka has a relatively satisfactory ratification record with regard to international human rights instruments, it has not ratified either the 1951 Convention or the 1967 Protocol, relating to the status of refugees.

As a member of the UN Sri Lanka is obliged to respect the protections guaranteed by the Universal Declaration of Human Rights (1948). However, Article 14 of the Universal Declaration merely recognises the right of individuals to "seek and to enjoy in other countries asylum from persecution". It does not delineate the obligation on the part of states to provide protection to refugees. The Convention against torture (1984) which was ratified by Sri Lanka in 1994 provides for the non-refoulement of persons to a country where the person would be in danger of being subjected to torture (Art 3). Although the parliament of Sri Lanka adopted enabling legislation to enforce the Convention, it does not contain provisions to enforce Article 3. In the absence of a legal framework of refugee protection, there appears to be an informal and ad hoc understanding between the Controller and the UNHCR to provide provisional protection to asylum seekers and those stranded.

The UNHCR as been informally "permitted" to take care of such persons exclusively at its expense and to make efforts towards their repatriation from Sri Lanka. However, those who seek asylum cannot regularise their stay in Sri

Lanka unless they can fulfil other legal recognised conditions for doing so. In the absence of grounds enabling them to do so, their stay in Sri Lanka, although protected by UNHCR, is technically illegal. Under the Immigrants and Emigrants Ordinance of 1948 (Cap. 2458 as amended) an alien (other than those aliens who are exempted by the law), aside from those possessing a valid passport, has to either obtain a visa or an endorsement by an authorised officer at the port of entry (Article 10,13 & 14). Where an airliner is obliged under ICA/IATA rules to take back passengers who are not admitted into the country, then such persons will be sent back, usually to the port of origin, without affording them an interview with the UNHCR at the airport.

If, on other hand, an airline is not obliged to take those who are not admitted to Sri Lanka, the controller permits the UNHCR to interview persons so stranded if they request protection. If not for this informal understanding between the Controller and the UNHCR, all those who are not admitted into the country and who are not accepted back by the airlines will be subjected to detention by the immigration authorities. Sometimes detention can be prolonged running into years unless UNHCR is informed of their plight and the need for protection.

Generally the UNHCR gets to know about persons needing protection from the airport immigration authorities, the detention centres at the request of the persons seeking protection or embassy staff and UNHCR officials who "discover" such persons at detention centres when checking the cases of others. The UNHCR states that the cooperation extended by the Controller in this regard is "excellent".

When the UNHCR takes over the persons seeking protection, UNHCR certificates are issued. They in effect operate as visas. All the needs of those under its protection have to be borne by the UNHCR. If for some reason a person receiving protection has a visa, and it has to be extended under prevailing laws, UNHCR has to obtain that extension as well, utilising its resources.

The UNHCR office in Colombo is able in some instances to make arrangements to resettle persons in its care in third countries through the embassies of those countries in Colombo. Example are Canada, Australia and Switzerland. Aside from that process, the UNHCR submits cases to other countries through the resettlement unit of the division of International Protection at UNHCR Headquarters.

However, the available number of settlement places tends to be few given the worldwide need. Those who are facing threats to physical safety, who are medically at risk, who are facing the danger of refoulement or are members of vulnerable groups receive priority in resettlement.

In the absence of a legal framework for the protection of refugees in Sri Lanka, provisional protection is afforded through informal and ad hoc arrangement between the Controller and the UNHCR. The latter has to bear the entire responsibility. This protection is extremely tenuous, as from a legal point of view those who receive UNHCR protection have no legal status in Sri Lanka. When compared with other countries in the subcontinent, such as India and Pakistan, the number seeking protection in Sri Lanka is very small. Yet, the need for a legal refuge protection regime is palpable from a human rights and humanitarian perspective. If not for UNHCR intervention those who seek asylum or are stranded in Sri Lanka will be an unknown group of humanity left to wither in detention facing an extremely uncertain future.

The irony is that India and Pakistan have received and continue to provide protection to thousands of asylum seekers, albeit without having legal provisions or process in place to determine refugee status and to provide for protection.

Given this situation, Sri Lanka should ideally

— ratify the international instruments for the protection of refugees;

— at the same time adopt a legal framework to authorise and provide guidelines to a competent authority (i.e., the Controller) to process asylum applications and to make determinations on refugee status in accordance with international standards;

— provide for a comprehensive protection framework including health care and schooling for young children;
— entrench the principle of non-refoulement in the legal system;
— provide necessary administrative infrastructure and facilitate coordination among various departments and ministries; and
— train relevant officials in how to handle refugee protection.

In the long run, of course, what is essential is the creation of a social and political environment, through policies and educational activities, which is sympathetic to and respects the needs of refugees.

The high intensity military for the retaking of the Jaffna Peninsula meant that the logistical systems that had been temporarily in place during the period of dual control for the transport and distribution of food and other supplies were initially disrupted. However, by June 1996, the government succeeded in effecting control over the entire Peninsula and security—transport, health, education and food distribution systems are improving in operation. Both the ports of KKS and Point Pedro are now functional. The implications of this change in the political and economic environment is that the government's obligation of providing relief and rehabilitation to the displaced has become easier and more practicable to fulfil.

Although precise information on numbers and the condition of the displaced in the Peninsula is difficult to come by on account of the prevailing tight censorship on news and movement of media personnel in the north, it can be presumed that as normalcy is restored the condition of the displaced will continue to improve.

The work of UNHCR along with the ICRS, MSF and other International NGOs working in the Northern Province has been considerably disrupted as a result of the conflict in recent months, and their services to the displaced have consequently been affected. UNHCR's activities in the fields, particularly after the liberation of Jaffna city by the military in February 1996, have been from Killinochchi but here too there have been restrictions on accounts of the delays in obtaining permission from the government, for high frequency radio transmitting facilities. Security considerations of the government have taken precedence over considerations of providing facilities to UNHCR and other external agencies which would have had the effect of relieving, to some extent, urgent needs of the displaced.

An important issue, new in the present phase of the conflict, but one of the major consequences in the past, especially in the period 1984 to 1991, is that of the possible "spillover" of the internally displaced to South India as refugees. Such movement in large numbers has potential destabilising effects on the bilateral relations between India and Sri Lanka. It has been the cause of friction in the past and can bring a new dimension to interstate relations in the future. According to official reports there apparently still remain in camps in South India about 50,000 refugees from Sri Lanka who went out with the outbreak of hostilities in June 1990. Another 50,000 or so are said to be out of the camps but yet residing in India. These are those who are not included in the repatriation which was conducted with some monitoring by UNHCR in the years 1992-1994. In these years the outflow was minimal owing to possibly three reasons: firstly the fact that UNHCR, a neutral party, was present in a practical way in overseeing the return and resettlement of returning refugees, in the overview of conditions at Welfare Centres and had initiated, in 'Uncleared area' the concept of the Open Relief Centres (ORCs); secondly, the fact that the Jaffna Peninsula which was under the virtual control of the LTTE constituted, at least for the Tamils internally displaced, a place of relative security; and thirdly, the fact that the then Tamil Nadu government was strongly discouraging the entry of more Sri Lankan refugees and had even threatened to close down the existing refugee camps.

Especially having regard to the important position that the DMK has in the present Indian cabinet and the well-known positive attitude of the present DMK government of Tamil Nadu to the LTTE in the past, the possibility of the

Tamil refugee question becoming a "casus belli" for straining Indo-Sri Lanka relations cannot be completely ruled out.

A careful perusal of the statute book of Sri Lanka reveals the total absence of provisions with regard to refugee protection. The laws governing immigration and emigration are silent on this subject. Neither the Controller of the Immigration and Emigration nor any other official possesses guidelines or authority to determine refugee status, to provide protection to asylum applicants and refugees or to enforce the principle of non-refoulement.

The strict controls imposed by the South Indian authorities on the intake of refugees may also deter their flight. The movement of refugees by boats to Tamil Nadu has remained a trickle with only a total of 200 reported as landing on the South Indian coast in the past fortnight. A spokesman for the Indian High Commission in Colombo said that although the Indian External Affairs Ministry had issued a brief statement noting the arrival of some refugees, he was not aware of any move by Delhi to raise the matter with the Sri Lankan government. According to some Indian newspapers and agency reports, the Tamil Nadu authorities are being very strict in their processing of applications for refugee status by the 200-odd civilians who have so far landed on the Rameṣwaram coastline.

The authorities were being strict in their investigation of refugee claims because of the need to prevent any infiltration by cadres of the LTTE, these reports indicated. Meanwhile, government officials in Vavuniya said that a further 64 trucks loaded with food and other relief supplies have moved north through Thandikulam. Details of the food, shelter and health needs of the refugees have been indicated and government and non-government relief agencies are now busy building up the relief operation required to cater to this new refugee problem. Government has denied permission to NGOs and other relief agencies, except ICRC, to set up relief camps at places close to Kilinochchi where thousands of civilians are arriving everyday following Operation Sathjaya.

3

Ethnic Violence

In South Asia, internal political, economic and social processes within countries are seen to affect the nature of relationship at both bilateral and regional levels. Therefore, ethnic conflicts within the countries of Asia generate internal pulls and pressures which affect interstate relations within the region.

The ethnic conflict in Sri Lanka has serious implications for India owing to the presence of Tamil multitudes in Tamil Nadu who sympathise with their brethren in Sri Lanka. India's perception of threat to its security in the Indian Ocean region is largely governed by political and military developments in Sri Lanka.

To trace back the Indian interests in Sri Lanka, the issue of expatriate Tamils had assumed importance for India even in pre-independence period. These Tamils of Indian origin who were employed in the tea and rubber plantations under the British colonial rule, have distinct socio-economic problems different from those of the Sri Lankan Tamils. The Indian Tamil political leadership has not been involved in the mainstream of Tamil politics in Sri Lanka and it does not support the cause of Tamil separatism. Hence, it has entered into some sort of alliance with the successive governments in order to secure the interests of the Indian Tamils. In this context, the issue of status and citizenship rights of Indian Tamils which arose in the post-independence period, was taken up by India who amicably settled the issue with the Sri Lankan government in later years.

Regarding the Sri Lankan Tamils who had raised the call for a separate state, as early as in 1976, the Indian government had remained aloof from such political development in Sri Lanka. Subsequently, with growing discrimination against Tamils and serious ethnic riots in 1983, India voiced its concern for the safety and security of the Tamils in Sri Lanka. So, when the riots broke out between the Tamil and Sinhalese communities in July, 1983, India found itself in a delicate situation. It felt that it had some moral responsibility in the safety and security of the Tamils in Sri Lanka. Moreover, in ensuring their safety, India had to impress upon interfering in the island's internal affairs.

However, in India, the ethnic riots of Sri Lanka had its immediate impact in Tamil Nadu where the government and opposition parties combinedly put pressure on the central government in New Delhi to intervene in Sri Lanka on behalf of the Tamils there. Hence, it is important to note that the Tamil Nadu parties have a long history of support for various causes espoused by the Tamils of Sri Lanka. In this context, they have supported the Tamil demands on language, federalism and even for the establishment of a separate state of Eelam in the Tamil-populated northern and eastern parts of Sri Lanka, in accordance with the political demand of the Tamil United Liberation Front (TULF) of Sri Lanka since 1976.

The Sri Lankan state faces a crisis of credibility, with its control over its whole northern territory—both the mainland north and the densely populated Jaffna Peninsula, which it took from the LTTE in 1995—in grave jeopardy. There have been a few indications recently of a stiffening of spine in the Sri Lanka Army, which has a major force advantage over the LTTE in the Peninsula.

However, it is handicapped by the inadequacy of air support and the inability of the Navy to control the seas around the Peninsula. The question is whether the Army in this decisive and crucial stage can be competently generalised, stay together as a fighting formation, mount an active defence, prevent the LTTE from advancing to place

Palaly within, say, a devastating 20 km gun range, and raise troop morale before counter-attacking to thwart the adversary's plans.

The key human question, of course, is how, in the event of major fighting in a densely populated region, civilian casualties will be avoided and a major influx of Sri Lankan Tamil refugees to Tamil Nadu in India prevented. The spectre that faces the small island nation, then, is the entrapment of over 25,000 troops in the Peninsula, with no way of escape by land, air or sea, and humiliating surrender by the Sri Lankan state to an extremist organisation that is determined to break up Sri Lanka in the name of 'national liberation'. Entrapment, surrender and an unprecedented political debacle for the Sri Lankan state may be the worst case scenario, but there is nothing inevitable about this.

The Sri Lankan government has maintained that, despite serious setbacks, the fight in the north is by no means over and that it is not considering evacuation of its troops from the Peninsula. On the other side, the LTTE has stepped up psychological pressure by announcing that it is "prepared to declare a temporary ceasefire... to facilitate the beleaguered government troops to be evacuated safely from the Jaffna Peninsula and warning that the Sri Lankan government will bear total responsibility for the disastrous consequences of heavy military casualties if it rejects our proposal for de-escalation and continues the war effort."

Along with the threat, it has held out a carrot: "A positive response, we are confident, will create cordial conditions for a permanent ceasefire, peace talks and negotiated political settlement for the Tamil national question." It does not require much political astuteness to realise that accepting the LTTE's offer of a ceasefire to "facilitate" abandonment of the Jaffna Peninsula is likely to prove suicidal for the Chandrika Kumaratunga government, which therefore has speedily rejected the proposal. In order to appreciate what is at stake, it is necessary to step back and view objectively what this government has attempted to accomplish, politically, over the past half decade or more.

If the ethnic conflict can be recognised as Sri Lanka's principal national question, then much of its independent history can be described as a story of two traps—the 'Sinhala Only' trap and, in reaction to and retaliation against this, the 'Eelam' trap. Both traps represent chauvinist or extremist responses to serious issues of ethnicity, democracy, socio-economic and political development, and justice. Cumulative entrapment in these two causes and modes of socio-political existence has taken an appalling toll of human life, entitlements, and welfare. To recognise this is in no way to take away from Sri Lanka's otherwise impressive and indeed enviable human development and social record, especially in comparison with its South Asian neighbours. The cruelty and hopelessness of double entrapment of a whole country and people can be expressed in another formulation whose truth has become increasingly obvious over the past decade or more.

The struggle for 'Tamil Eelam', led uncompromisingly and with Pol Potist concern for human life and well-being by V. Prabhakaran's LTTE, is a pipe-dream. For one thing, it will not be tolerated geopolitically—it can be seen to be profoundly inimical to India's national and democratic interests. On the other hand, the attempt to suppress the armed struggle for 'Eelam' by military force is incapable of success even in the medium term. Against such an unrelenting background, the devolution-along-federal-lines component of the constitutional package that the Kumaratunga administration has tried to put in place as an enduring solution to the ethnic conflict must, from an enlightened Sri Lankan Tamil standpoint, be recognised as the best on offer for over half a century.

It represents a genuine break with Sinhala-Buddhist chauvinism that landed the island state in the 'Sinhala Only' trap. It builds on the conceptual advance made in the failed Bandaranaike-Chelvanayakam Pact of the late 1950s and, more importantly, on the paradigm shift brought by the Indo-Sri Lanka Agreement of 1987, which could not achieve its objective. President Kumaratunga's constitutional and political package for the Tamils can be improved upon, but it has the potential to overcome the burden of a benighted history if it is given a fair chance. Unfortunately, non-cooperation and obstruction by the main opposition party, the United National Party, combining with unrelenting extremism by the LTTE have denied it that chance.

The Sri Lankan government has, legitimately and un-surprisingly, sought India's material assistance to protect the island state's unity, sovereignty and territorial integrity. But thus far, the LTTE under Prabhakaran has shown absolutely no inclination to talk seriously about, let alone accept, any solution short of 'Tamil Eelam'.

The organisation, which was banned as a terrorist entity in India following its assassination of Rajiv Gandhi under orders from Prabhakaran who is wanted in India as accused No. 1 in the assassination case, has shown a great deal of resourcefulness in using ceasefires, lulls and swings in the military balance to raise false hopes, generate illusions and take governments for a ride.

The worsening of the situation in Sri Lanka has confronted India with a strategic dilemma. Past experience does not provide adequate guidance to meet the challenge. It was relatively easy for External Affairs Minister Jaswant Singh to declare in parliament that the present government does not propose to "go down the IPKF road". That is as it should be and Jaswant Singh went on to outline a sound-enough framework for India's Sri Lanka policy: "The Government of India will be guided by its continued commitment to a negotiated peaceful resolution of the conflict, within the framework of Sri Lanka's unity and territorial integrity; a united Sri Lanka where all communities can realise their aspirations," and "it is India's hope that peace will soon return to Sri Lanka, a country which is a close and friendly neighbour."

However, under pressure from the Tamil Nadu political parties within the ruling National Democratic Alliance, Prime Minister Atal Behari Vajpayee has back-tracked from the implications of his External Affairs Minister's statement and ruled out, not just military intervention but any supply or sale of arms to the Sri Lankan government regardless of the situation. However, with Chief Minister Karunanidhi graciously allowing him a "free hand", the Prime Minister has announced that "humanitarian assistance" may be provided if a request comes from the Sri Lankan government. If the military and political situation deteriorates further in Sri Lanka, there will be no soft options left for India. There will be the real prospect of the involvement of external forces and this will clearly be to the detriment of non-aligned and democratic India's interests in the region. It will be pointless for the Indian government to wake up to the implications of the crisis at that stage and come up with a 'hands-on', 'proactive' policy.

The assumption of a mediatory role by India in the Sri Lankan ethnic conflict started as the initiative was taken up with the visit of the then External Affairs Minister, P. V. Narasimha Rao, to obtain first-hand information about the July ethnic riots. On his return, the Minister informed the then Indian Prime Minister, Mrs. Gandhi, about the serious situation in Sri Lanka and the failure of the Sri Lankan government to bring the ethnic violence under control. He also confirmed media reports that the Sri Lankan government had sought military assistance from the United States, Britain, Pakistan, and Bangladesh to meet the crisis. In response, the Indian Prime Minister, while hoping for an early restoration of normalcy, candidly expressed disapproval of the Lankan move in seeking foreign assistance professedly to meet a non-existent Indian intervention. Later, in a statement to the Indian parliament on 5 August 1983, Mrs. Gandhi clarified that India did not pose any threat to Sri Lanka and it had no desire to interfere in its internal affairs. But she warned that any external involvement would complicate matters for both the countries. Further, she expressed India's wish for unity and integrity of Sri Lanka but emphasised that, in dealing with developments in Sri Lanka, India was directly concerned and Sri Lanka could not "treat India as just any country."

So, in response to Mrs. Gandhi's stand on the Tamil issue in Sri Lanka, the Sri Lankan President Jayewardene took swift diplomatic steps by sending his brother H. W. Jayewardene as his personal emissary to India. In his message, Jayewardene demanded that the Indian government should stop the Tamil militant groups based in Tamil Nadu from operating against Sri Lanka. The visiting emissary also conveyed to the Indian Prime Minister, Mrs. Gandhi, that Sri Lanka was ready for talks with Tamil leaders and would accept India's offer of good offices. Taking note of the good intentions of the Jayewardene government, Mrs. Gandhi told parliament that India was opposed to a separate state for Tamils in Sri Lanka. She also informed the House that President Jayewardene had expressed willingness to make major concession to the TULF if it renounced its separatist demands.

As a result, the TULF leader, Appapillai Amritalingam met Mrs. Gandhi on August 14. Initially, though he refused to renounced the demand for a separate homeland for the Tamils, he expressed readiness after a second meeting with her to negotiate with the Sri Lankan government without preconditions and to consider any reasonable offer that Sri Lanka was prepared to make to meet the Tamil demands. After having obtained the agreement of both sides for a dialogue, the Indian government went ahead to prepare the ground for a negotiated settlement to the ethnic conflict. So, Mrs. Gandhi appointed G. Parthasarathy as her special envoy who was entrusted to play the mediatory role in bringing about a solution to the ethnic conflict. In his shuttle diplomacy, Parthasarathy undertook four separate missions to Colombo to discuss possible solutions to the island's ethnic problem. The discussions centred around the devolution of power and the unit of devolution in Tamil areas. He held talks with President Jayewardene, as well as with political parties, religious organisations and interest groups in Sri Lanka. Consequently, the Sri Lankan government convened an All-Party Conference (APC) in which all the recognised political parties participated including the TULF and several Sinhala Buddhist religious and non-political organisations.

So, the substantive issue before the APC was the devolution of power to local units and the Parthasarathy formula as "Annexure C" which was to serve as the basis of discussion. Under this conceptual paper, "Annexure C", the regional councils would replace the existing District Development Councils (DDCs) with a fair degree of autonomy. This proposal faced a strong opposition from the Sinhalese Buddhists who were in no mood to concede anything beyond the DDCs. The Buddhists saw the concept of regional councils as India-inspired and strongly opposed it. Though it was jointly drawn by India and Sri Lanka, the President did not appear to take either credit or responsibility for his part in reaching an agreement on the above plan. Moreover, he made insufficient efforts to press for its acceptance by the Sinhala Buddhist groups. So, the APC ended in failure and was dissolved in December 1984. One of the more fruitful results of the APC of 1984 was the decision regarding the granting of citizenship to Indian plantation workers who were 'stateless' persons in Sri Lanka. Once this recommendation was accepted in principle, the government enacted necessary legislation granting citizenship to stateless persons in the subsequent years.

After the failure of the APC, the Indo-Sri Lankan relations deteriorated as the Sinhalese hard-liners were critical of India. Quoting the media reports which cited the presence of training camps and facilities for Tamil militants in Tamil Nadu, some Sinhalese leaders charged India with harbouring Tamil terrorists from Sri Lanka. Prime Minister R. Premadasa's statement in June 1984 that the Tamil militants could not attack Sri Lanka without New Delhi's complicity caused an uproar in India. The Sri Lankan National Security Minister, Lalith Athulath-mudali's visit to Delhi in April and President Jayewardene's meetings with Mrs. Gandhi in June and July did not pave the way for an improvement in bilateral relations. Unfortunately, in his statement at a press conference in India, President Jayewardene gave a mild jolt to Indo-Sri Lankan relations by saying that the Tamil problem is an internal matter of Sri Lanka and hostile propaganda emanating from Indian territory was alienating public option in Sri Lanka. Hence, this atmosphere of mutual fear and suspicion continued for some time till new moves were taken by both sides.

In the meantime, the 'Tamil Nadu' factor considerably influenced the formulation of the Indian foreign policy towards Sri Lanka. The arrival of thousands of Tamil refugees in Tamil Nadu with their tales of atrocities by the Sri Lankan army against the island's Tamil population aroused passions in Tamil Nadu.

The two major political parties in Tamil Nadu sufficiently politicised the Sri Lankan issue and exerted pressure on the central government to deal more firmly with Sri Lanka including direct military intervention, if necessary. The central government, however, rejected the Tamil demand for military action against Sri Lanka but refrained from dislodging the Tamil militants from Tamil Nadu. The militants were allowed to build up communication facilities and move freely between India and Sri Lanka. It is, however, wrong to assume that India's Sri Lanka policy during this period was solely guided by Tamil Nadu politics. Though New Delhi voiced concern for Sri Lanka and offered relief to refugees from the island, a distinction was made between the Indian perspective and the Tamil perspective of the situation in Sri Lanka. The Indian perspective was concerned with the security interests of India considering the geopolitical fallout of the ethnic crisis and the resultant foreign involvement in Sri Lanka. On the other hand, the Tamil perspective saw the Sri Lankan crisis in strictly ethnic terms and demanded a more direct involvement to the extent of intervention by India. As would be seen, the distinction between these two perspectives got eroded with the worsening of ethnic situation on the island.

Gradually, with Rajiv Gandhi replacing his mother as India's Prime Minister upon her assassination, Indo-Sri Lanka relations showed definite signs of improvement. The Sri Lankan diplomats and senior cabinet ministers who met Rajiv Gandhi in the early months of his Prime Ministership, came back positively encouraged, if not enthused. A meeting between Rajiv Gandhi and the Sri Lankan Minister of National Security, Mr. Lalith Athulathmudali, in February 1985 was described as very constructive. The Indian government took two important steps that seemed to convince Sri Lanka of Rajiv's genuine interest and sincerity of purpose in solving the ethnic problem. First, the Foreign Secretary, Mr. Romesh Bhandari, was appointed in the place of G. Parthasarathy as the Prime Minister's special envoy dealing with the Sri Lankan problem. As Parthasarathy had not gained the confidence of Sri Lanka, this was a right move in the proper direction. A second and more important step taken by the Rajiv government was to curb Tamil militant activity in India. Indira Gandhi's reluctance to discourage the Tamil militants had been a major irritant in Indo-Sri Lankan relations. Hence, the curbing of the Tamil separatist activity was an important prerequisite to convince Sri Lanka of India's sincerity in serving as an honest broker. In this direction, Rajiv Gandhi took some prompt action against the Tamil militants and it was appreciated in Sri Lanka.

Subsequently, the visits of Romesh Bhandari to Colombo succeeded in obtaining a new peace package from Jayawardene in April 1985 that included a general amnesty for Tamil rebels, release of detainees, confinement of security forces to barracks and resumption of negotiation to settle the Tamil issue. A summit meeting was also arranged between Rajiv Gandhi and Jayewardene. It took place in June and produced some positive results. India promised to take more effective steps to curb Tamil militant activities on its soil and the flow of arms from India to Sri Lanka, while Sri Lanka agreed to minimise the atrocities in the Tamil areas. An important outcome of this meeting was the acceptance by the two leaders that there was no alternative to a political solution and so, the military onslaught to quell Tamil militancy needed to be abandoned. It was also recognised that no final solution to the ethnic conflict could emerge without the agreement of TULF and other militant groups.

On the basis of talks with India, the Sri Lankan government took the initiative to start a fresh round of negotiations to seek a solution to the ethnic problem. Hence, a new round of talks began in the Bhutanese capital, Thimpu between the Sri Lankan government and most Tamil militant groups under Indian supervision. The

Thimpu talks did not make any headway, with no fresh proposal from the Sri Lankan government as the terms offered were not much different from those offered at the APC in 1984. The Tamils, on the other hand, showed their intransigence by their demand for the right of self-determination. Though the talks failed to resolve the ethnic conflict, yet it showed the constructive role played by India in bringing together two parties with irreconcilable views for a political dialogue. In this context, the Indian policy was one of persuasion by creating goodwill.

Gradually, the worsening ethnic conflict in Sri Lanka worried India who made another bid to find a political solution. So, an Indian delegation headed by the Minister for Internal Security, P. Chidambaram, visited Sri Lanka and succeeded in committing the Sri Lankan government to the principle of Provincial Council as the basic unit of devolution. The provincial structure envisaged in this proposal took on the aspects of states of the Indian Union with a Governor and Provincial Council but with powers that fell short of those in India. These proposals were discussed in the government-convened Political Party Conference (PPC) in which the political parties and the TULF participated. Though there was some progress in the deliberations for a compromise between the demands of the Tamil separatist groups and the Sri Lankan government, yet there was no consensus on the basic Tamil issue. Since the TULF and some of the Tamil separatist groups continued to press for the creation of a single regional unit encompassing the northern and eastern provinces as a Tamil ethno-region, this was unacceptable to the Sri Lankan government as it was firmly opposed to the idea of a single Tamil linguistic unit.

So, the outright rejection of the Colombo proposals very much annoyed the Indian government which felt that the Tamil militants were approaching the matter of political solution with a wholly negative attitude and with no concrete suggestions of their own. So, it tried to put pressure on the militant groups based in Tamil Nadu through the state negotiation process. Later, on the eve of the SAARC Summit in Bangalore, a meeting was held between Rajiv Gandhi and Jayewardene to discus the modalities for a solution to the Tamil problem. Moreover, the LTTE supremo Prabhakaran was flown to Bangalore at the instance of the Tamil Nadu Chief Minister who expressed confidence that he could secure Prabhakaran's agreement to the provincial council proposal if Jayewardene offered more concessions. In response, the Sri Lankan President offered to trifurcate the existing Eastern province into a Tamil-majority Batticaloa Province, a Sinhalese-majority Trincomalee province and a Muslim-majority Amparai province with each having its own Provincial council. Mr. Prabhakaran was offered the Chief Ministership of Jaffna in the latest proposal. The Indian response was favourable to this set of proposals. But all Tamil groups rejected it as there was no offer to merge any part of the Tamil-speaking area in the Eastern Province with the Northern Province.

However, in the aftermath of the SAARC Summit, the Indian mediation efforts continued with the External Affairs Minister, Natwar Singh, and Chidambaram. The major objective was to seek a middle ground between Tamil insistence on the merger of the Northern and Eastern provinces and the Sinhalese opposition to it. This was achieved in the consensus that emerged between Sri Lanka and India and it came to be known as the "December 19" proposals. According to it:

> The proposals essentially involve formation of a new Eastern Province by excising Sinhalese majority areas (Amparai Electoral District) from the existing Eastern Province and creation of two Tamil Provincial Councils in the Northern and the reconstituted Eastern Province. The two Councils would have institutional linkages for coordination between the two so as to make them acceptable to all concerned.

Moreover, these proposals provided for some sort of institutional linkage between the Northern and Eastern Provinces through the establishment of a common university, a common planning commission, an inter-ministerial committee to coordinate functions and a national lands commission. Although the Sri Lankan President supported the above proposals, yet the government expressed reservations and was unprepared to implement it. As a result, India could not proceed with its mediatory efforts on the basis of the above proposals.

But the ethnic crisis in Sri Lanka entered a new phase when the LTTE started carrying out its plans to take over the civil administration in the north which was under military control. This provoked the government to impose an economic blockade on the Jaffna Peninsula in January, 1987. Simultaneously, the government stepped up military action both in the north and the east against the Tamil guerillas. So, the military offensive and the embargo on the supplies of fuel and other essentials to the north caused scarcity and hardship to the civilian population in the Jaffna Peninsula.

Gradually, the worsening situation in Sri Lanka compelled India to express its concern for the sufferings of the Tamils in Jaffna. Indian Prime Minister Rajiv Gandhi sent Dinesh Singh as his personal emissary on 13 March 1987 to deliver a message to President Jayewardene. In his message, Prime Minister Rajiv Gandhi said that India was suspending its good offices and demanded that Colombo lift the economic blockade of Jaffna and affirm its commitment to the "December 19" proposals. If these steps were not taken and the military option was continued, Mr. Gandhi had earlier warned that with prolonged fighting, the situation might escalate. Though there was a positive response to the Indian proposals, yet the Sri Lankan government carried out its military campaign against the Tamils. With both the LTTE and Sri Lankan government ignoring the Indian persuasion to stop fighting, the situation further deteriorated in Sri Lanka. India expressed serious concern at the continued aerial bombing of Jaffna. But President Jayewardene was determined to pursue the campaign against the Tamil guerillas as he said; "We have decided to fight them and that will go on until they win or we win."

The primary aim of this military operation was to secure Vadamarachchy, the north-eastern corner of the Jaffna

Peninsula. But the government, taking note of India's concern, tried to justify its action against the guerillas as the Minister of National Security said, "We will prove to them they cannot possibly achieve their aims by violence and, by doing so, hope that they will see the wisdom of political settlements."

In the meantime, the response in Tamil Nadu was instant. The Chief Minister of the state condemned the attacks on Jaffna as inhuman, uncivilised and serious violation of fundamental human rights. He urged Prime Minister Rajiv Gandhi to prevail upon Colombo to suspend the offensive. Moreover, the Tamil Nadu government announced a monetary grant of 3.2 million US dollars for the Tamil militants in Sri Lanka to be used for their food, clothing and medicine. Under these circumstances, the Vadamarachchy Operation came to a halt on 31 May with heavy civilian casualties in Jaffna and the entire Vadamarachchy area come under the control of the Sri Lankan army.

The Indian government, on its part, announced that it was sending shipments of food and petroleum to Jaffna which it claimed was facing a serious shortage of these items though a blockade by the Sri Lankan forces. So, on 3 June, India sent relief supplies for the people of Jaffna in a flotilla of nineteen fishing boats flying the Red Cross flag. The Sri Lankan government rejected the supplies and blocked the Indian flotilla's entry into Lankan territorial waters. Condemning Colombo's act, India once again warned that it would not remain an indifferent spectator to the plight of the Tamils in Jaffna.

In a drastic move, on 4 June, five Indian Air Force planes, escorted by Mirage 2000 fighter jets entered Sri Lanka's air space and dropped twenty-five tons of relief supplies in and around Jaffna. Sri Lanka condemned this Indian action as gross violation of its independence and an unwarranted assault on its sovereignty and territorial integrity. However, gradually, it softened its stand by lifting the six-month embargo on Jaffna and ceasing military operation. Finally, with the conclusion of the Indo-Lankan Accord, it normalised its relations with India.

Following renewed diplomatic activity between India and Sri Lanka in the aftermath of the Indian air-dropping of supplies on northern Sri Lanka, an agreement was signed by Rajiv Gandhi and Jayewardene on 29 July, 1987 in Colombo to establish peace and normalcy in Sri Lanka for the resolution of the ethnic conflict. The agreement, commonly referred as Indo-Sri Lankan Accord, granted a substantial and powerful role to India in the process of settling the ethnic conflict in the island.

The agreement provided for the immediate cessation of hostilities with surrender of arms by the Tamil militants and withdrawal of the Sri Lankan army to its barracks within a specific timeframe. Further, it provided for the recognition of a single administrative unit and the setting up of a single provincial council covering both Northern and Eastern Provinces. There was also a provision for a referendum to be held before December 1986 in the Eastern Province to decide whether it should remain merged with the Northern Province as a single unit. Also, according to the agreement, elections were to be held before December 1987 to the Northern and Eastern Provincial Council under Indian observation.

Moreover, under the Indo-Lankan Accord, India got obliged to provide military assistance as and when requested by the Sri Lankan government for the implementation of the agreement. In this matter, it provided for the presence of an Indian peace-keeping military contingent to guarantee and enforce cessation of hostilities if so required. Subsequent to the conclusion of the agreement, there was an exchange of letters between President Jayewardene and Prime Minister Rajiv Gandhi on matters of concern to India. Hence, both parties agreed to reach an early understanding on the employment of foreign military and intelligence personnel with a view to ensuring that such presence would not prejudice Indo-Lanka relations. Sri Lanka undertook not to make Trincomalee or any other port available for military use to any country in a manner prejudicial to India's security interests and ensure that foreign broadcasting facilities on its soil serve only public and not any military or intelligence purposes. In return, India agreed to deport all Sri Lankan citizens engaged in separatist or guerilla activities from the Indian soil and also to provide military training facilities and military supplies for Sri Lankan security forces.

The signing of the Accord came as a surprise to the public an was greeted with mixed feelings in India and Sri Lanka. Though the Indian government succeeded in bringing various Tamil groups around to accept the agreement, yet the LTTE leader Prabhakaran complained that there were several shortcomings in the Accord and the Tigers would not accept it. Subsequently, in the process of implementation of the accord, the Tigers flouted the agreement on the slightest pretext. It made a very poor surrender of arms to the Indian Peace-Keeping Force (IPKF), killed members of rival Tamil groups and deliberately buried the proposed Interim Administrative Council (IAC) for the Northern and Eastern Provinces in which India and Sri Lanka were willing to give the LTTE maximum representation. Finally, by declaring war against the IPKF, it gave a new dimension to India's role in the Sri Lankan crisis.

On the other hand, from the Sinhalese point of view, the accord had little impact on the masses. Though the international response to the Indo-Lanka Accord was quite positive, yet within Sri Lanka, it faced serious criticism and protests. The announcement of the Accord was met with violent protest marches in Colombo organised by the militant Buddhist sections. Already the anti-government sentiments had reached its peak with the re-emergence of the JVP or People's Liberation Front in the south. In the wake of the Indo-Lankan accord, it sought to mobilise "anti-Tamil feelings and anti-Indian sentiments to build support wherever it could." But with the introduction of curfew throughout the country, the government adopted some ruthless measures to suppress the JVP uprising which took the form of a civil war in the south. With the IPKF fighting the Tamil Tigers, the Sri Lankan government could use all its military muscle to bring the situation in the south under its control in late 1989. However, it became evident that the

JVP had grown to be a serious threat to the Jayewardene government. In this light, the Indo-Sri Lankan Accord had serious military and political implications for Sri Lanka. From the economic point of view, the expenditure in conducting the war against the guerillas had reached serious proportions which severely curtailed the development programmes of the government. So, this economic fallout had far-reaching political consequences in terms of left-oriented JVP uprising and the government found some economic relief with India taking over the responsibility of fighting the Tamil separatists. Moreover, as the aid by foreign countries and international organisations had been given contingent to a political settlement of the ethnic issue, there was a strong economic compulsion behind the conclusion of the Indo-Lankan Accord. Above all, the internal situation in Sri Lanka had deteriorated to such an extent that President Jayewardene found the Indo-Lankan Accord as the only alternative to his regime's stability.

From the above analysis, it can be assessed that the Indo-Lankan Accord was a positive development in the bilateral relations which guaranteed the security and stability of Sri Lanka. But as the Indian government underwrote and guaranteed the resolutions in the implementation of the accord, it got totally entrenched in the Sri Lankan crisis, because neither the Tamil separatist nor any other Tamil political organisation became a party to the accord. India had to play the role of a guarantor and peace-keeper on behalf of the Tamils. For Sri Lanka, the accord was the only viable alternative in the face of serious internal threats to its security. Moreover, it wanted India to do the job which it was unable to meet. As the National Security Minister, Lalith Athulathmudali, observed, "While we are sad about the involvement of India in our ethnic issue and are disappointed over it, what was important was how we extricate ourselves from the involvement." India would get tied up in the solution to the problem after bilateral accord.

On India's part, the Indo-Sri Lankan Accord defining the major framework for the resolution of the ethnic conflict had serious implications, because in India's view, "the internal conflicts within the region are a security concern for the Indian state, and all efforts would be made to arrive at accords, wherever there are threats to regional stability." In this context, the Indo-Sri Lankan Accord was a positive development for India, as it assured an active and responsible Indian role in the Sri Lankan affairs.

Regarding the nature and degree of the Indian involvement in Sri Lanka, the IPKF seriously got on to the job of ensuring peace and security in the Tamil-dominated areas of the north and the east. It stated relief work by supplying the essential commodities and medicines to the people, repaired roads and restored electric power. But the IPKF in its military role, encountered difficulties in implementing the provisions of the accord as there was no cooperation from the Tamil groups. For the cessation of hostilities, the Tamil militants were to surrender arms to the Sri Lankan government under Indian observation and the Indian peace-keeping contingent was to enforce the cessation of hostilities. But in the implementation of such provisions and others, the accord from its beginning, ran into several major problems. First and foremost, with a token surrender of arms by the Tamil militants, the Indian troops could not disarm the LTTE within a reasonable period of time. The Tigers, on their part, showed little intention of complying with the accord and decided to continue their war for a separate state. They sought to unleash a renewed wave of violence against Sinhalese civilians and the Sri Lankan army in the north and the east of Sri Lanka. Initially, they did not fight the IPKF as the latter enjoyed the confidence and support of the Tamil masses. Gradually, with the complexities of peace-keeping, the IPKF started its military campaigns against the Tamil guerillas who had attacked other Tamil groups supporting the Indo-Lankan Accord. The Indian armed contingents launched a military operation to drive away the Tamil guerillas from their hide-outs. Hence, most of the guerillas from north and east moved to the Jaffna Peninsula where it had dug into very planned defences. So, the IPKF launched "Operation Pawan" in the Jaffna Peninsula on October 10, 1987 which lasted about fifteen days before the IPKF could flush out the militants and capture the Jaffna town. The LTTE put up stiff resistance with both sides suffering heavy casualties. The civilian population in Jaffna had to undergo certain hardship in the wake of these military operations.

The Indian involvement in military terms was very limited as the IPKF was fighting under certain constraints. It was under instructions to inflict minimum damage to civilian lives and property. Another major problem was the IPKF's unfamiliarity with the LTTE's mode of fighting against its enemy. As an urban guerrilla force, the Tigers easily merged with the local population after attacking the IPKF soldiers behind the compound walls of houses or from inside the houses. So, the Indian troops carried out cordon and search operations in houses and it caused certain hardships to the civilians. Gradually, with the growing intensity of the military operations, the civilians became alienated from the IPKF and shifted their allegiance back to the Tamil militants. Therefore, the hostility of the local population was a serious impediment to this counter-insurgency operation.

Generally after the capture of the Jaffna Peninsula, the IPKF launched "Operation Trishul" and "Operation Viraat" between April and June 1988, spreading across the entire Northern Province from Mannar to Mullaitivu and from Elephant Pass to Vavuniya. The soldiers "drove out the LTTE militants from the population centres and had them bottled up in the scrub jungles of Vavuniya and the thick tropical forest of Mullaitivu on the eastern seaboard." In the meantime, the continuous fighting in the north brought immense hardships to the civilian population. So, there was a complete transformation in the attitude of the Tamils towards the IPKF with the image that "the Indians had changed from the garlanded heroes of the hour to the hated tormentors of the Tamil people, they had come to resume, as they too swept through Jaffna Peninsula in military operations against the Tigers".

From the Indian side, there was some ambivalence in the politico-military strategy as the Indian government lacked a well-defined and consistent policy towards the Sri Lankan crisis. India had not conceived of a situation where its armed forces intended for peace-keeping, would be drawn in to a protracted armed conflict with the LTTE. Moreover, the IPKF was severely constrained by confused signals from the political centre in Delhi which wanted that room should be kept open for the LTTE to join the democratic process. In this light, the cessation of hostilities between the armed guerillas and the IPKF and the former's willingness to participate in the political process became "imperative with over-riding questions".

As the first anniversary of the Indo-Lanka accord drew near, the Indian government sought for some sort of negotiations regarding the elections to the provincial councils, because at home, the opposition parties in Indian severely criticised the government's policy of military engagement in Sri Lanka which brought rising casualty figures among the India troops and escalating economic costs of the military involvement. But the government justified the IPKF presence in Sri Lanka as the fulfilment of the provisions in the Indo-Lankan accord. Hence, it initiated a political process for the holding of elections to the provincial councils in the north and the east of the island. President Jayewardene further accelerated it by announcing the merger of the two Tamil provinces to form a newly designated North-Eastern Province. This was an improvement on the Indo-Lankan Accord which had provided for the merger of the two provinces only after they had elected their councils.

So, with the announcement of elections to the North Eastern Provincial Council, the Indian government followed a two-pronged policy of simultaneous military pressure and political dialogue to bring the LTTE under submission. Meanwhile, the unacceptable high rate of casualties created some rumblings within the Indian army command which felt that either there should be a full diplomatic initiative or the IPKF should be given a free hand to take on the LTTE. There was also a general feeling in India that it was a war by proxy and the government should order a unilateral ceasefire and bring talks with the LTTE. But after weighing his options, Rajiv Gandhi decided in favour of vigorous military operations against the LTTE in the wake of provincial council elections. Therefore, the dual approach of talks alongside military pressure gave way to a coercive policy. But it was not surprising; because India's options were limited in the sense that it could either withdraw the IPKF pleading that it could not implement the Indo-Lanka accord or it could enforce the accord by destroying the LTTE. The first option would have meant the loss of India's credibility internationally and so, the second option was chosen. However, it offered certain concessions to the Tamils in the hope of building confidence among them.

In October 1988, elections were held to the North-Eastern Provincial Council as provided in the accord. Beforehand, the IPKF carried out some military operations in the north and the east to perempt any sabotage of the election process. Hence, under the IPKF supervision, elections were held without the participation of the LTTE. The EPRLF and its ally, the ENDLF, won the majority of seats in the newly constituted provincial council and the EPRLF leader, A. Varadaraja Perumal, became the Chief Minister. Though the election was formal in nature, yet the IPKF did a commendable job by initiating the political process in the north and the east, as according to one of the IPKF's top-most commanding officers, the successful elections demonstrated the faith and confidence of the majority of Tamils in the Indo-Lankan accord and their intrinsic desire for peace and democracy.

In the meantime, there was a growing JVP menace in the south of Sri Lanka with widespread violence, killings and terror. The JVP in its ultra-nationalist stand had created an anti-India propaganda in Sri Lanka by using the accord as a symbol of Sinhalese humiliation and hence it tried to "mobilise ethnic fears, prejudices and dark jealousies." The JVP had posed a serious problem to the continuance of President Jayewardene who finally announced his decision to retire from politics. Subsequently, during the presidential election of December 1988, the two main contenders, Prime Minister Ranasinghe Premadasa and the opposition SLFP leader, Sirimavo Bandaranaike, were pledged to send the IPKF back. Both opposed to Indo-Lankan accord in substance, but Premadasa was less hawkish in demanding its replacement by an equitable friendship treaty.

In India, with growing criticism of the IPKF's role in Sri Lanka, the government maintained that the provincial elections were a step towards autonomy for Sri Lanka's Tamils and the IPKF would stay on until all the other provisions envisaged in the devolution package had been fulfilled. The Foreign Minister announced that the IPKF was there under a bilateral arrangement and so, neither India nor Sri Lanka could decide unilaterally on its withdrawal.

Generally, with the situation brightening up for the IPKF in Sri Lanka, India started thinking of pulling out the IPKF in a phased manner. The then Prime Minister, Mr. Rajiv Gandhi, told at a meeting of the Army commanders on April 25 that India was seriously thinking of getting back the build of the IPKF from Sri Lanka as soon as possible while preserving the gains that had been achieved. But the next day, in a surprise development which upset the existing equation, the LTTE's political, adviser A.S. Balasingham, began talks with the Sri Lankan government. It became clear that the cementing factor between the LTTE and the Colombo was their common demand that the IPKF leave the island.

The LTTE in its dialogue with the Sri Lankan government put forth its demands which included the abolition of the north-eastern council, the holding of fresh elections in the Tamil provinces, no referendum to ratify the merger of the Tamil provinces, recognition of Tamil identity and above all the withdrawal of the IPKF from the island. Premadasa carried on the dialogue with the LTTE in a calculated move to rope in the JVP for negotiations in order to ensure peace and order in the south. Subsequently, despite Indian Prime Minister Rajiv Gandhi's assurance that the bulk of the IPKF would be de-inducted as soon as possible, President R. Premadasa demanded that India withdraw all its troops from the island by 29 July 1989 which coincided with the second anniversary of the Agreement.

However, the Indian government refused to withdraw its peace-keeping force from Sri Lanka on the ground that the withdrawal required the concurrence of both the governments. It added that the Sri Lankan government had failed to proceed with devolution of power to the Tamils as provided in the accord and so, the IPKF had no choice but to stay on. None of these arguments were "truly tenable since the IPKF was on the island at the invitation of the Sri Lankan President and the Accord did not specifically call for India to guarantee the devolution of power to the Tamils." All the same, as a result of high-level talks in September 1989, India and Sri Lanka issued a joint communique stating that all efforts would be made to accelerate the de-induction of the IPKF to complete the de-induction by December 31 1989.

Subsequently, the IPKF suspended its military operations and maintained a symbolic presence. Later, with the new government coming to power in India, the time-limit for the withdrawal of the IPKF was mutually extended up to 31 March 1990. But before this deadline, the phased withdrawal of the IPKF was completed by 24 March, 1990. So, in the ultimate analysis, the Sri Lankan involvement was too costly for India, as "after 967 days in Sri Lanka at the cost of a reported Rs. 300 crores and at a loss of 1,155 lives with three times as many wounded, the Indian Army was home."

Thus, from the military standpoint, the IPKF operation was a grim counter-insurgency campaign fought in a tragic setting which saw the Indian troops fighting against the very people whom they were to protect. It was obvious from the fact that "any counter-insurgency campaign undertaken in a foreign country has historically been a politico-military haemorrhage for the intervening power as in recent cases of Afghanistan and Kampuchea." Moreover, the IPKF's setbacks could be attributed to the confused political thinking which bogged down the military operations. The lack of a clear-cut politico-military aim of the Indian policy makers led to ad-hocism, dithering and utter confusion. Despite this, the overall performance of the IPKF was largely satisfactory in the sense that it created a conducive climate where the diplomatic initiative could be undertaken.

From the foregoing analysis, it becomes clear that the Indian involvement in Sri Lanka had serious implications for both the countries. India was primarily guided by its long-term security interests in the region. In order to preserve and promote this, the Indo-Lanka accord served as a guarantee in bilateral and regional context.

Consequent to the bilateral relations, India had to support the legitimate interests of the Tamils in Sri Lanka within the framework of Sri Lanka's unity and territorial integrity. In pursuing these objectives, India's approach and moves were conditioned by the developments in Sri Lanka's ethnic situation and the Sri Lankan government's foreign and defence policy initiatives and moves. In this context, the Indo-Lanka Accord was the high-point of bilateral understanding and cooperation between the two countries.

In the final analysis, the role of India in the Sri Lankan conflict, despite some lapses and misgivings has been one of constructive engagement. It shows a close link between India's willingness to guarantee the peace and security of Sri Lanka in return for the accommodation of its security concerns. In this direction, the Indo-Lankan Accord has served its security concerns and also, as a step towards the peaceful resolution of the conflict.

Ethnic riots represent an event which is not normal in civilised society. The violence perpetrated at the time of an ethnic riot can be horrendous. It can include hacking people to death, or burning them alive. Retaliation and punishment meted out to members of other communities may include violence against children, old people and women.

There is a feeling of disbelief and horror, especially at the manner of the violence; the evil seems central, yet liberal opinion tries to hold on to the idea of goodness of human nature. If human nature is bestowed with an innate goodness, then the tendency is to regard communal riots as an aberration and to search for culprits who can be held responsible for perpetrating the horrendous violence one encounters during communal riots. This is not to deny the importance of fact-finding commissions and of recording such events. Such records are important for political activities concerned with the protection of human rights.

As in other parts of South Asia, in Sri Lanka too the recurrence of communal riots is seen as a manifestation of communalism. Riots are considered to reflect the irrational passions of backward sections of society. Thus the liberal, modernist tradition uses the opposition of reason and passion to distinguish between the progressive course of history within which the processes of nation building and development take place, and the occasional regressions reflected in isolated outbursts of the passions of what are considered communal-minded and backward people.

In this kind of analysis such aberrations are to be condemned and the culprits punished so that the normal processes of nation building and development can proceed. The point is that, within this approach, ethnic riots are isolated events, discontinuous in time, and reflective of an outdated, false consciousness. Opposed to the view of ethnic riots as isolated incidents is the suggestion that we look at them in relation to the changes in society in which they occur. The main issue is whether ethnic riots are a manifestation, in an acute form, of the very structures that characterise normal society.

As Sri Lanka moved towards independence, the multi-ethnicity of the state became a central issue in defining state structures. Although in the late twenties some of the political leaders and representatives of certain ethnic groups put forward the idea of a federal constitution for Sri Lanka, what was introduced into the Constitution of Sri Lanka at the time of independence was the mechanism of trying to safeguard the rights of minorities through checks at the centre.

Some of the measures adopted were the distribution of seats in parliament so that minority voices could be heard, multi-member constituencies where there were pockets of minorities, a second chamber into which minority representatives could be appointed, and clauses in the constitution to safeguard minority rights.

The political history of post-independent Sri Lanka shows the ineffectiveness of these safeguards at the centre which appeared in the face of the emergence of Sinhala Buddhist nationalism as a dominant political force. The electoral process helped to brıng these pressures on the state. The elections in 1956, by which a government with a hegemonic Sinhala Buddhist ideology came to power, was a turning point in this process. Although the influence of this ideology was seen immediately after independence, when a section of a minority was disfranchised, it was after 1956 that Sinhala Buddhist nationalism became the dominant ideology of the ruling class. It is from this point onwards that a class block similar to the class block of Kelecki's intermediate regime came to dominate state power.

One result of this was the institution of state-dominated populist development policies within a capitalist framework. The other development was the hegemony of Sinhala Buddhist ideology and the systematic dismantling of the safeguards for minorities that had been introduced at the time of independence. This process shows the contradictions of a bourgeois-democratic system in a multi-ethnic society.

Due to the importance of numerical strength within the bourgeois-democratic framework, the Sinhalese Buddhists came to occupy a dominant position. Further, the minorities began to feel that they did not have the numerical strength to exercise power within the system. Thus, ethnic issues began to dominate the electoral process and came to occupy an important position in mass consciousness. Even the bourgeoisie, whose objective interests within an internationally operative capitalist system is to overcome narrow ethnic nationalism, begins to play politics with it in order to stay in power.

Thus, in Sri Lanka all the major parties identify themselves with a Sinhala Buddhist ideology. This does not mean that ethnicity in politics is only a result of the manipulation of the ruling classes, for ethnic consciousness has a real basis within popular consciousness. This is true of all ethnic groups. Both the rulers and the ruled form part of a society where ethnic consciousness has come to dominate. The response of the minorities to the process of emergence of Sinhala Buddhist ideology into dominance came from the Sri Lanka Tamils who form the numerically biggest minority. Tamil political leadership agreed to the safeguards at the centre at the time of independence, although the demands of some of them were more than what was agreed upon. These demands soon changed to one based on concepts of regional autonomy.

In the mid-fifties the major Tamil party put forward the demand for a federal system of government and by the early seventies this had escalated to the demand for a separate state. The escalation of these demands also saw the emergence of a new political leadership within Tamils and a change in the form of the political struggle. The social background of the leadership was more of a petty-bourgeois character. They were less Westernised than the earlier leadership, and had a regional base in the northern province, where there is a concentration of Tamil population. Armed struggle became the dominant form of struggle of the political movements led by this group. In some ways they are a mirror image of the Sinhala petty bourgeoisie which spearheaded the ethnic nationalism of the south.

Enactment of the First Republican Constitution in 1972 saw the beginning of the emergence of armed groups within the Tamil social formation. This constitution removed the earlier safeguards for the minorities in the previous constitution, gave pre-eminence to Buddhism in the constitution in addition to the Sinhala language, and concentrated all power in the Sinhala-dominated legislature.

The early seventies also saw the aggravation of ethnic issues on account of the introduction of new admission schemes for entrance into the university. These schemes had discriminatory elements against Tamil students. All this led to the emergence of a separate state demand from the Tamil minority.

Therefore, by the time the United National Party (UNP) was getting ready for elections in 1977, the ethnic contradiction was aggravated. This resulted in the Tamil United Liberation Front (TULF)—the organisation that spearheaded the demand for a separate state—not only winning the elections in the north and to a lesser extent in the east with a separate state demand, but also becoming the major opposition party. For the first time in Sri Lankan history, parliament reflected the ethnic polarisation in the country. While the United National Party (UNP) with a five-sixths majority obtained largely from a Sinhalese majority, was on the government side, the TULF was leading the opposition after winning the Tamil vote on a separate state demand.

In contemporary situation of capitalist growth, Sri Lanka's development policies are internationally determined. This determination emerges not only because of the greater intervention of bodies like the IMF and the World Bank, but also because international capitalism as an objective historical force determines these policies. What we are observing now is the greater influence of this international system in the economies and societies of not only Third World countries, but also in the Second World.

The international bodies began to advise on the economic affairs of Sri Lanka in 1952. Then, in 1965, this took a new turn by the establishment of the Aid Ceylon Club under the auspices of the IMF, and since then its influence has grown. At the moment, IMF/WB influence in policy formation in Sri Lanka is significant. This is parallelled by greater penetration of the international capitalist system as a fact into all forms of production in Sri Lankan society.

Today, even the cultivation process of a small farmer in a remote village area of Sri Lanka is touched by forces that can be traced to an international system. The post-1977 economic policies of Sri Lanka are influenced by recommendations of the IMF and the WB (World Bank). These in turn are influenced by what has come to be known as monetarist theories of economic development, and some authors have referred to Monetarist/IMF/World Bank (MIW) policies. The MIW-type recommendations may be summarised as being in favour of economic liberalisation, export-led growth and fiscal balance: "Great faith is placed on the market mechanism as a panacea for economic ailments, and government intervention in the economy is opposed in almost any form."

These policies have two aspects, namely, structural change and stabilisation. The structural policies recommended are liberalisation of trade and financial dealings with the world, the development of financial institutions and money markets, and the reduction of the state. As regards stabilisation, balanced budgeting and maintaining a stable growth in money supply are emphasised.

These recommendations are based on well-known tenets of free-market theories that emphasise market forces, comparative advantages, reliance on private capital (local and foreign), balanced budgets and control of money supply as the principal means of economic growth. These more liberalised economic policies, implemented now for ten years, have to be understood in the context of the socio-political forces within which these policies are implemented.

The basis of all political problems in the ethnic issue is related to the fact that it is the majority Sinhala community that enjoys state power in Sri Lanka. Thus, the state that emerged in post-independent Sri Lanka was heavily biased in favour of Sinhala interests.

The intervention of the state in the economy and other spheres of society carries with it the interests of the majority community. This is a dimension largely ignored in the discussions of policies that came to dominate in Sri Lanka after 1956. The expanded role of the state in the economy introduced three main mechanisms that could go against the interests of minority ethnic groups:

1) State's expansion of the economy could mean taking over areas of economic activity by the state in which the minorities had been involved. If the state sector creates monopolies in such areas, it could mean a continuous shutting-off of the minorities from such sectors.

2) Expansion of state regulations in the economy also mean the introduction of systems of quotas, permits and licenses even in economic activity in the private sectors. Political patronage plays a significant role in granting these licences and permits.
3) The state becomes the major avenue of employment, with the expansion of the state in the economy. Here too political patronage becomes critical. Loyalty to political parties that come into power becomes extremely important.

The Kalecki's model of intermediate regimes can be used to explain the political economy of state-dominated populist policies that emerged in the Sri Lanka. Intermediate regimes have a state with a multi-class character. In this class coalition, middle-level landowning class and petty-bourgeois sections play a key role. The petty-bourgeois will include many others, like sections of the trading class, those employed in minor positions within government, and the vernacular intelligentsia. Their role is crucial in intermediate regimes.

The economic policies adopted by the UNP government after 1977 had implication for ethnic relations in Sri Lanka. The policies make political stability an important prerequisite. The ethnic issue was the main candidate as a destabiliser when these policies were initiated. With relatively little importance being attached to the state sector the policy framework had the potential of reducing the importance of ethnically-biased structures that the earlier state interventionist policies had brought into prominence.

A government which had in mind a strategy of development based on a greater integration with international capitalism could not afford to ignore the contradictions arising out of ethnic relations. The policy depended heavily on foreign sources of finance. Attracting foreign investment is a cornerstone of these policies, and for foreign investors, political stability is a *sina qua non*.

Thus, liberalised economic policies have built-in pressures for political stability. The strategy of the UNP leaders in facing this issue was to try and arrange an accommodation with the representatives of the Tamil bourgeoisie and the traditional Tamil leadership. This was not a new thing for the UNP, whose previous period in power was a coalition with the leading Tamil political party—the Federal Party.

The UNP itself had Tamil members as well as Tamil-speaking Muslim members from the eastern province—a province dominated by the minorities. The UNP was also able to get the participation of the leader of the Ceylon Workers Congress (CWC). The CWC is virtually the sole representative body of the Indian Tamil community. As revealed by the leader of the CWC in parliament, the UNP held discussions prior to the elections with representatives of the Tamil minority.

The result of these discussions was the acceptance by the UNP, in its manifesto, that several grievances of the Tamil people were legitimate, as well as the promise of an all-party conference to resolve the issues. The leader of the CWC, Mr. Thondaman, joining the government and becoming a minister, was another by-product of this process. This was a very useful step for the UNP to prevent contradictions arising out of the ethnic issue spreading to the estate areas where the bulk of the workforce is Indian Tamil.

The UNP government was more aware of the issue, mainly because of the self-interest of capitalism, which needed political stability. The UNP government's attempt at accommodation with the Tamil leadership continued, even after it came to power.

One of the first measures of the UNP government was the removal of standardisation from university admission policies. Although this was replaced by a different formula that had some disadvantages *vis-a-vis* Tamil students, the removal of standardisation was significant in appeasing Tamil grievances. The new constitution enacted in 1978 gave Tamil the status of a national language. Perhaps the high point of this accommodation process was the enactment of the District Development Council Bill (DDC) in order to give a certain measure of autonomy to the districts. The removal of controls that accompanies a closed economy will remove the influences of forces dominant in state power from the economy. Thus, a liberalised economy will give less chance to ethnic factors becoming influential. The dynamics of the economy will be determined more by economic considerations.

Reduction in the role of the state within the economy will be accompanied by a lessening of the power of Sinhala nationalism. Being the dominant force in state power, it could use its power for it own economic ends within a context of a state-dominated, controlled economy. This becomes more difficult within a liberalised economy. Thus the rational capitalist element of the UNP and their foreign collaborators had a self-interest in overcoming the contradictions of ethnicity. However, the UNP also had, within itself, populist as well as Sinhalese nationalist elements. Being a creature of the electoral process and also being dependent on it as a vehicle of power, the UNP adapted very fast to the changing situation *vis-a-vis* the Sri Lankan electorate after 1956.

Sinhala nationalism and ethnic chauvinism were the dominant prevailing ideologies among the electorate. In some sense the UNP had to catch up with the SLFP, which was the party that had greater recognition as the representatives of the majority community—the Sinhala Buddhists. Thus, opposition to accommodative policies with the Tamil minority was also found within the governing party itself and from the very inception of this government one can see an interaction between these two opposing tendencies. The attempt at accommodation was also nullified because of the growth of Tamil militancy.

If the expressions of Sinhala nationalism in its extreme forms, both within the government and outside, could be kept in check by the ruling sections because of state power, there was nothing to check the growth of Tamil militancy. The accommodative attitude of the government was directed more towards the moderate Tamil leadership. Militancy was met by harsh repression. The repressive action of a highly Sinhalised army spilled over to the Tamil civilian population, which in turn created a social basis for Tamil militancy.

More liberalised economic policies had to be implemented in a society which was ethnically polarised, while the majority community enjoyed state power. Since the liberalised policies had the potential to dismantle some of the structures that gave special benefits to those enjoying state power, they were bound to evoke a reaction among Sinhala extremists. This reaction could take the form of an ethnic riot.

ANTI-TAMIL POGROM OF 1983

In Sri Lanka, most of the large-scale events of ethnic violence since 1977 have occurred against a backdrop of various kinds of political moves which were attempts to begin a process of dialogue and discussion. What preceded the August 1977 riots were the pre-election discussions and dialogue between the UNP, representatives of the Tamil bourgeoisie, and the traditional leadership. The post-election incidents of violence in July 1977, during which members of the opposition were attacked, continued into anti-Tamil riots. The August 1981 attack on Tamils occurred within a context of the first District Development Council elections, which was a measure agreed upon as an interim solution by the moderate Tamil leadership. However, the brunt of the attack in these riots was borne by the Indian Tamil community.

The July 1983 riots also coincided with an attempt at calling an all-party conference to settle the issue. This was first called only to discuss the so-called terrorist problem, but later its scope was expanded to include the entire issue of ethnic conflict in Sri Lanka. The expanded scope of this consultation even had such issues as the removal of the draconian Prevention of Terrorism Act and the limiting of the role of armed forces in the northern and eastern provinces. This consultation was to be held on 27 July.

The July 1983 event started on 23/24 July. Therefore, all instances of anti-Tamil violence since 1977 coincided with various attempts by the system to come to terms with the contradictions. This is necessary for the system for its own self-interest. However, it generates a reaction from Sinhala chauvinist elements. These elements could be found both within the government and outside, although it seems that those who are in positions of power within the government have a greater chance of perpetrating violence and yet escaping the consequences of their actions. The large-scale ethnic pogroms were the organised reaction of Sinhala chauvinism whenever the government tried to accommodate the moderate Tamil leadership.

The event that provoked the July 1983 violence was the killing of soldiers by Tamil militants who had been waging a guerilla war with the objective of setting up an independent state, Tamil Eelam. Militants had lured out the army with false information, and they were ambushed around 11.30 p.m. In this incident thirteen soldiers were killed. On the same day, the army had begun certain operations to remove some of the state Tamil population that had been settled in the predominantly Tamil districts of Manner, Vavuniya and Trincomalee. These were refugees of the August 1977 and August 1981 riots who were later settled in these lands. The settlement of these people, who were victims of ethnic riots, had been strongly opposed by Sinhala chauvinist elements. A former cabinet minister of the regime in power led this opposition.

According to a statement issued by the Ceylon Workers Congress, around 600 people were removed from this area in the early hours of the morning of 23 July and brought to Nuwara Ellya district, where there is a preponderant Indian Tamil population. The role of the army is an important factor in the anti-Tamil pogroms of Sri Lanka.

In the case of the July 1983 outbreak, this seems to have begun from these actions by the army against the Indian Tamil population. Just after the soldiers were ambushed in Jaffna, the army retaliated against Tamil civilians. During this retaliation, which took place in Tirunaely and Kantharamadu area, a number of people died. The figure is 20 according to official sources, 51 according to TULF sources, and over 70 according to others. Similar incidents seem to have taken place in the Trincomalee area. In these incidents the navy was involved, but the toll is not known.

By the afternoon of Sunday, 24 July, 1983, the news of the ambush reached Colombo. A crowd, including the relatives of the soldiers, had gathered at the General Cemetery, Colombo, for the burial of the soldiers. The government was to bury the soldiers with full military honours, and even high-level representatives of government were to attend the funeral. But the bodies of the dead soldiers could not be brought to Colombo in time, mainly on account of conditions prevailing in Jaffna, where the government was finding it difficult to control the army that had gone on a rampage against Tamil civilians. Ultimately the bodies were brought to army headquarters and handed over to the relatives; but that was later.

By the evening of Sunday a large crowd had gathered expecting the bodies of the soldiers, and some began to become unruly. Police officers who were trying to control the crowd were attacked, and some of the shops and houses at Borella belonging to Tamils were stoned and set on fire. This is the area where the General Cemetery is situated.

However, it is also clear that Tamils living in other parts of Colombo, and especially in the suburbs, were not aware of what happened at Borella on the previous night. Many left their homes for work on the following morning and children went to school as well. The systematic attack on Tamil property seemed to have begun a little later on Monday. All the Monday morning papers carried the story of the ambushing of soldiers, with full banner headlines, despite the press censorship which had been imposed a few days before, on 19 July.

On Monday, 25 July at about 10.30 a.m. there began what seemed to be a carefully organised attack on Tamil property. By the time the government imposed a curfew at 2 p.m., hundreds of buildings and factories had been set ablaze by thugs. Along with the organised elements, the lumpen proletariat of the city joined the fray. Curfew was on from 2 p.m. on Monday until 5 a.m. on Wednesday. On Monday night, according to official sources, about 300 to 500 prisoners broke out of their cells, overpowered the guards and beat and stabbed 35 Tamil detainees to death with spikes, clubs and ironrods. This was at the Welikade Prison, Colombo's maximum security prison, which held 800 convicts and 73 extremist suspects detained under emergency regulations. The looting and arson which started on Monday continued on Tuesday despite the curfew.

On Wednesday at 5 a.m. curfew was lifted to enable people to shop. Food was scarce in the city as many Tamil wholesale and retail shops had been burnt. Many Tamils were streaming into hastily opened camps. On Wednesday violence spread to other parts of the island and curfew was imposed at 4 p.m. Tamil detainees were killed at Welikade Prison, in the same manner as on Monday night. The victims included Dr S. Rajasunderam, Secretary of the Gandhian Movement, a social service organisation.

It was on 28 July, that President Jayewardene spoke publicly for the first time in brief on radio and TV in both Sinhala and English. He neither condemned the rioters nor offered consolation to the victims. He laid blame for the mayhem on the Tamils for demanding a separate state; he further announced that a constitutional amendment banning separatism would be put into effect. But the speech did not seem to placate the Sinhalese as, on the next day, there was fear and panic among the Sinhalese over the rumour that the Liberation Tigers were in Colombo. Rumour spread in Colombo that the Liberation Tigers were invading the city to exact revenge. Mobs beat to death Tamils who strayed from the security of the refugee camps or their homes. About 100 persons were reported killed.

On Friday, 29 July, the security forces took serious measures against looters, shooting or arresting some. This was the last wave of violence in Colombo.

According to official sources the number of dead was around 400 and 100,000 were rendered homeless. Outside Colombo there were 175,500 refugees. An estimate of the damage to trade and business establishments was done by a government task force. It covered 116 industrial establishments that had been damaged within a 30-mile radius of

Colombo. In addition it estimated that 492 trading establishments had been damaged at Pettah.

The first response of the government to the riots was contradictory and showed the confused position of the government on the issues. On the one hand the government said and did a lot to appease the sentiment of the Sinhala Buddhist majority. This began with the head of state saying that the riot was a legitimate expression of anger by the Sinhala Buddhist majority. The ministers who followed gave assurances that the government would do all it could to safeguard the rights of the majority. This culminated in legislation which made espousing the cause of separatism illegal; it resulted in the removal from parliament of legitimate representatives of the Tamils.

The government made an attempt to find scapegoats from the left as elements behind the riots. Several theories of conspiracy were floated. One talked of an attempt to promote conflicts between different ethnic groups of the country, starting from Sinahala and Tamil. This was expected to lead to general destabilisation. This same speculation extended to a coup theory in which sections of the army were also supposed to be involved.

Therefore, for the government, on the one hand the riot was a legitimate expression of Sinhalese anger, and on the other it was an attempt to overthrow the government: a classic contradictory situation reflecting a crisis.

The event of July 1983 ended a week after it began. But similar pattern of events continued within the context of intensifying ethnic conflict in Sri Lanka. Such a pattern of events was characterised by a backlash on the Tamil civilian population provoked by the actions of militants. The army was involved in several such incidents after July 1983, showing how institutions of the state themselves became the perpetrators of violence and lawlessness. It was hoped that the Indo-Sri Lanka agreement signed on 27 July 1987 would be able to break the cycle of violence. However, immediately after signing the accord, there were violent protests all over southern Sri Lanka.

The government responded with massive police operations against the JVP, the major militant group opposed to the accord and against concessions to Tamil demands for self-government. The Indian Peace-Keeping Force (IPKF), which was charged with keeping peace in the Northern and Eastern Provinces, launched military operation against the LTTE to disarm them. In the offensive several charges of human rights violation were made against the IPKF. The victims were mainly Tamils in Jaffna and the Sinhalese in Trincomalee.

4

Ceylon to Sri Lanka

The unfortunate change of Sri Lanka from a peaceful, idyllic Ceylon to a synonym for macabre ethnic violence is the story of a majority community's attempt to fashion a nation in its own image through monopolisation of the state and of the consequent emergence of a secessionist ethno-national movement. Despite claims of ancient enmity and eternal difference, this ethnic conflict is a depressingly modernist tale. The effacement of alternative imaginations of the self and their attempted replacement by a single view, one based on a modern, sovereign nation-state in Sri Lanka are unremarkable in the sense that such things have been happening everywhere for some time now.

The idea of the nation is heavily interlaced with the notion that it is a special land because it is consecrated by the Buddha and its manifest destiny is preservation of the Buddhist faith.

The liberal-democratic idea of the fundamental equality of all citizens within the national space runs directly counter to the idea of Sri Lanka as ultimately the abode of the Sinhala Buddhists, a space divinely ordained for the preservation of their faith. Political leaders are self-conscious about the need to employ their lives as coherent and redemptive narrators. This was certainly the case with Jayewardene, who in his various writings and speeches is acutely conscious that the manner in which his life is recounted is critical to both his own fashioning of a self-identity and the way he will be judged by history into the next century.

One of the more interesting texts authored by Jayewardene is a glossy and slickly produced book titled *Golden Threads*. Based on the ancient Pali chronicle *Mahavamsa,* Jayewardene dates the "origin" of Sri Lanka to 544 B.C. and the arrival of King Vijaya and his men from Northern India to the island. The past is thus the period from the founding of the dynasty of Vijaya all the way to the Kandyan Convention of 1815, when the Sinhala chiefs signed over the Kandyan kingdom to George III of Great Britain.

The present, intriguingly, is the period that spans both the period of British colonial rule and post-colonial Sri Lanka from 1948 to 1977. This configuration effaces the year of independence, something very rare in post-colonial recollections. The year 1977 is the one during which the Jayewardene-led United National Party (UNP) defeated the Sri Lanka Freedom Party (SLFP) at the elections and assumed power. It thus becomes the terminus of the present and the beginning of the future.

To date the beginning of Sri Lanka on the basis of the *Mahavamsa,* besides forever tying Sri Lanka with Buddhist cosmology, effaces both the prior and the non-Buddhist populations of Sri Lanka. By anchoring the origins of Sri Lanka in a Buddhist, Pali chronicle, Jayewardene pushes to the margins the Tamils and other ethnic and religious communities who have no comparable mythic charter of their presence. Further, it ignores the fact that even if the chronicle is true, according to the *Mahavamsa* itself Vijaya's seven hundred men, including the king himself, populated the "new" space by marrying women from the Tamil, Pandyan kingdom of Southern India.

Perhaps most important, this origin myth, as currently disseminated, establishes a hierarchy of authenticity within Sri Lanka, the Sinhala Buddhist perched at the apex and the other ethnic and religious groups reduced to supporting positions, but only if they behave themselves. In a sense, Jayewardene passes up on an opportunity to inscribe Sri Lanka at the very outset with the miscegenation of its population and thus irrevocably to ambiguate the purity of its origins. This move is suggested by at least three of Sri

Lanka's most prominent scholars, Stanley Tambiah, Leslie Gunawardana, and Gananath Obeyesekere although each stresses different aspects of the issue. It is a fairly large concession to state that the so-called founding fathers of Sri Lanka populated the realm with women from the Tamil kingdom of the Pandyans. Now, one could counter that miscegenative act with the principle of patriarchal lineage. That is to say, no matter who the founding mothers were, the fact that lineage is tracked through the male suffices to establish the Sinhala character of the origins of this realm.

The Sinhalese, according to this founding myth of the *Mahavamsa,* descend also from the thousand families who accompanied the spouses of Vijaya's men. These people are to stay momentarily within this artificial discourse of racial purity, to begin with wholly non-Sinhala and their incorporation into the broadened category of Sinhala is effected minimally through their learning of the Sinhala language. Thus, it is by virtue of linguistic incorporation, and not by descent, that they would have become Sinhala.

Physically the Sinhalese and Tamils cannot be differentiated. Though the initial Sinhalese migrants were probably Indo-European language speakers who arrived over 2,500 years ago, practically all later arrivals were South Indians (mostly Tamil speakers) who were assimilated into the Sinhalese Buddhist community. This important argument has many parallels in the context of South Asia, especially in dispelling the racist mythography of those who would point to the Aryan origins of the region's upper castes.

The glorious Theravada Buddhist civilisation of Anuradhapura ended, according to Jayewardene, with the conquest by the miasmic forces from southern India and the beginning of a medieval dark age in the Rajarata. Jayewardene avers: "In the first quarter of the thirteenth century from South India came Magha—the Tiger."

In fact Jayewardene's interpretation of the entire issue of post-colonial Tamil-Sinhala ethnic relations is boiled down to the following: "Terrorism a world phenomenon raised its ugly head in the North and East, and some Tamils joined them to press for separation. In 1980 these activities increased and killing of Sinhala security forces in the North in 1983 were followed by Sinhala-Tamil riots throughout the island."

Any rational agency on the part of the Tamil and the possibility that Tamil grievances may be genuine—based on discrimination and violent exclusion at the hands of the Sinhalese majority—are eliminated here. Instead, the so-called terrorism is naturalised through a metaphor of unpredictable and irrational bestiality. It is estimated that in the pogrom of July 1983 anywhere between 2,000 and 3,000 Tamils were killed, property worth about $ 300 million was looted or destroyed, and more than 100,000 were rendered homeless and became refugees in their own land. The pogrom is justified by Jayewardene; however, as a response to this insensate phenomenon.

Overwhelmingly directed against innocent civilians, systematically organised by individuals high in the ruling political party, and often conducted in the presence of the Sinhala-dominated police and armed forces, the pogrom is further justified as a response to the killing of security forces in the North. Having diminished the ethnic question to a problem of terrorism, one further reduced as a non-particular world phenomenon, and having homogenised the nation into a supportive realm, Jayewardene can turn his attention in the last part of *Golden Threads* to the question of his country's tryst with the future: its moment of arrival as an ersatz Singapore.

At the concluding lines of *Golden Threads* Jayewardene notes, "We have no time to waste. The future urgently beckons.... We must participate in this revolution of technology and information if we ever hope to catch up with the developed world. We need to know all about it before we can participate or catch up. It was during the late-colonial period that societies such as India and Sri Lanka were for the first time brought under the regime of censuses, national agricultural yield and land-revenue data collection, trigonometric surveys of territory, fixed and demarcated political boundaries, and, increasingly, the classification of the population into definable groups such as castes, races, languages, religions, and the like.

The interaction between categories such as Sinhala Buddhist or Tamil Hindu and the requirements of competitive, electoral politics based on universal suffrage in the post-colonial period has been predictably explosive and violent, which ought to indicate that Sri Lanka's ethnic strife is not born out of any atavistic and primordial attachment to traditions, one that would go away if it was force-fed modernity in ever-increasing doses. The ethnic violence that wracks the country today is the definitive indication that Sri Lanka has arrived as a modern nation.

Jayewardene built his political career upon intransigent opposition to any concessions to the Tamil minority when he was trying to gain power and upon stonewalling, dissembling, and complicity with annihilatory violence against them when he was in power.

Jayewardene is an extremely well-read man, conversant in ideas of secularism, liberalism, multiethnic societies, nation building in plural societies, and the like. Moreover, as he and many another Sinhala political leaders would hasten to add, not only do they count many Tamils, Burghers, and Muslims as close friends, but their own families have married into these communities.

The *Golden Threads* represents a story that crystallises the sense of an originary hierarchy of authenticity: there are some to whom this island is home; the others are permanent guests who live in Sri Lanka at the behest of the majority community. They can continue to live here provided they remember their place. Viewed against this hierarchy, the periodic pogroms and explosions of violence against the Tamils in Sri Lanka represent efforts to put them back in their place on grounds that they have become too assertive and need to be taught a lesson, according to an oft-used phrase.

It is hardly coincidental that the bouts of collective violence in recent times have all occurred immediately after or during efforts to open a dialogue on redressing minority grievances in Sri Lanka. The *Golden Threads* acquire social efficacy because they provide the moral and mythic charter that redeems and encourages anti-minority violence. Violence becomes a form of tough love for the majority community, a cathartic experience that reasserts the nation. Indeed, one could argue that a concept such as tough love does capture significant elements of majority/minority relations in much of South Asia.

5

Battle for Jaffna

As the battle for control of Jaffna peninsula raged on Thursday May 11, 2000 in Colombo, a senior Sri Lankan armed forces officer monitoring the string of surprising gains being notched up by the rebel Liberation Tigers of Tamil Eelam (LTTE) observed: "The difference is that our soldiers fight to live, the Tigers fight to die." Perhaps that statement comes closest to explaining why an army that has pitted four of its elite divisions consisting of 25,000 well-armed men should be struggling to stave off a determined push by just 7,000 LTTE fighters, many of who are, as another officer despairingly dismisses them as "Just women and school children".

The Tigers had staged an awesome comeback into Peninsula after being driven out by the army in 1995. The LTTE had overrun key Sri Lankan military posts, including the strategic Elephant Pass linking the Peninsula to the mainland. As the Tigers engaged in a virtual hand-to-hand combat with Sri Lankan soldiers in the suburbs, just a day's fighting on Thursday, May 11, 2000, left over 100 dead and scores wounded with each side claiming more "kills" than the other.

The Army had imposed a round-the-clock curfew on the town's half a million residents, some of whom called up their friends in Colombo to report they could hear sounds of regular gunfire and mortar shelling. The LTTE had earlier broadcast messages over its widely heard radio station, the Voice of the Tigers, asking Jaffna residents to vacate the town to avoid being used as human shields by the soldiers.

Meanwhile. Sri Lankan Air Force jets, Israeli-built Kfirs, strafed LTTE positions in the Peninsula in a bid to put the rebel forces on the defensive. But it appeared only a matter of days before the town fell to the Tigers. It is a symbolic victory and the Tigers know it. To claim complete control over Jaffna Peninsula the LTTE had to first defeat the Sri Lankan forces guarding the nearby Palali Air-Force base and the Kankasanturai Naval port. Both these strategic military positions control movement of food supplies to the town apart from ammunition and reinforcements. For Sri Lankan President, Chandrika Bandaranaike Kumaratunga, who in a broadcast to the nation had vowed to protect the town at whatever cost, the Tiger's rapid advance has sent her credibility plummeting. It was also a major psychological blow to the already beleaguered Army.

The President's response to the crisis was to acquire even more sweeping powers that she had arrogated to herself after declaring a national emergency. She moved desperately to still political dissent by prohibiting all gatherings, even arresting scores of right-wingers who threatened to violate her order in Colombo. The government then tightened the already stringent press censorship laws by banning live telecasts and broadcasts. Still, with no credible information coming out, wild rumours did the rounds including one that the LTTE had recruited schoolgirls to act as suicide bombers in Colombo. That saw police stop and check children in several schools, especially those dominated by Tamils.

Meanwhile, the government desperately shopped for arms and ammunition to rush to the troops. Having hurriedly restored diplomatic relations with Israel after a gap of 17 years, the Sri Lankan government asked it to ship five Kfir fighters on an emergency basis. With India ruling out military intervention or selling arms to the island nation, the Lankan government approached Pakistan, China and Russia for purchasing artillery shells and mortars apart from armoured vehicles. It may already be too late. Kumaratunga and her government are much to blame for allowing the LTTE not only to regroup but to return with such ferocity that the current battle may prove to be the most decisive of the ongoing ethnic war that has seen over 20,000 dead in the past two decades. When she had launched Operation Riverisa, a major military offensive against the LTTE six years ago, Kumaratunga had grandly called it the "War for Peace". She and her chief adviser General (retd) Anuruddha Ratwatte, Deputy Minister of defence, had hoped that by weakening the striking power of the world's most ruthless terrorist organisation she could isolate it politically and ram through a settlement that would ensure the rights of the Tamil minority without compromising on the territorial integrity of Sri Lanka.

Some defence experts even then questioned Kumaratunga's policy of going for the "head of the beast", or trying to regain full control over the North and East Provinces (which the Tigers claim as Eelam or Tamil homeland). They warned that such a tactic could result in the army overstretching itself by wresting military real estate from the Tigers that may prove hard to defend. Miraculously, for a while Kumaratunga's strategy even appeared to succeed. She not only evicted the LTTE from the Jaffna peninsula in 1995—not a mean task considering that the Tigers had held it for the previous five years—but had its feared leader Velupillai Prabhakaran on the run in the jungles of Wanni. But the Lankan government had underestimated Prabhakaran's fighting skills again. For, the LTTE chief, realising that he could not match the army's superior artillery fire, withdrew to the jungles with his entire armour intact and began to regroup his forces.

Contrary to rumours that the Tigers were weakened because of internal conflicts, Prabhakaran began recruiting a new commander, at least 10 years younger than him, and put them in charge of major regiments. To match Sri Lankan armour he knew he had to acquire an artillery that could rain as much fire-power if not more. For that he had to have access to the sea to land the guns clandestinely purchased from other countries. By then the LTTE was rumoured to be involved in smuggling narcotics and other contraband to help fund its battle. On July 18, 1996, he launched Increasing Waves-1, a meticulously planned operation to storm-capture the strategic Lankan Army base at Mullaitivu on the east coast. Apart from a major land battle, the LTTE involved its Naval arm, the Sea Tigers, to encircle the base. The attack began at 1 a.m. and within hours the surprised Army base was routed. Besides a major psychological victory the LTTE got a rich haul of arms and ammunition, including two 120 mm howtizers and a huge range of mortars. To match the Tigers' spectacular success at Mullaitivu, a week later the army launched operation "Sath Java" (True Victory) in a bid to open an alternative supply route to Jaffna on the A9 highway that had for long remained under Tiger control. Initially, the army made impressive gains and captured Kilinochchi town bringing almost an 80 km stretch under its control and linking it to Jaffna.

Emboldened by the success, the army triggered "Operation Jaya Sikuru" (Ture Victory) designed to not only ensure that the highway remained under the forces' control but also to clear the Tigers from the surrounding jungles of Wanni. This is where the Tigers had lured the Indian Peace-Keeping Force (IPKF) to battle and had bogged it down for months. The army employed massive fire-power and did make substantial inroads. But in retrospect it stretched its resources too far and too thin and consequently found it difficult to defend the gains made.

The LTTE knew that and planned its next move meticulously. A year later the Tigers decided to regain Kilinochchi and launched Unceasing Waves-2. Within three days of intense fighting the rebels gained control of the Kilinochchi-Elephant Pass axial road that had taken the army over a year to capture.

The Tigers were in no hurry to take Jaffna and for their final assault on the Peninsula they prepared for a war. In his mid-40s, Prabhakaran had put on weight and was much the family man in the jungles. He lived with his wife and three children, constantly moving locations. The young firebrand, with a penchant for Western movies and admiration for Netaji Subhas Chandra Bose had grown into a mature leader. He continued to be a good listener and his soft voice belied the image of a ruthless fighter. He remained supreme commander of his force, plotting all their moves. Says D. Sivaram an LTTE analyst: "He still has the reputation of being one of the few Tamil leaders who hasn't sold out to the cause. His aim was to build a conventional army that could ensure an independent Eelam." By November 1999, the LTTE was ready to make its final assault on Jaffna, called Unceasing Waves-3. They began by capturing strategic towns on the A-9 highway and over-running Sri Lankan bases guarding them. Then on March 22, 2000, the cadres mounted their assault on Elephant Pass. In a brilliant manoeuvre, they cut off the drinking water supplies to the two divisions stationed in and around the pass and encircled them.

The attack on Elephant Pass caught the Army napping, and forced the government to make desperate changes in the army brass. In a major blunder, the dehydrated divisions were ordered to withdraw at high noon under a scorching sun. In what is considered the defining moment of the battle on April 27, 2000, the LTTE overran Elephant Pass. Many of the 800 Sri Lankan Army casualties were a result of dehydration. There were also reports of mutiny and large-scale desertions. With the fall of Elephant Pass it was clear that the LTTE would go for the jugular. Equipped with captured artillery and equipment purchased clandestinely from outside, the LTTE is in a position to match the Army's fire-power. That is why the Kumaratunga government panicked and desperately appealed to other countries, including India, for help.

Now the war over Jaffna has become a do-or-die battle not just for the 25,000 troops stationed in the peninsula but also for the Kumaratunga government. To boost the sagging morale of the army, the President has decided to suspend all developmental work and focus on defence. But with defence expenditure already constituting 34 per cent of the annual budget the economy is headed for trouble.

Taking Jaffna will give Prabhakaran tremendous bargaining power when he sits for peace talks which are certain to resume after the battle is over. Talks for devolution of power which Kumaratunga had initiated by suggesting that the North and East Provinces get more autonomy and possibly making Sri Lanka a federal state rather than a unitary one has broken down. India has stepped into the diplomatic void and offered to mediate with "all the parties" concerned if they are agreeable. It is certain to be a tortuous process but something that is absolutely necessary.

As rebel incursions into the northern Jaffna Peninsula sent the nation into a state of alarm, the territorial, political, military and diplomatic consequences of the latest offensives by the separatist Liberation Tigers of Tamil Eelam (LTTE) are considerable. With daily rebel advances towards government-held positions in the Peninsula, imponderables confront the island on several fronts.

The territorial implications of the latest LTTE offensive conjure up an alarming picture. The Tigers have perforated Army defence lines along southern coastal Jaffna and permeated themselves across the Peninsula. Multi-pronged in their attacks and actively present in at least three sectors, the LTTE is in a position to take the offensive into the government's strongholds in the Peninsula. The worst-case scenario is one of Sri Lanka being forced to pull out its soldiers from the north and losing territorial control over the Peninsula. At best, the situation could be contained to a lower level of insurgency—an attempt which has been relentlessly going on for the past five years. If the Tigers were to wrest territorial control from the Sri Lanka Army (SLA) in the north, the situation in the east becomes unpredictable, with the Tigers already holding a part of Batticaloa district. The offensive has had a debilitating effect on the armed forces, and that is what it aimed to achieve. The entrapment of nearly four divisions of the Army would be a telling blow on the security forces.

The indubitable reasoning behind Prabhakaran's siege over the Peninsula appears to be to emaciate the Army totally. The big change from the past is that the guerillas would capture the Peninsula with the significant addition of the Lyakachchi-Elephant Pass gateway garrison, from which the earlier Jaffna operations to push the LTTE into the jungle tracts commenced. The offensive also marks a territorial high-point of Tamil separatist militancy, which has been on since the late 1970s.

Several incidents over the past decades, if seen together, give a clear picture of the slow but steady distancing of the northern Peninsula from the mainland. If the 1984 bombing of the Yal Devi train to Jaffna set off the serious disruption of transport services, the stoppage of rail services since the 1990s has meant the loss of a vital lifeline of a nation. Road links to the Peninsula have been disrupted in the fighting beyond the northern Vavuniya town.

The LTTE's control over the seas off the Peninsula has resulted in a reluctance on the part of private transport operators to ply their vehicles. The minimal air traffic between Colombo and Jaffna has also remained hampered. In addition to this severed logistics situation, the various checks brought in by the government to control terrorist movements has made the hiatus between the Tamil-majority north and the rest of the island near-complete.

Entry for all civilians is restricted between rebel-held territories in the four northern districts—Mlinochchi, Mullaitivu, parts of Mannar and Vavuniya. The media and the non-governmental organisations are banned from entering these areas. The fact that there has been neither the decadal census updates nor the annual collation of vital economic and social statistics by the Central Bank from Tamil-majority areas portrays the stark distancing within the island. This has also resulted in place names such as Jaffna, Mullaitivu, Mannar and to a lesser extent Batticaloa, remaining just images for a vast section of the people, mainly the Sinhalese. The vocabulary of the island also now reflects the us-and-them syndrome, with terms such as 'war', 'border villages' and 'occupation' gaining widespread use.

There are three plausible scenarios now:

1. An Eritrea-type of situation where claim and control over land precedes secession;
2. The Tigers agree to head to the negotiating table; and
3. A situation of containment, under which the LTTE's activities are curbed to the north, the government takes control over the east and ensures normalcy in the south.

Whatever the situation, the future portends a phased period of extended agony: international, more specifically, regional pressure is not loaded in favour of an Eritrea-type situation; all prior attempts at talks had turned out to be breathers before a next round of offensives and experience has proved that containing the Tigers in the north does not necessarily result in normalcy being maintained in the south. Therefore, as the Tigers claw their way into the Peninsula, military action and diplomacy move in tandem.

The Sri Lankan conflict, more than anything else, has been a conflict in attrition—both politically and militarily. The few proactive efforts at conflict resolution since the 1950s, such as the various pacts between governments of the day and Tamil political parties as well as the latest initiative at rewriting the Constitution remain unimplemented owing to a lack of political consensus.

The Tigers are back on the prowl five years after losing control over the Peninsula to Army advances. Closing in from several pockets on Jaffna's civilian, military and logistics strongholds, they have unleashed a series of offensives, keeping the Army guessing about their next move. After the security forces pushed the Tigers back to the Vanni jungles in 1995 in a three-pronged offensive, the LTTE vowed to retake Jaffna—a seemingly difficult task then, given the balance of manpower and military hardware between the standing Army and the rebel forces.

Continued bickering between the ruling People's Alliance (PA) and the Opposition United National Party (UNP) have skewed the political approach towards conflict resolution. The northern offensives are taking place at a time when parliamentary elections are on the horizon, with political players choosing to view the unfolding events through the electoral telescope.

The UNP, which declined to offer any support to the government's efforts at peace-building through a draft Constitution aimed at providing greater powers to the region, seems all set to gain political mileage from the latest setbacks suffered by the PA regime. Given the escalated bullet-ballot dynamics in the Sri Lankan polity, battlefield realities have a direct bearing on poll outcomes. If winning elections are all about success stories, the Chandrika Kumaratunga government would be on a weak footing, notwithstanding the considerable improvement on the human rights front as well as its measures to bring in a more liberal political mindset in a nation which has witnessed brutal parliamentary majority as well as degrees of authoritarianism among their past leaders. If the PA regime reached its high-point in 1995 by retaking Jaffna from the Tigers and putting in place a draft constitutional reform package, it seems to have touched a nadir in 2000—politically and militarily. Since December, the third phase of the LTTE's 'Operation Oyatha Alaigal' has been in force, lashing the island's political and military landscape with relentless fury. That the government had initially brushed aside the Vanni debacle under the political carpet by accusing the UNP, sections of the media, sections of the Army and the LTTE of conspiring to ruin the chances of Chandrika Kumaratunga in the December presidential election, is an indication of the politicisation of the island's battlefield. As a result, the military outcomes of the offensives are set to influence the political agenda as the island heads for parliamentary elections.

The political ramifications of the battlefront developments are set to emerge as critical factors that will guide the immediate future. Voter preferences are more likely to be divided along the lines of military expectations than realpolitik. The PA's insistence that the war would continue, contrasts with the UNP's rather ambivalent attitude which prepared the ground for pushing the concept of a 'phased de-escalation' even during the run-up to the presidential election. The UNP is all set to take the electoral offensive into the PA camp by ascribing the losses to the ruling party's handling of the ground situation. While the PA accuses the opposition of spreading rumours about an already delicate military situation, the official line of thinking is that painting the present setbacks as a debacle would be akin to treason.

Seemingly perfect, the broad plan, however, remains elusive on all three counts. With daily advances that take the battle into government positions, the LTTE is far from being a militarily weakened force. The broad consensus which the present leadership hopes to achieve, despite decades of failure to do so, remains as elusive as ever. And the expectations from an external interlocutor are drastically different from what they were in February, when Norway took upon itself the challenge of initiating direct talks between the government and the Tigers. On the diplomatic front, matters remain in flux. Neither side being in a position as they were, say a year ago, to emphasise the 'internal' nature of the conflict, nor willing to call for an externalisation, the island's foreign policy is, for all practical purposes, linked to the battlefield realities. So is that of India and other nations which are watching the unfolding politico-military dynamics in the island. The island's underlying desire to consider the conflict an internal matter was also apparent when Kadirgamar told the first official press conference after the military developments and External Affairs Minister Jaswant Singh's offer of mediation if invited by the government of Sri Lanka, that India's offer was a very young offer.

The nuanced Indian offer, suffixed with a diplomatic 'if invited', set the island-nation debating on who should extend the invitation to resolve the crisis. "It is for the patient to go to the doctor, not *vice versa,*" said the former Chief Minister of the North-Eastern Province, A. Varadharaja Perumal, who was elected the first, and till date, the only Chief Minister of the north-east, when the Indian Peace-Keeping Force was present in the island in the 1980s. Perumal left Sri Lanka along with the IPKF in 1990, and, after a decade-long self-imposed exile in India, returned to the island last year. He has been an active advocate of Indian intervention. As diplomacy moved in tandem with battlefield developments, Sri Lanka kept its option for assistance, including humanitarian assistance, open but ruled out inviting foreign combatants. The external involvement would be confined to facilitating a dialogue with the rebels.

India has "ruled out military assistance, but has not ruled out humanitarian assistance". India's decision to extend the ban on the LTTE, was "not a fatal impediment" to the possibilities of a resumption of negotiations with an Indian initiative. He was also cautious about the multiplicity of offers made by states to resolve the island's crisis. That India was accorded primacy. Sri Lankan Foreign Minister Lakshman Kadirgamar while commenting on the visit of the Norwegian Special Envoy Erik Solheim to New Delhi, told the Norwegians that "India must be kept informed" about the developments of the Oslo initiative, which seeks to initiate talks between the government and the Tigers.

To a question whether India had prevailed upon the Tigers to contain the offensive, Kadirgamar said, "I reject absolutely and totally that the Indian government has anything to do with the LTTE behind our back." He also said that "we are totally convinced" that India does not want a separate state in the north and east of Sri Lanka.

Admitting that the military situation had necessitated the resumption of diplomatic ties with Israel, Kadirgamar said the island was paying for all the military purchases it was making from seven countries.

Concerns of sovereignty have been dictating the foreign policy of the island ever since the sovereignty-human rights conundrum gained importance on the United Nation's agenda.

Expressing confidence that "the Chinese and the Russians will not allow the Security Council to get involved in Sri Lanka," he said, "this is our internal situation. We appreciate the help of friendly countries, but we must maintain dignity and self-respect, however small a country we are, whatever difficulties we have got ourselves into, our position is still that sovereignty is paramount."

On the request for Indian humanitarian intervention, he said, "By consent, a friendly government can ask a friendly government to help. Our sovereignty is our sovereignty. A Security Council decision is not necessarily by consent. That is a decision that can be imposed on a state." The Indian policy of restricting its assistance to the humanitarian level has engaged much attention: A visible sadness among the Sinhalese that an active Indian military involvement is missing, contrasts with a subtle satisfaction among the Tamils. On the Indian official response to the Sri Lankan developments, Kadirgamar said, "It is perfectly understandable that the government of India would take time to reach decisions on the Sri Lankan question."

To the advantage of Sri Lanka's external policy is the near-total international posturing against separatism. However, given the international attention on the Jaffna offensives, and the drastic changes it could bring about in the island's polity, Sri Lanka would have busy days ahead on the diplomatic front. Even as the battlefield manoeuvres continued, Chandrika Kumaratunga and Opposition Leader, Rand Wickremasinghe, held separate all-party confabulations on the unfolding scenario.

A confident Chandrika Kumaratunga told the political leaders that she was determined to go ahead with the constitutional reform proposals, with or without support from other parties. She said she was holding discussions with various political parties on the draft constitutional reforms and was determined to introduce the devolution package. On the LTTE's recent offer of a temporary cessation of hostilities, the President said that the offer was turned down as the Tigers were "not sincere". The government was open to genuine talks but ruled out withdrawal of security forces from Jaffna.

The left-radical Janatha Vimukthi Peramuna (JVP), which walked out of the meeting protesting against a delay in starting it, made a six-point representation. The JVP called upon the government to abandon its devolution package and treat all communities as equal citizens.

Wickremasinghe, who stayed away from the meeting convened by the President, called upon the government to accept the Indian offer of mediation if invited. He called upon other political parties to urge the government to accept the offer. Holding the view that the nation was going through a "crucial moment", he demanded a political solution. Sri Lankans are war-weary. Although there is a semblance of normalcy, apprehensions run deep: the repeated pleas for the war to end, merely address the issue at a symptomatic level.

Decades of division, enhanced by entrenched militarisation, has left the society wishing for salve, yet it realises that the path to a solution is rough.

Geographically, Jaffna is the name for the northern peninsula. It is also the name of the district. Jaffna district consists of all the areas in the Peninsula and the outlying islands except for the Pachchilaippalli Assistant Government Division (Taluk). The latter belongs to Kilinochchi district. Jaffna and Kilinochchi districts together comprise the Jaffna electoral district. There is also the Jaffna electoral division. Then there is Jaffna city. Jaffna city or municipality consists of the Jaffna electoral division as well as areas from the adjoining Nallur electoral division. Ariyalai and Colombothurai, for instance, are part of the Jaffna municipal area. So technically the LTTE is in Jaffna city after entering Colombothurai or Ariyalai.

After the fall of Elephant Pass, the LTTE went on to take Pallai on the Jaffna-Kandy road or the A-9 highway. It also took areas towards the north-east and Puloppalai to the north-west of Pallai. The Tigers also went further north on the A-9 to reach the southern outskirts of Eluthumattuvaal. They also advanced up the south-western coast to reach Kilali. On the eastern coast, the LTTE targeted Nagar Kovil.

The Sri Lankan armed forces began strengthening their defences in a diagonal line that extended from Kilali to Nagar Kovil via Eluthumattuvaal. At the same time, the LTTE had also established fixed positions in Keratheevu and southern Tanankilappu, south-west of the Peninsula. Also, it had a presence in Eastern Ariyalai in the places around "Munai", or point, including the settlement scheme called "Poompuhaar". The Elephant Pass debacle along with the LTTE's clear-cut military ascendancy had caused grave apprehensions about the future of the Sri Lankan armed forces in the Peninsula. If the LTTE succeeded in advancing further and besieging the Palaly-Kankesanthurai base complex, the military supply lines between Jaffna and the rest of the country would be placed at great risk.

After the recent change in the military equation, Palaly airport and Kankesanthurai harbour were the only viable entry and exit points for air and sea communication. If the LTTE juggernaut rolled on relentlessly and interdicted this link, the physical safety of 38,000 troops in Jaffna would be in peril. Even as a controversy arose in India about this issue, the LTTE offered a "temporary ceasefire". The Tigers stated that their ceasefire would enable the Sri Lankan government to evacuate the "beleaguered troops" safely through the good offices of the International Committee of the Red Cross and avoid further "escalation of violence and a bloodbath". Calling upon the Sri Lankan government to "respond positively without delay", the Tigers also hinted at "a permanent ceasefire" in the future that would "create cordial conditions for peace talks and a negotiated political settlement".

The LTTE also held out a warning that the government will "bear total responsibility for the disastrous consequences of heavy military casualties if it rejects our proposal for deescalation and continues the war effort." Whatever the motives behind the LTTE offer, it seemed to open a "window of opportunity" for the de-escalation of the conflict. While the government could not be expected to accept all the terms of the offer, analysts felt that Colombo would accept a ceasefire in principle, and then negotiate further. But the government reacted quickly and defiantly. The offer was rejected out of hand as "psychological warfare".

President Chandrika Kumaratunga attempted to restore morale by issuing a special message of enthusiastic hope to the soldiers on the battlefront. Deputy Defence Minister Anuruddha Ratwatte announced in Parliament in Sri Jayewardenepura that "we would fight to the last man". Analysts point out that the LTTE "offer" had been drafted in a manner that offered no face-saving way out. It was an ultimatum demanding total surrender without explicitly stating so. The government could just not cave in. Also the retention of Jaffna was of paramount importance to the political fortunes of the People's Alliance (PA) government. The PA's record of governance has been dismal, and in recent times the only effective "plus point" had been the taking of Jaffna. It was the PA's "jewel in the crown". If the government was seen as abandoning Jaffna it was likely to affect the PA in the parliamentary elections to be held after August. Besides, if the government was perceived as letting go of Jaffna without a fight there was a possibility of anti-Tamil violence breaking out in the Sinhala-dominated areas.

Apart from these reasons there was a view in government circles that the LTTE had overstretched its limited resources. It was felt that the Tigers lacked the wherewithal to sustain the current levels of pressure. Also, that it was short of the manpower and firepower needed to take over the greater part of the Peninsula, including Jaffna city and the Palay-Kankesanthurai base complex.

Therefore, the ceasefire offer was interpreted as a stratagem of the LTTE to cover up its deficiency and a bold gamble aimed at getting the Army out without fighting. There was also optimism that after obtaining fresh arms and armaments, the military situation would tilt against the LTTE. The Sri Lankan government also unleashed a massive aerial bombardment within and without the Peninsula. The bombing was ostensibly aimed to prevent the LTTE from inducting its cadres from the mainland into the Peninsula. More important, it was also a "search-and-destroy" mission against LTTE heavy artillery. In recent times, the Tigers have used long-range artillery and armoured cars extensively and successfully in combat. The Air Force scoured the skies in search of these. The objective was to destroy these before the LTTE could move them and reach positions within firing range of the Palaly-Kankesanthurai base. In spite of intensive bombardment there have been no claims by Colombo of targeting artillery or armoured cars.

Observers have detected a "pause-and-pounce" strategy in the LTTE campaign. The Tigers do not fight on continuously. Instead they conduct intermittent assaults, resting in between. These temporary lulls in the LTTE offensive were misinterpreted in Colombo as signs of weakness.

In a dangerous exercise of self-delusion, sections of the Colombo media projected the view that the LTTE "wave" had ebbed. The pause-and-pounce pattern was seen as signifying the LTTE's decline. There was a confident assertion that the critical period for the government had passed and that it had "turned the corner". Events that unfolded proved how dangerously wrong this assessment was. The temporary calm before the storm ended on May 10. In a three-pronged deceptive exercise, LTTE cadres attacked simultaneously the Kilali, Eluthumattuvaal and Nagar Kovil defence lines. The assault in Kilali was particularly severe as the main camp was assailed from three directions. But ultimately these manoeuvres proved to be part of an elaborate diversionary tactic.

The "real" action was close to Jaffna city. This was also on three fronts but within proximity of each other. A simultaneous offensive was launched on all three fronts. The first was when LTTE cadres crossed the western parts of the lagoon from Kalmunai on the mainland in the Pooneryn area and reached Ariyalaimunai on the Peninsula. These cadres advanced further through Poompuhaar and attacked the Army detachment at Maniyan Thottam in Ariyalai. As the Army retreated, the LTTE moved through Ariyalai's interior and reached the Nedunkulam junction on the Jaffna-Kandy road. Technically, the Tigers were now in Jaffna city, 2 km from the Jaffna road leading to the Jaffna district secretariat at Chundikuly. They moved along Mambalam junction and reached Pungankulam junction where another Army detachment was stationed at a community centre-cum-library. Fighting ensued and the Army withdrew. There is, however, a very large camp at the Old Park premises opposite the Jaffna secretariat. Personnel deployed there also entered combat. The LTTE had not moved beyond Pungankulam junction.

The second front was at Navatkuli on the outskirts of Jaffna city. A very long causeway-cum-bridge across the lagoon, known as the Navatkuli palam, is situated on the Jaffna-Kandy road here. It is of strategic importance as it links the Thenmarachchi sector with Jaffna city. Navatkuli has large military installations. Buildings such as a government warehouse and granary, and private shrimp processing and hardware manufacturing plants are now part of a military complex. The third front was at Tanankilappu.

The shortest points between the Peninsula and the mainland on the western lagoon is Keratheevu and Sangupiddy respectively. The LTTE already held both. A road runs from Keratheevu and reaches Navatkuli along the coast, somewhat parallel to the A-9. The road branches off at Tanankilappu junction, where one branch goes straight on to Navatkuli through Kovilaakkandy while the other goes to Chavakachcheri, which incidentally is the largest town in the Thenmarachchi sector. LTTE cadres moved in great numbers from Sangupiddy to Keratheevu and then launched a two-pronged attack on the defences at Tanankilappu on the one hand, and Kovilaakkandy on the other. As fighting progressed, the LTTE claimed successes over both the Tanankilappu and Kovilaakkandy bases.

The LTTE could have moved further up the Tanankilappu road towards Chavakachcheri town. Doing so would have made the Tigers vulnerable to Sri Lankan artillery and aerial attacks as the winding road passes mostly through wide open spaces. Instead of taking that route the LTTE moved towards Navatkuli. After a lull, the LTTE went along the axis of the Navatkuli road and attacked the smaller camp at Thachanthoppu on the way. Troops withdrew after skirmishes. Then came a ferocious onslaught on the Navatkuli base with the Tigers encircling and attacking it on three points from Thachanthoppu, Ariyalai and Navatkuli bridge. After some fierce fighting, the LTTE announced the capture of Navatkuli. Meanwhile, another LTTE contingent came across in a flotilla of boats from Nachikuda in the mainland and landed at the Colombothurai jetty in the Peninsula.

From Colombothurai, the Tigers moved to adjacent Pashaioor and from there to Karaioor, now known as Gurunagar. The LTTE met with stiff resistance in both places but succeeded in proceeding quite a distance on the coast. At the same time, it has not moved into the interior of Colombothurai, Pashaioor or Gurunagar but has maintained its presence only along the coast, at least for now. This is what has led to conflicting claims: the government says these areas are in its possession, while the LTTE says it moved along the coast and took these places. Both sides are partially correct. The balance, however, would alter drastically if and when the LTTE decides to move into the interior of Jaffna city in a decisive manner.

More significant and from Colombo's perspective, fatal strides were made in the Thenmaratchchi sector. After taking Kovilakkandy, another LTTE column went along an interior road through Maravan Pulavu and reached Kaithady situated between Navatkuli on one side and Mattuvil/Nunavil on the other. The village is about six miles from Jaffna city centre and consists of areas on either side of the Jaffna-Kandy road. A sprawling Army camp consisting of several houses in the vicinity has been set up at Kaithady junction. Technically it may not be defined as a "base" but it is certainly a key and vital military installation set up at a strategically important spot.

Branching off from Kaithady northwards is the Kaithady-Kopay road. This road, bordered by Chemmani, winds its way through sections of the lagoon, paddy fields, palmyra groves and open spaces until it reaches the Irupalai junction in Kopay on the Jaffna-Point Pedro road. If one were to proceed straight further along, one would reach Urumpirai junction, on the axis of the Palaly-Jaffna road. With a slight change of direction and covering a short distance one would reach Punnalaikattuvan on the outer perimeter of Palaly complex. If one turns at Irupalai junction in the direction of Point Pedro, then the villages of Puthoor, Neervely and Atchuvely can be reached along the Point Pedro-Jaffna road.

All of them provide access through the interior to reach vantage points, rendering Palaly vulnerable. If one were to turn in the direction of Jaffna one can cover Kopay, Kalviyan Kaadu and Nallur on the Jaffna-Point Pedro road. This would enable the LTTE to move in on Jaffna city from other directions too. Thereafter, the rebels have progressed some distance along the Kaithady-Kopay road and reached the large area known as Kopayveli, 12 km from the Palaly base. They have targeted 122 mm artillery guns with a range of 17 km at Palaly.

The first shells fell in Punnalaikattuvan north and then in Vasavilaan. All these areas have been acquired by the state and incorporated as part of the Palaly base. Nearly 12,000 acres (4,800 hectares) of prime agricultural land in the Valigamam north AGA division have been annexed to the Palaly-Kankesanthurai complex in order to ensure territorial contiguity between airfield and harbour. The expansion of the base also ensured immunity from LTTE attacks, it was felt. But the LTTE was now targeting Palaly with its long-range artillery.

By May 20 it seemed certain that the Tigers could target Palaly effectively. The LTTE claimed that the air traffic control tower at Palaly was hit and damaged. It also claimed that its shells had fallen on the runway as well as on several buildings and barracks within the Palaly base, killing a number of personnel. Significantly, the government denied that the shells had men on the runway but was silent about the other claims. The LTTE also claimed that shells were now falling in the Kankesanthurai harbour area, about five km from the airport. LTTE media outlets abroad claimed on May 20 that the government had suspended air and sea traffic at Palaly and Kankesanthurai after its shells fell in those places. It was also clear by May 22 that the Palaly-Kankesanthurai base was not dysfunctional as claimed by the Tigers. Even though Tiger shells were falling in the airport and the harbour, air and sea traffic continued. In spite of the pressure, the supply lines had not been disrupted—at least not until May 22.

Significantly, the LTTE seemed to have moved some of its artillery closer to Palaly, presumably along the interior of the Jaffna-Point Pedro-Palaly roads. LTTE-fired shells were now hitting places beyond Kankesanthurai to its west, places such as Senthankulam and Illavalai Mathagal. This made Army positions on the northern and north-western coastal sectors vulnerable and increased pressure on Kankesan-thurai. If and when the LTTE dominates the entire Thenmaratchchi sector, it would be in a position to move in full force into the Vadamarachchi and various zones of Valigamam. Also, it would be possible for the Tigers to use the Wanni mainland as a rear base and move to and from the Peninsula without big problems. In the meantime, Air Force planes kept searching for LTTE artillery positions. Even though many bombing forays were conducted, nothing tangible seemed to have been achieved by May 22.

A small group of LTTE cadres also infiltrated the Valigamam west sector and were seen in the area with heavy weapons. The Army had closed down several camps in this sector in the aftermath of the fall of Elephant Pass. These included the ones at Chankanai, Vaddukkoddai and Sithankerni. Upon receipt of information that the Tigers were seen in these places, a large number of troops converged on Vaddukkoddai, Sithankerni and Chankanai and conducted a cordon and search operation. No Tiger cadres, however, were netted. The fighting in and around Jaffna started an inflow of displaced persons into this sector. The possession of Kopayveli as well as progress on the Kaithady-Kopay road has afforded the LTTE a major advantage vis-a-vis Palaly. Apart from reaching strategic positions by proceeding along the road, the Tigers can also use the Kopayveli "Plains" bounding the all pervasive lagoon and reach Kappoothu in the Vadamarachchi sector, Mattuvil in the Thenmarachchi sector, Vatharavathai-Puthoor and Sirupiddy-Neervely in the Valigamam sectors. By May 20, reports indicated that the LTTE was pursuing at least one of these options successfully. A small road—Chappattiaan Kulam road—running through parts of Kopayveli links Kaithady north with Mattuvil north. The Tigers proceeded along this road and passed beyond the Mattuvil landmark, the Pandrithalaichi Amman temple. Thereafter comes the Mattuvil-Sarasaalai junction.

The importance of Kanaganpuliady junction renders its control essential to both sides. Five roads lead out of Kanaganpuliady. First, there is the Madduvil-Kaithady road. Secondly, the Sarasaalai-Kappoothu-Kaligai-Point Pedro road. Thirdly, the Sarasaalai-Vembiraai junction road that mounts the Jaffna-Kandy road between Meesaalai and Kodikamam. Another road from Vembiraai junction goes through Manthuvil and joins the Neeliaddy-Kodikamam road at Varany. Fourthly, there is the Chavakachcheri post office road through Kerudavil (not to be confused with Kerudavil near Valvettithurai) and Perunkulam that reaches Chavakachcheri town. Fifthly, there is the Sarasaalai south road that reaches the Puthoor area after crossing the Vannathi Paalam bridge. It is also possible to travel through Mattuvil and reach the Jaffna-Kandy road at Nunaavil.

The vast potential and possibilities of the strategic Kanaganpuliady and to a lesser extent, the Vembiraai junctions, makes the fighting quite intensive. If and when Kanaganpuliady falls to the LTTE and the Tigers take over all linking roads, the Army will have to vacate Chavakachcheri town and its environs. If the LTTE proceeds downwards from Chavakachcheri, then the greater part of the Thenmarachchi sector will come under its control. The armed forces will have no choice but to move out from places like Kilali, Eluthumattuvaal, Kodikamam and Kachai. Already the LTTE is asking the civilians to move out from the Chavakachcheri sector. In addition to Thenmarachchi, the Tigers can move far more easily into Vadamarachchi and Valigamam sectors apart from edging closer to Jaffna city from other directions and increasing pressure on Palay-Kankesanthurai.

In comparison with the swift pace at which the LTTE progressed in earlier campaigns, the current fight seems slow. This is mainly due to logistical reasons. The LTTE needs time to move its cadres and armaments in sufficient numbers into the upper portions of the Peninsula. This is particularly so in the case of relocating its artillery. Heavy camouflaging is needed to prevent it being targeted aerially and destroyed. Also avenues for speedy mobility have to be ensured because the secret of Tiger successes has been its ability to move heavy guns quickly from point to point in combat. Also, fighting positions like bunkers, pill boxes and trenches have to be constructed at vantage points.

Ideally, the LTTE would have preferred to "pause" for longer periods, prepare adequately, and then "pounce", but circumstances have compelled LTTE supremo Velupillai Prabhakaran to expedite his moves after the Elephant Pass victory. First, the LTTE leader knows that more than any other factor his recent victories were owing to the widespread demoralisation that has set in within Army ranks. Therefore, he wants to extract maximum advantage out of that demoralised mood. To pause too long may give the troops time to restore at least part of their lost morale and regain a fighting spirit. As such the LTTE has to keep its military pressure on relentlessly. Secondly, the LTTE has to reach within striking distance of the Palaly-Kankesanthurai complex as soon as possible. By achieving this proximity, the LTTE can start and sustain an intensive artillery barrage. An "encircle and enfeeble" strategy similar to the one adopted at Elephant Pass, seems somewhat an ambitious project at this juncture, but maintaining an artillery barrage is imperative. This would help disrupt supplies to Jaffna and retard the Army's logistical equilibrium. It would also unnerve the troops, reduce morale and increase panic. Also with Colombo embarking on an expedited worldwide shopping binge for arms and armaments, the LTTE wants to prevent those from reaching Jaffna by a pre-emptive decommissioning of its one and only conduit—the Palaly-Kankesanthurai base complex.

Another factor causing accelerated movement is the international dimension. The LTTE knows that at some point international pressure or possibly intervention will compel both parties to suspend fighting and start talking. If and when that moment comes, the Tigers want to have as much real estate as possible in addition to contracting and undermining Palaly-Kankesanthurai. The LTTE may have scant regard for the rule of law, but it knows that "possession is nine-tenths ownership".

The weekend of May 20 and 21, 2000 saw a spurt in action in the Thenmarachchi sector. The LTTE moved from Kaithady into the Mattuvil-Sarasaalai areas and targeted the strategic Kanakanpuliady camp at the Skandavarodaya school. After heavy fighting the Tigers overran the camp as well as some smaller camps in the vicinity. Thereafter the Tigers followed through on one route and attacked the camp at nearby Vembiraai junction.

The Army abandoned it and readjusted its defence lines. Utilising the geographic advantage accruing to them as a result of dominating Kanakanpuliady, the Tigers launched a multi-pronged attack on the main Thenmarachchi town of Chavakachcheri which, incidentally, is also the second largest town in the peninsula, next to Jaffna.

In the process, the LTTE took over the areas of Mattuvil, Nunavil, Sangathanai, Kovil Kudiyiruppu and Sarasaalai. After some heavy fighting, the soldiers pulled back to positions near Meesalai and Kachchai. Even though the Tigers were claiming Chavakachcheri, the government was denying the claim on the strength of the fact that some soldiers were in occupation of certain spots in the general area of Chavakachcher, even though not in the town. Even as the armed forces began withdrawing from Thenmarachchi into the Vadamarachchi areas, the LTTE mounted attacks on the remaining Army camps in the Thenmarachchi sector. These were in Kodikamam, Kachchai, Meesalai, Mirusuvil, Eluthumattuvaal and Kilaly. By May 22 it was apparent that the most intensive attack was on in Kilaly. One tragic consequence of the fighting in Thenmarachchi was that a number of civilians were affected. The most horrifying incident took place in Kaithady when shells hit a home for the aged: 16 senior citizens were killed and 31 injured. The Tigers are impelled to go slow in actual fighting, particularly in the case of densely populated places such as Jaffna or Chavakachcheri. Ironically, similar factors cramped the Indian Army when it confronted the LTTE during "Operation Pawan" in 1987 to take over Jaffna.

The Sri Lankan Army was not constrained in this manner when it took Jaffna during "Operation Riviresa" in 1995. Lt. General A.S. Kalkat, who commanded the Indian Army in Jaffna in 1987, explained this clearly in an interview to N. Ram of Frontline in 1995. Kalkat said that unlike the Sri Lankan Army that followed a broad front strategy to take Jaffna, he was hampered by concern for loss to civilian life, limb and property. The Indian Army had to avoid civilian casualties and destruction. It could not simply reduce everything to rubble for territorial gain. This "handicap" faced by the Indian Army was exploited by the LTTE then.

Now the LTTE finds itself in a somewhat similar position. The Tigers project themselves as freedom fighters and describe the current war as one seeking to "liberate their homeland from alien aggression". So the LTTE cannot simply launch an all-out offensive and simply march in. The Tigers, who claim to be fighting on behalf of the Tamil people, must demonstrate their concern for the civilians. They cannot fire artillery at random or destroy buildings. They also cannot endanger civilian lives unnecessarily.

There are also logistical reasons. Propagandists in Colombo may "scream" about the Tigers having unlimited firepower and manpower to the extent of sacrificing cadres in waves. All knowledgeable military observers know this is incorrect. Judicious and economic usage of artillery coupled with unbelievable flexibility and mobility has allowed the LTTE to gain maximum advantage from its artillery. A close examination of the LTTE leader's recent war strategy demonstrates that great care is taken to ensure prevention of loss to Tiger lives. Apart from its strategic superiority and tactical brilliance the element of economical management is also evident. It is a case of extracting maximum gains out of minimum resources—material and human. All these factors restrain the LTTE from conducting an all-out onslaught. Even if it wins pitched battles, the LTTE would suffer immense losses, making the victor a Pyrrhic one. The overwhelming concern, however, is for civilians. If the LTTE succeeds after demolishing and destroying much of Jaffna or Chavakachcheri and after causing immense civilian casualties it will be accountable to some level at least to international and Tamil public opinion.

Instead of moving to Chavakachcheri byway of the main Kandy road, it is adopting a more elaborate tactic of encirclement that would enable it to take the town with minimum damage and losses. Likewise, it has scrupulously avoided fighting in the thickly populated interior of Jaffna city. Instead it is encircling the Jaffna municipal area.

These are in comparative terms sparsely populated. Although civilians have started moving out from Jaffna to areas like Manipay, relief organisations estimate that 75 per cent of the population still remains in Jaffna. The LTTE has issued a one-week deadline for the Army in Jaffna city to surrender "with dignity and honour". If they lay down arms they are promised safe passage out of Jaffna within 24 hours under the auspices of the Red Cross. This message is being relayed in Sinhala over the LTTE radio—"Voice Of Tigers"—and also blared over loudspeakers. The armed forces remained apparently oblivious to the LTTE demand. The overall commander of the armed forces in the north, Maj. Gen Janaka Perera, announced over television that there was no question of surrendering and that the armed forces would fight to the last man if necessary. He also asserted that the Army could push the LTTE out of Jaffna in due course.

With Jaffna coming under pressure from the Liberation Tigers of Tamil Eelam, behind-the-scenes diplomatic efforts relating to the situation have intensified. In a significant change in the Indian government's stated position on the situation, Prime Minister Atal Behari Vajpayee said on May 20, 2000 that India was "ready" to take any step "if necessary".

Defence Minister George Fernandes, however, said there was "no question" of military intervention or supply of arms to the Sri Lankan Army. He said India was ready to provide humanitarian and other assistance, including help in the evacuation of troops and stranded civilians, which may be "sought by all sides". Sri Lanka hopes that the Indian concept of humanitarian aid would encompass the evacuation of Sri Lankan troops, if the need arose. Sri Lankan Deputy Foreign Minister Lakshman Kirialla said in Chennai during a visit on May 20 that Colombo and New Delhi had worked out the details of the assistance India would give to his country's troops.

Sri Lankan diplomatic sources, however, confirm that not even a single bullet has been received from India since the onslaught on Jaffna started. They say that Pakistan and China were among the first nations to step in. Israel has also been supplying arms, according to highly placed sources, but reports about their quantity and level of sophistication are apparently exaggerated. For instance, reports about the deployment of eight Israeli Kfir fighter planes on the warfront are not true, according to the Sri Lankan sources. Until the third week of May, the jets had not arrived in Sri Lanka. The Israelis believe in a "cash and carry" policy, and Sri Lanka is facing a financial crunch. Sri Lankan officials say that humanitarian or military aid after the fall of Jaffna will be of no avail. If Jaffna falls, the backlash against India will be tremendous.

The Sri Lankan Joint Operations Chief, General Rohan De Silva Daluwatte, made a four-day trip to India during while he was in Chennai, Bangalore, Kochi and Thiruvananthapuram. Neither Indian nor Sri Lankan officials were forthcoming about the real purpose of his visit, coming as it did when the war was escalating. Senior Indian officials claimed that Daluwatte's visit was concerned only with spiritual matters; the General was in Bangalore to seek solace in the ashram of Sai Baba of Puttaparthi.

Other reports indicated that Daluwate's visit was connected with preparations being made by the Indian Navy for the possible large-scale evacuation of Sri Lankan troops and Tamil refugees from Jaffna and its surrounding areas. The Navy had reportedly moved eight battleships to Chennai and two to Visakhapatnam.

The Indian Air Force was also reportedly on stand-by alert in Thiruvananthapuram. The Navy and the Coast Guard appeared to have enforced an informal blockade in order to prevent an influx of refugees to Tamil Nadu and to stop the transfer of any smuggled arms to LTTE cadres.

Meanwhile, India extended its ban on the LTTE for two more years, while insisting that the ban would not impede its efforts to mediate between the Tigers and the Chandrika Kumaratunga government.

India was yet to receive any formal request for diplomatic intervention from the Sri Lankan government. President Chandrika Kumaratunga maintained that she would take a decision on India's offer of mediation only after receiving an official intimation about it from New Delhi. As things stood at the end of the third week of May, the only international peace effort was the Norwegian initiative. India, despite some initial scepticism supports the quiet diplomacy mode of Norway and other European countries in South Asia, at least for the time being.

A delegation led by Erik Solheim, special adviser to the Norwegian government on Sri Lanka, arrived in New Delhi in the second week of May to hold consultations with the Indian government. Both sides agreed that there were no basic differences in approach in their respective peace moves with regard to Sri Lanka. They also agreed that a meaningful peace would be one that respected the aspirations of the minority peoples within a united and sovereign Sri Lanka.

The Indian Ministry of External Affairs said in a statement that the two sides had agreed that the parties to the conflict should find a solution "in a manner by which all communities can realise their aspirations within the context of the unity, sovereignty and the territorial integrity of the country." Solheim reassured India that his country "recognises India's legitimate interests in Sri Lanka" and that no obstacles would be placed in the way of any Indian initiative. He said that his country's effort was a "low key" one, primarily aimed at staying in touch with all the parties concerned.

Before coming to India, Solheim had briefed the US administration about Norway's willingness to broker peace. The US supportive of Norway's effort to facilitate negotiations between the warring parties, is keen that India participate in the initiative.

The Clinton administration's trouble-shooter, Under Secretary of State, Thomas Pickering, was planning to visit Colombo after holding consultations with Indian officials. Solheim had met him during his visit to Washington.

In recent months, the US has expressed a desire to play a major role in the South Asian region. In this case, the US. State Department said that Washington would facilitate a mediation process "if we are asked". Informed sources in

New Delhi said that Washington wanted a collective international effort to restore peace in the island. According to them, the US wants India to take the initiative in this regard. However, a piquant situation prevails in that the Norwegians are in the forefront of the diplomatic initiative while the Israelis are the conduit for arms supplies to Sri Lanka. In a major boost to Sri Lanka's diplomatic campaign against the LTTE, the European Parliament adopted a resolution recommending a ban on the LTTE by member-states. The European Union (EU) had earlier issued a strong statement calling upon both Colombo and the LTTE to cease hostilities and restart talks. The EU statement expressed deep concern over the increasing intensity of the conflict. It urged both the parties to "cooperate with the Norwegian Government in its endeavour to facilitate a negotiated settlement."

Reports indicated that Sri Lanka was not too happy with India's reluctance to play a more active role. New Delhi had not acceded to Colombo's request for arms. India wanted an open appeal for help. Sri Lanka was reluctant to do so as India gave the impression that it was caught in a dilemma on the issue of supplying arms and providing other tangible forms of support.

Sri Lankan Foreign Minister Lakshman Kadirgamar said that events may force India to play a key role in the conflict. He indicated that India "was gearing itself up for assuming a role". For a change, he praised Tamil Nadu Chief Minister M. Karunanidhi's latest stand on the LTTE, describing it as "very significant and clear".

On May 11, Karunanidhi had stated that his party would be happy if the LTTE achieved the goal of Tamil Eelam. In a clear flip-flop on May 15, he distanced himself from the LTTE, accusing the organisation of indulging in fratricide. "Our support to Tamil Eelam and the tears we shed for the Sri Lankan Tamils could not be construed as support to all the activities of the LTTE," he said in the State Assembly.

Harkishan Singh Surjeet, General Secretary of the Communist Party of India (Marxist), said that India's current stand is detrimental to "our national interests and allows our security to be jeopardised." He added that the US was using countries such as Israel as a front to further its own agenda in the region. "It is high time the Government of India reasserted its firm position on the Sri Lankan issue, steered clear of chauvinism and came to the help of the Sri Lankan government in finding a negotiated and principled solution to the ethnic question."

Britain is in favour of United Nations' intervention in Sri Lanka. It reportedly considered moving a resolution in the Security Council on this, citing the precarious humanitarian situation there. Russia and China were opposed to the move. Britain for the time being has been dissuaded from seeking UN intervention.

The Pakistan government said that "the charters of the United Nations as well as of the SAARC make it incumbent upon all members to respect the sovereignty and territorial integrity of other states. Interference in internal affairs is impermissible under international law."

The Sri Lankan Tamil issue, which had a major, emotional impact on Tamil Nadu in the early 1980s, continues to cast its shadow over the state's politics. So much so that no party, however limited its political presence and ambitions, can afford not to take a stand on the emotive issue of "Eelam".

From 1983, when ethnic strife broke out in Sri Lanka, to Rajiv Gandhi's assassination in May 1991, every Sri Lankan Tamil group enjoyed the backing of one major political party or the other in the state.

The Tamil Eelam Liberation Organisation (TELO) under Sri Sabaratnam had the patronage of M. Karunanidhi, the leader of the Dravida Munnetra Kazhagam (DMK), while Tamil United Liberation Front (TULF) had Chief Minister M. Karunanidhi. Liberation Tigers of Tamil Eelam (LTTE) leaders were supported by Chief Minister M.G. Ramachandran of the All India Anna Dravida Munnetra Kazhagam (AIADMK). But the LTTE, ruthlessly liquidated its political rivals, starting with Sri Sabaratnam in 1984, and arrogated to itself the role of sole champion of the Sri Lankan Tamil cause.

Tamil Nadu, besides being a sanctuary, offered the LTTE financial and material support. The LTTE painstakingly created a clandestine network of smugglers, fishermen, political activists, transport operators, businessmen and officials. This network proved especially useful to the Tigers after it was proscribed. The heinous act of killing Rajiv Gandhi and the revulsion it caused among the people dramatically changed the major political parties' perception of the LTTE and also the larger question of resolving the ethnic crisis.

Most parties rejected the extreme, terrorist approach of the LTTE and favoured a solution within the framework of a united Sri Lanka. A few who believed that a separate Tamil homeland was the only solution maintained a tactical silence in view of the ban on the group and the overwhelming public opinion against it. But pro-LTTE groups became active in Tamil Nadu once again after the Supreme Court confirmed the death sentence against four of the accused in the Rajiv assassination case in November 1999. Under the guise of rallying against the death penalty, these chauvinist elements tried to neutralise the revulsion towards the LTTE and "revive sympathy for it by portraying the assassins as heroes," as pointed out by the CPI(M) Polit Bureau member Prakash Karat. Now, with the LTTE's string of victories since November 1999, the supporters of Tamil Eelam, mostly belonging to chauvinistic parties such as the Marumalarchi Dravida Munnetra Kazhagam (MDMK), the Pattali Makkal Katchi (PMK) and a few fringe groups, have expressed open support to the militant outfit's demand for Eelam.

6

Political Dimension

The Liberation Tigers of Tamil Eelam (LTTE) began a long expected offensive against military positions in the Jaffna Peninsula on December 10, 1999. As the fighting progressed, it became apparent that the LTTE's war strategy for the Peninsula was different from its earlier tactics that proved successful in the northern mainland of Wanni. Instead of launching all-out and frontal attacks on premier military installations, the Tigers seemed to be engaging in piecemeal operations that had the cumulative effect of gradually undermining key targets.

The Jaffna peninsulas chief link with the mainland is the isthmus known as Elephant Pass. After a highway and a railway line were constructed during British rule, Elephant Pass assumed importance as the road as well as the rail line to and from the Peninsula passed through this narrow strip. The military camp at Elephant Pass gained strategic importance after the conflict escalated, as its location enabled the control of all ground transport to Jaffna.

In 1991, the Tigers conducted a full-fledged onslaught, named "Operation Tharai, Kadal, Aahayam" (Land, Sea, Air), to capture the Elephant Pass camp. Although the camp was besieged for several weeks, the LTTE failed in its bid because the Army succeeded in establishing a beachhead at Vettrilaikerni on the south-eastern coast of the peninsula and sent in reinforcements. The Army's counter-offensive was called "Balavegaya" (force). The LTTE suffered over 600 casualties and was beaten back.

Realising the strategic importance of Elephant Pass, the security forces expanded the Elephant Pass camp into a gigantic base complex. Two big camps were established at Vettrilaikerni along the coast and adjacent Kattaikaadu to the interior.

The main camp itself was enlarged through the acquisition of buildings and the area belonging to the once flourishing Elephant Pass Salterns. Midway between Vettrilaikerni and Elephant Pass another big camp was established at Pullaveli. Thus a supply route from Vettrilaikerni to Elephant Pass was set up. Ships ferried supplies and personnel from Trincomalee to Vettrilaikerni. Another camp was set up at Iyakkachi on the main A-9 Highway within the peninsula. This was the western gateway to the Elephant Pass camp. Another camp was established south of Paranthan on the mainland. All these camps were linked as part of the Elephant Pass base complex.

In terms of area the Elephant Pass base is perhaps the largest in the north as Paranthan on one end is four miles away from the central main camp while Vettrilaikerni at the other end is 13 miles away. The Elephant Pass complex houses the whole 54th Division of the Army. Since it was obvious that the fall of Elephant Pass could well enable the LTTE to regain the Peninsula from which it was driven out in 1995-96, it was thoroughly fortified. After the Tigers marked a string of military successes in the Wanni from November 2, 1999, anticipating a frontal Tiger assault on the entrance camp to Jaffna, the Army was lying in wait at Elephant Pass. The Tigers, however, had other ideas.

LTTE cadres travelling by boats from the Mullaitivu coast infiltrated the areas surrounding Vettrilaikerni and Kartaikadu. They attacked both camps simultaneously. The Army was forced to alter its defence lines and withdraw. Thereafter the Tigers overran the camp at Pullaveli. This was followed by a successful attack on the Paranthan camp housed in what was earlier the Chemicals Corporation. The camp at Iyakkachi was being attacked fiercely by the Tigers. If and when Iyakkachi falls, the main camp at

Elephant Pass would be isolated and made vulnerable. Already it is facing artillery pounding. The LTTE strategy of cutting off all "lifelines" by eliminating the surrounding camps could gradually weaken the main camp to the point of capitulation. If the LTTE strategy succeeds in Elephant Pass, it would be a triumph; the Tigers would have achieved their objective with minimum losses and bloodshed. Had the Tigers rushed headlong into the fortified Elephant Pass, they may have sustained heavy losses. All the gains made in the Wanni would have been nullified. Also, the likelihood of overrunning Elephant Pass in a direct confrontation was slim. The innovative strategy adopted instead of the expected conventional one has raised LTTE hopes of an ultimate victory at Elephant Pass.

The LTTE also conducted amphibious assaults on the southern coast of the peninsula. Trained commandos of the LTTE's "Siruthai" (leopard) unit along with Sea Tiger cadres crossed the Kilaly lagoon and made swift raids. A radar station at Thanankilappu was demolished and the equipment seized. The Tigers captured Kerathivu on the peninsula and Sangupiddy on the mainland. These were the points of entry for the Pooneryn ferry service that has been suspended for some years now.

The LTTE fired long range artillery from the mainland at targets in the then maratchy or southern sector of the Peninsula. It was preceded by an announcement calling upon civilians along the coastal areas and in the proximity of military camps to move to the interior. The LTTE claimed that the shells had hit the brigade headquarters of 512 and 514. It was claimed that the artillery points of the Army on the coast were destroyed. Some shells hit civilian positions including a hospital. One person was killed and 18 people were injured.

After taking Vettrilaikerni the LTTE proceeded. northwards along a coastal road that ends up at Point Pedro, the northernmost point of the island. The LTTE succeeded in capturing the army camp at Maruthankerni and adjoining villages such as Uduthurai and Aaliyavalai. The next military camp along this road is at Thalaiyadi where a major confrontation is expected.

Another contingent of the LTTE turned westwards at Maruthankerni and are proceeding along a road that merges at the Puthukaddu junction on the Jaffna-Kandy road north of Iyakkachi. If the Tigers reach their destination, then they would have formed a rectangular swathe of territorial control above Elephant Pass. Thus it would be interdicted from all other possible strategic points on the Peninsula. If the quick successes of the Wanni are the standard to measure LTTE progress, then in the Peninsula the pace is slow in comparison. But the strategy employed by the Tigers seems to be "cost-effective".

The Tamil people of the north and east constitute a distinct nation, equal to the Sinhalese. As such they have the intrinsic and inalienable right of self-determination, which includes the right to set up their own independent and sovereign state. In accordance with Leninism, this right is to be supported by Marxists unconditionally and unreservedly. However, like the right to divorce, it is one thing to support this right and another to support, at a given time, its exercise in the form and modality of separation.

From 1976 onwards, when the Tamil United Liberation Front (TULF) adopted the Eelam slogan, up to roughly 1985, it was possible, indeed incumbent, for socialists to champion the right of the Tamil people to national self-determination, including the right of the secession and furthermore to support the Tamil effort to exercise that right to the fullest in the specific form of setting up of an independent, sovereign (hopefully socialist) Tamil Eelam State.

The key link in Sri Lankan politics was the Tamil national question and the central question of the Sri Lankan revolutionary left strategy at the time was in fact the Tamil national question. However, Lankan progressives and democrats can no longer support the exercise of the right of Tamil self-determination in the concrete form of a struggle for an independent, separate state. In other words they can no longer support the struggle for Tamil Eelam. It is in fact in the best interests of the Tamil and Sinhala masses and the democratic forces in the entire subcontinent, that the struggle for self-determination not be exercised in the form of this option. The turning point came in the period between 1985 and 1986. In May 1985 the attack on Anuradhapura took place in which at least 200 innocent, unarmed, non-combatant, entirely uninvolved men, women and children of all ages were slaughtered in cold blood by the LTTE. It was the Anuradhapura massacre that brought home two facts—firstly, the character of the LTTE and secondly, their hegemony within the Tamil Eelam liberation struggle.

Until May 1985, the Tamil Eelam liberation struggle did not target noncombatant civilians. So there was, in that sense, a compatibility between Left/revolutionary activity among the Sinhalese people and the defence of the Tamil Eelam demand. It was a non-zero sum game between the mass base of Sinhala progressives and the mass base of the Tamil liberation movement. But this changed qualitatively in 1985. May Day was commemorated by the LTTE with the brutal slaughter of TELO militants in the streets of Jaffna. This indicated that the LTTE was metamorphosing from a national liberation movement into something else. That metamorphosis has now been completed and the Tigers have degenerated into a fascist force. This is not to say that there is no Tamil nationalist or even national liberationist aspect to their struggle, but this is no longer the primary aspect.

'Militarily defeated' does not mean that the LTTE can be defeated by military means alone. They must be politically isolated and militarily contested. Political isolation necessarily means the granting of a genuine measure of autonomy to the Tamil people, i.e., meeting at least part-ways, the right of self-determination of the Tamil Nation. This perhaps does not hold true for national struggles in the subcontinent in general.

The Tamil struggle in Sri Lanka, given its present leadership, i.e., that of the fascist LTTE, should not be carried to the extent of the struggle for an independent state as that would have been profoundly destabilising with retrogressive effects throughout the subcontinent. By destabilisation, one does not refer solely or even primarily to the stability of the capitalist system. In this global period of the retreat and recession of socialism, sub-nationalist and anti-systemic movements will be looking around for a new role model. If the LTTE succeeds, that would deal a death blow to the possibilities of a rational-socialist renewal in the subcontinent. In this period of globalised communications, it would have a demonstrative effect which is negative, in other parts of the world as well.

Capitalism will survive the setting up of separate state by the Tigers, because the relations of production in such a separate state will inevitably be capitalist (at first it will be petty bourgeois but it will certainly evolve, perhaps rapidly, into full-fledged capitalism). But the radical democratic forces and in particular the socialist forces will be very badly damaged in the subcontinent and perhaps even throughout the Third World, by a victory for the LTTE.

This analysis is based on the assumption that of all the threats to democracy and to democratic forces, the most dangerous comes from fascist and Pol Potist organisations. And in Sri Lanka today, after the defeat of the JVP, the LTTE remains the most dangerous foe. The JVP was potentially more dangerous because it posed a threat to state power at the centre. The late Ranjan Wijeratne was one of those who simplistically equated the JVP with the LTTE. Though this is incorrect, the nationalist appeal of the LTTE 'only' means that far more, qualitatively more, than in the case of the JVP, attention will have to be paid to assuaging the national feelings of the Tamil people.

The struggle of the German Communists and the Italian Communists furnish certain lessons of relevance. Fascism in those instances was not a foreign fascism; it was a fascism which had strong national roots, a very strong nationalistic appeal. That did not mean that those Marxists did not consider 'their' national fascism to be other than their primary enemy. The German Communists were, of course, not successful.

The maximum momentum to be imparted to the anti-Tiger was only if the democratic forces bring psycho-political pressure to bear upon them. The larger and more generous the political package and the faster it is made available, the bigger will be the contribution to the anti-Tiger war. The more powers the state devolves, the more powerful will be the shove it administers to the Tigers.

The more generous and faster the designing of the devolution package, the swifter will be the fall of the Tigers. This is primarily because the Tamil people, who have begun to have doubts as to the success of the Eelam struggle, will decide that it is not worth continuing the armed struggle when a large measure of self-rule is on the table and is obtainable if they simply give up the war. Such altered thinking on the part of the Tamil masses of the north cannot but manifest itself as pressure from below upon the Tigers. Such pressure may even cause fissures in the ranks of the Tiger leadership, resulting in internal killings. This will finish off the Tigers and end the war in fairly short order.

One cautionary note is needed here. If the Tamil people are to be re-inducted into the democratic mainstream, that mainstream itself has to change. At the very least it must change back to what it was when the Tamil community felt itself to be part of it; before the Tamil community felt alienated from it. In short, to pre-1956, before SWRD Bandaranaike, when official discourse and official political culture was not weighted with the symbols and rituals of any one ethnic or religious community. Today though, when the Tamil community watch Colombo-based TV listen to Colombo radio and read southern newspapers, can they believe that the mainstream which they are being invited to join is one in which they will be treated as equals? On the contrary, it would seem that the mainstream is as (or almost as) iaden with symbols and rituals of the dominant culture and the majority religion than before.

A visibly pre-eminent place given to one religion—specially to one which almost no Tamil belongs, be it in the north-east, the hill country or Colombo—is simultaneously taken to be discrimination against the Tamil community. In short, the very high profile given to the majority culture and religion, does not render the mainstream very attractive for the alienated Tamil community to rejoin. Premadasa used to point out that the Tigers had been in the jungles for

17 years and therefore the democratic leadership and the system should make the necessary concessions to help them adjust. That thinking was wise and correct, though there were errors and delays in implementation.

The Tamil community has been 'in the jungles', that is to say, alienated from the mainstream, for a much longer period than the LTTE—for at least 35 years. After all, it is that community and that alienation which gave birth to the Tigers! How much greater then, how much more far reaching, should be the changes (of and in the mainstream), in order to reincorporate this community? Prabhakaran makes the point that his struggle is a continuation of forty years of Tamil nationalist politics in its various forms and thrusts. This is basically true, though his struggle is a distorted, debased and fanatical extension of that political phenomenon. Since the Tamil people have been exposed to these politics for so long, it is easy for Prabhakaran to win their support or sympathy or at least to secure their neutrality. It is like the JVP having grown on the SLFP propaganda about the Accord.

This being the case, what have Sinhala democrats done to contain or neutralise the Tamil nationalist political content of this struggle? What concessions, what reforms have been made to split off and co-opt that component? In the case of the JVP, we have witnessed a number of initiatives—Provincial Council, Presidential and parliamentary polls, the candidacy of Premadasa, sending off the IPKF, the Land Task Force, the Youth Commission, the Janasaviya, and so on. But what of the LTTE and the phenomenon of Tamil insurgency? In fact the state needs to enact more far-reaching reforms in order to undercut the LTTE, since ethno-nationalism is a far more powerful phenomenon than the forces and factors that created the JVP. Ironically though, the state's psycho-political reform efforts on the Tamil issue have been far fewer. So far, almost all Sinhala politicians seem to have underestimated the emotional depth of this phenomenon. Making Tamil a national language is, taken by itself, 'too little, too late.' In any case, Tamil nationalism has graduated from a language question to one of territorial autonomy and self-rule.

Therefore, reforms have to commence in the sphere of regional autonomy. The day a substantial autonomy package is passed by parliament and becomes law, that day will be the beginning of the end for the LTTE, because the support base for the insurgency will begin to wither.

The best option by far therefore was—and is—to move swiftly on the autonomy issue together with the non-LTTE Tamil groups. The military is likely to be far more amenable to a political deal with the non-LTTE Tamil groups which are its current allies—especially since such a deal would bring victory and peace, closer. If it is a stark choice, the Sinhala public would probably prefer a deal with the anti-Tiger groups than with the Tigers.

In 1977 the UNP manifest promised to address Tamil grievances through a round table discussion process. It didn't do so, thereby squandering away a golden opportunity, given the Government's strength and popularity at that time. J. R Jayewardene had a chance-given the margin of the UNP victory—to solve this problem which dates back at least to 1956, if not to the 1920's and 1930's. It is because Lanka mishandled this question that it never fulfilled the promise shown at the time of independence and especially after the Korean boom. The same thing happened just before the anti-Tamil riots of July 1983.

In 1952 Dudley Senanayake won the elections, but one year later came the hartal of 1953, followed by the language cry of 1955 and the defeat of 1956. The UNP's victory of 1965 was followed by policies which led to the birth and rapid growth of the JVP. In a mere five years, Rohana Wifeweera, a young man in his twenties, built a movement which launched an insurrection that made worldwide news. Even Prabhakaran's rise was not as swift and dramatic. There must have been something very wrong indeed with the policies of the Senanayake regime especially in the rural sector, since Senanayake's popularity in those areas only masked the growth of a rural youth rebellion. Even the galaxy of brains and experience in the seven-party coalition government of Senanayake could not foresee or forestall this.

The 1970 victory of the SLFP-LSSP-CPSL United Front couldn't forestall the 1971 insurrection. Their 1972 Constitution laid the foundation for the Eelam movement while their policies and practices almost ruined the economy, destroyed their own credibility and paved the way for nearly two decades of UNP rule. All this in a mere seven years unthinkable in 1970, at the time of their victory. So this seems to be a rigid pattern in our politics, almost an iron law. The common root of these grave failures seems to be a blindness to core problems; the belief of these governments that since they were so popular electorally, nothing really serious could go wrong; that they were past the worst challenges; that ethnic or youth issues could be dealt with. In other words, electoral victory gave them an illusion of possessing impregnable strength.

Facing and outmaneuvering India, fighting the LTTE, etc., would fall into these categories in today's context. It is possible that this distinction in politics corresponds with the difference between 'government' and 'state'—with high intensity politics related to issues of the state and problems of statecraft, rather than with those of governance (particularly those problems of the state which have an external dimension). Or to put it differently, victory in electoral competition between parties, success in party politics, seems to have always blinded Sri Lankan government to more deep-seated, basic and fundamental crises in its structures and system. The question then is how could successive governments avoid this deadly error and use their electoral triumph as a means to address out deep-rooted structural and systemic crisis? One keeps thinking of Gorbachev's great political sagacity land ideological insights and yet the collapse of the USSR occurred during his term of office. It is incumbent on the state, therefore, to design a political component and corollary of its military actions. The war must not be fought as an ethnic war. It cannot be allowed to lapse into what it used to be—namely, a war with an ethnic character. If the state permits the war to become an ethnic one, we shall surely lose. It is vitally necessary to distinguish the war against the Tigers, from our response to the Tamil national question. That question requires and will always require a political solution, a solution that meets the legitimate national aspirations of the Tamil people.

Lankan democrats simply must come up with and put in place a package of substantial political reforms, which can meet the just grievances and aspirations of the Tamils. What are the components of such a political package? The repeal of the Sixth Amendment is indubitably one such component.

The Tamil people must feel and see that Tamil nationalists, even the most extreme Tamil nationalists, can voice their sentiments within the Sri Lankan parliament and its other democratic institutions. If our institutions can house extreme Sinhala nationalists, many of whom are chauvinists, one simply cannot see why their Tamil counterparts should be excluded from these fora. The repeal of the Sixth Amendment would therefore give Lankan political institutions and practices the kind of flexibility and elasticity they so badly need. In other words, it is a question of stretching our political institutions so as to accommodate the demands and aspirations of the majority of the Tamil people, at this advanced stage of the development of their ethno-national consciousness.

With out deep-seated and wide-ranging political reforms the state will be unable to drive a wedge between the terrorists and the Tamil people. It must be able to win over, or at the very least neutralise the Tamil masses. All efforts, any sacrifice, any concession or compromise is warranted in pursuit of this objective, which is a vitally necessary corollary of military action. There is a view that the political package should be shelved until the military task has been accomplished. On the contrary, the political efforts must undergird the military. The strategy must be two-track. The repeal of the Sixth Amendment and, of course, genuine autonomy to the provincial councils are a necessary part of the political track. The non-repeal of the Sixth Amendment did not drive the Tigers to war. None the less, it should have been repealed because its continued existence on the statute book provides the Tigers with an argument to do what they always wanted to.

The repeal of the Sixth Amendment will not give the Tigers anything they do not have already. In fact, the repeal would deprive them of something, i.e., of one of the arguments in their propaganda armoury. They pushed for it in 1990, not because it mattered to their pride. They chose to make an issue of it at this time precisely because they understood that, given the balance of power in parliament, the government would find its repeal problematic.

At the time the Sixth Amendment was brought in, the Sinhala establishment (both government and opposition) was heading in a policy direction quite the opposite, to the direction in which it should have gone. Its strategy at that time should have been to split the Tamil moderates from the extremist secessionists. All it achieved with the Sixth Amendment was the very opposite, namely, to drive the TULF and, much more important, its mass base out of the democratic process, transforming them into a virtual diplomatic-cum-propaganda arm of the guerrilla groups, thereby enhancing the international legitimacy of the latter. Therefore, the Sixth Amendment was a disaster. Brought into appease the rampaging Sinhala mobs, whose mindless destruction some senior UNP politicians in the party leadership probably thought would amount to a mere rap across the knuckles of the Tamils.

Coming as it did in the immediate aftermath of the July 1983 riots, the Sixth Amendment heaped insult upon injury. No wonder even the Tamil moderates could not stomach it. The position of the Tamil moderates had been gravely undermined, while that of the extremists had been greatly enhanced. It is no surprise, therefore that the moderates could not, and did not, even feel inclined to swear their loyalty to the unitary state. If a women, having been badly mauled by her husband, is disinclined to swear her fidelity to him and their marriage on the day after the beating, and indeed seriously contemplates divorce, who one earth can one blame her? It was utterly hypocritical of Sinhala politicians to criticise the TULF on this score.

The Sixth Amendment is something that even an enlightened democrat should be unwilling to stomach, because it deprives an individual or group from advocating a different constitutional and political model. It is like the right of divorce. The marriage vows or civil code should not explicitly preclude the right of divorce.

For instance, SWRD Bandaranaike was a committed federalist in 1925/26. He believed that a unitary state was totally unsuitable for a multi-ethnic polity such as ours. At that time it is possible that he may have refused to swear loyalty to a unitary state. So long as a Tamil politician or group does not resort to arms in furtherance of secession, he/it should have the perfect right to peacefully advocate secession. If Sinhala politicians can advocate a unitary state, but still be honourable members of parliament or honourable ministers, why should a Tamil not be able to do the same? After all if socialist revolution can be advocated in parliament, why insist that one must religiously worship a unitary or even a united state?

It is cause for amusement that Sinhala politicians sound quite bewildered and hurt wondering why the Tamils are so 'unreasonable' as not to accept the notion of an undivided Sri Lanka and feel themselves part of it. When we changed over to calling ourselves Sri Lanka from Ceylon in 1972, we did so as part of a move that did away with Section 29c of the Soulbury Constitution with its safeguards for the minorities, while also ignoring the TULF's six-point letter which sought a discussion on the proposed new constitution. In other words, we made clear that Sri Lanka was co-terminous with Sinhala, and indeed Sinhala Buddhists. We invested it with an ethnic content, and then we are appalled that Tamils have a problem about considering themselves Sri Lankan. The same goes for our army. Our politicians, our editorialists, what to know, why the Tamils object to the Sri Lankan army being stationed in Tamil majority areas—and we ask this, having transformed the Sri Lankan army over the decades, into a Sinhala army.

The greatly belated recognition by the Tamil organisations of the specificity of the Muslim identity and the concomitant necessity for sub-unit devolution (autonomous areas) for the Muslim people of the east is most welcome. However, an electoral deal with the Muslim organisations, if it is perceived by the Sinhalese to be at their expense will only reactivate the dormant anti-Muslim component of Sinhala chauvinism.

The electorally defeated Sinhalese will remain within the north-east as an embittered minority; a veritable antibody, striving for Enosis with the Sinhala areas across the border. The only solution is perhaps to remove as much as possible of the aforementioned 'inflammable material'. The way to do this is by re-drawing the boundaries of the north-east in such a manner that the Sinhala majority areas are excised. These areas in Vavuniya can be attached to Anuradhapura, those such as Seruwila to Polonnaruwa, and as we suggested in the Chidambaram proposals of December 1986, Amparai should be excluded from the merged province. As for Trincomalee town, one could permit the central government control not only of the harbour but also of the inner ring of Sinhala populated areas within the town.

The Sinhala objection of the re-demarcation proposal is that it results in the creation of an ethnically homogeneous, i.e., a purely Tamil/Tamil, speaking province, which is easily rendered a launching pad for Eelam. The Sinhala presence in the Eastern Province today is seen as a handle for the central government.

Taken together, the objection to a merger of the two provinces as they are currently constituted and this critique of redemarcation, comprise one of the many Catch-22s of Sinhala consciousness. The larger and longer Lankan crisis, dating from at least the 1960s, is rooted in the contradiction of maintaining a racist capitalism, that is to say, the contradictions inherent in the expanded reproduction of a capitalism that is dependent and transnationalised globally, integrated together with a political superstructure, symbolism and an ideology that are rooted in Sinhala hegemony.

In 1977 J. R. Jayewardene was a man with a hegemonic project. Its foundation was the 'open economy'—heralding a new stage of dependent capitalist growth—while its edifice was the presidential system. Jayewardene was an ideological politician who had enunciated his 'general line' in the 1960s, in contradiction to the softer, more welfarist line of the then UNP Prime Minister, Dudley Senanayake. While the left had expected Jayewardene's new model to generate a social backlash and therefore go into political crisis fairly swiftly, these hopes were belied at least until 1982—and it might be argued, permanently.

Jayewardene crushed a general strike in July 1980 with a tidal wave of sackings and did so without any visible diminution of the UNP's stability or indeed popularity. In October 1982 he won the presidential elections in a relatively violence-free and unrigged poll, albeit flawed by the enforced absence of the UNP's traditional rival Sirimao Bandaranaike from the contest. The crisis of the hegemonic project came later and differently, with the riots of July 1983. Is one to conclude then that crises are never generated along the economic or even the socio-economic axis and are always 'over-determined' by the superstructure? And is over-determination not in fact inevitable, inextricable as it is from uneven development? Is overdetermination conjun-ctural while uneven development is structural? Or is it that given the historicity and structure of the Lankan formation it was inevitable that the crisis would unfold along the ethnic fault lines?

If one's focus is narrower and closer, one may conclude that the undoing of Jayewardene's hegemonic project, and subsequently that of Premadasa's, lay in the realm of the political—and more specifically in the lack of structures and practices by which political contradictions can be correctly handled. These constitute not only those institutions conventionally referred to as 'think-tanks' for analysis, public-policy oriented research, conflict prevention and resolution and crisis-management, but also a political culture in which these inputs are made at the apex of the decision-making process.

Though seemingly American, this political practice is present as far afield as Malaysia, Pakistan, India and Bangladesh. Ironically, the presidential form of government is usually far more conducive than the parliamentary, to this arrangement and process, Sri Lanka has throughout remained one of the few exceptions, despite its older democratic political institutions, its higher levels of literacy and its greater economic modernity than all other South Asian states—and many Third World ones. This absence stems from the absence of a meritocratic and modernist political culture and culture in general.

Does chauvinism come from 'top-down' or from the 'bottom up'? Are the bourgeois political parties and leaders in fact responding to the sentiments of the masses? Or does this chauvinism originate neither from the 'top' or the 'bottom' but from the intermediate strata, the petty bourgeoisie and its organic ideologies, the clergy? And what is the pattern of interaction, the directional thrust? Is it 'middle' to 'bottom' to 'top'?

In July 1983, one wondered why our society had not produced an anti-racist or peace movement as in the USA or even Israel. One tentative answer was that we had an unfree media. If the Sinhala people really knew, one thought, they would be behaving differently. Later one realised that, while true, this was not the whole truth. Even in the absence of censorship, editors and journalists were putting across only one side of the story. So that problem then was one of racism and consequent self-censorship rather than one of the big bad capitalist state or monopoly capitalist ownership of the press. This in its turn brings up the question of the class character of chauvinism. Was it bourgeois or petty bourgeois? The problem is that petty bourgeois chauvinism is sometimes not only non-capitalist but also anti-capitalist.

Using Marx's typology in the Communist Manifesto, one can identify this sectors ideology as that of the traditional petty bourgeoisie, based on those sectors of the economy and society that were being swamped by the rapid growth of dependent capitalism. This ideology is thus a backward looking, reactionary one. This identification of the class character of racism points to another problem. Is national chauvinism bound up with capitalism or is it pre-capitalist as well? Lenin thought the former, but Stalin in 1912 touched on the latter. For his part, Lenin, who almost always spoke of bourgeois nationalism, once spoke of it as the most deep-rooted petty bourgeois prejudice. This sub-theme in Lenin and Stalin needs to be developed.

For over a decade after 1958, Sri Lanka was ruled intermittently under emergency laws. The laws were introduced in 1947, and used first in 1953 but more prominently during the race riots of 1958. They were re-imposed in 1966 and continued till 1970 under the UNP regime of 1965-70.

The SLEP-led UF's years of emergency lasted from 1970 to 1976. Then came the UNP regime and the operation of the Prevention of Terrorism Act. This process of permanent emergency is something of a contradiction in terms. Emergency in this sense, has become the norm in Sri Lanka. This process of near-permanent emergency has some structural implications, in terms of the evolution of what is called in Latin America, the National Security state. Now if the Indian state, one of the most powerful bourgeois states in the Third World, could be used by the Tamil militants as a lever—albeit in pursuance of its own interests, because it had to give something to the Tamil people, particularly after the IPKF operations, and also because of Tamil Nadu public opinion—then the polity and centralised Lankan state could be prised open and structural reforms could also be effected.

After all, Sri Lanka unlike India, does not have a big landlord class, which is the social class that usually resists democratisation. Unlike in most Third World societies, there are hardly any feudal residues. Capitalism is not only the dominant but, arguably, almost the exclusive mode of production in the Sri Lankan social formation. The agrarian revolution is not the main aim of the democratic revolution here. These externally induced reforms of the state structure could be seen as analogous to the land reforms under Douglas Mac Arthur in post-war Japan. Such was the thinking, the perspective of the Left after the Accord.

Irony, therefore is in command and contradictions abound. The various struggles for peace, against racism, for autonomy, against authoritarianism, against capitalism, against fascism, against imperialism, the struggle for national reconciliation and unity, the struggle for national independence and sovereignty, diverge, collide and contend. Far from being able to effect the necessary articulation of the anti-racist, anti-authoritarian and anti-fascist struggles, these get concretely dearticulated. The struggle for the recognition of 'diversity in unity' comes up against that for 'unity in diversity'. The struggle for democracy itself split up between those against authoritarianism (anti-regime), for devolution and against fascism.

The anti-fascist struggle necessitates alliances even with authoritarian, pro-imperialist capitalists and chauvinists—the very targets of the earlier struggle! The struggle for peace, for autonomy and against chauvinism, necessitated a bloc with pro-imperialist bloc can therefore be neither 'national' nor 'popular'. Since neither the SLFP nor the UNP are liberal or consistently democratic forces (the former being semi-feudalistic in superstructure and the latter, semi-authoritarian), the 'anti-fascist bloc' is not the equivalent of a 'democratic bloc'. Finally, since both the SLEP and the UNP have factions which appease the JVP, a distinction had to be drawn between an 'anti-fascist bloc' and 'a non-fascist' one.

The Marxist-Leninist EPRLF, representing interests of the proletariat, was ensconced in the camp of the Indian army, representing the interests of the Indian big bourgeoisie! In the south, the Left parties, not to mention the revolutionary groups, were closer to the dependent capitalist UNP at that moment, than to the anti-imperialist, plebian JVP. Similarly, the Marxist EPRLF is farthest away from the plebian nationalist LTTE and the Marxist EROS and is closer to the nationalist TELO class struggle, but which classes against which? How could the Left get out of this back on to the 'correct class struggle track'? Is there any such straight and narrow path? At the present moment what alternative strategy is possible or more correct? How do we prevent this from causing a deviation of long-term consequence? Class struggle is not like some football match with just two teams, clearly identifiable in their jerseys. 'Classes' do not 'struggle' that way. It is 'blocs' that contend, and these blocs consists of class and non-class social groups, connected in certain changing patterns of hegemony and subalternity. In other words, one is talking about politics, though not inevitably and totally in opposition to class struggle.

After the Anuradhapura massacre, a young Sinhalese boy or girl was no longer just interested in the history of oppression of the Tamils by the Sinhala bourgeoisie—all they wanted was to do something and as far as they were concerned the government was not doing anything about the Eelamist affront. So they signed up with the JVP. There was a real continuity, in a politico-historical sense, between the JVP and those who blocked the Bandaranaike-Chelvanayakam Pact in 1957 and the Dudley Senanayake-Chelvanayakam Pact in 1966. The JVP became the armed vanguard and the new generation on the selfsame social-cultural forces that thwarted a revolutionary (i.e., power sharing) settlement of the Tamil national question from 1955 onwards, thereby causing a separatist armed struggle for two decades and Indian intervention three decades later. When there was agitation against the pact of 1957 and the pact of 1965 causing the abrogation of both, there was no 'open economy' and the referendum of 1982 had not taken place. One cannot deny the other causes of the massive anti- Accord rioting of 29 July, 1987, i.e., that socio-economic and democratic streams of dissent fed into this, but the Accord was simply 'the straw that broke the camel's back'. The forces of Sinhala-Buddhist hegemonism have an autonomous existence, and cannot be reduced to socio-economic causes.

It must be emphasised though that bourgeois democratic reform (devolution) was a result of 15 years of armed struggle against the bourgeois state and successive albeit rival bourgeois regimes. This reveals something about the character of the Lankan state. So much struggle, suffering and sacrifice to win this basic bourgeois democratic reform!

Some may think that the Sinhalese (JVP) and Tamils (LTTE) should and could have united to oppose Indian intervention, but there was little chance of that really happening. They opposed Indian intervention because they wanted to get at each other's throats. It was the IPKF that should in the way. Both the JVP and the LTTE opposed that Accord and the IPKF but for two different and divergent reasons.

The JVP wanted to get rid of the IPKF and the Accord and wanted all the concessions granted to the Tamils under the Accord rolled back. The question cf the JVP, though they are very similar in their behaviour and though they may even collude temporarily, will eventually contend, because they are both exclusivist, hegemonist and supremacist in ethnic terms. They are also incapable and perhaps this is the key of political power-sharing. From a strictly scientific point of view one cannot agree with the terms 'Indian imperialism' or 'Indian expansionism'. The terms 'hegemonism' and 'interventionism' are more accurate.

There is a notion that Rajiv Gandhi was duped by Jayewardene into doing his dirty work while another notion is that there was a much deeper Indian design. Both interpretations are correct. It is true that Rajiv Gandhi had been taken for a ride by Jayewardene when it came to actual implementation of the Accord. Rajiv would have preferred to have the Accord implemented in full. But the structural question remains the India state, the nature of the India state and its role. It has aspired to recognition as a 'sub-super power' and it had always been recognised as such by the erstwhile Soviet Union from the time of Khrushchev.

The problem with the Americans was that they failed to concede it until after Bangladesh. However the US could concede it relatively unproblematically on the question of Sri Lanka. This was not so the question of Pakistan, where the American commitment goes back three decades. But on Sri Lanka, American stakes are sufficiently low, it is a non-zero sum game, because it can concede India's regional pre-eminence (only?) on this question. On the Accord there was an 'agreement' between the United States and India.

The role of the Indian state is very much like the role of a Bonapartist state. It is a regional Bonapartism, relatively autonomous of the contending forces (Sinhala and Tamil), tilting to one side and then the other and finally attempting to impose a settlement, a Pax India, on both. At one time, it tilts to the Tamils, equips them, then it tilts to the Sinhalese and raps the Tamils. What must be understood is that in the latter part of the 1980's, this 'regional Bonapartism' acted through the 'domestic Bonapartism' of the Jayewardene government which was balancing between the Sinhalese and the Tamils; the fractions of his own party and government; the left and the ultra-conservatives. He was relatively autonomous of these forces and cracked down alternately on each.

Just as, given the individualistic nature of Sinhala society, we need a strong leadership, the history of this island also points to the need for a strong state with a degree of centralisation if its sovereignty and therefore territorial integrity are to be defended. The recent experience of Yugoslavia and even Canada underscores that point. It is also necessary to prevent any Tamil political formation being tempted to link up with Tamil Nadu, Delhi or even the West.

However, the problem is that the over-centralisation of our state also resulted in the Eelam war. What then is the way out of this dilemma? Perhaps the main problem is not so much over-centralisation, but the non-secular nature of the state. If the state is not perceived as Sinhala-Buddhist-oriented, perhaps the Tamils and other minorities would not mind a degree of centralisation. So, possibly, the answer is a trade off—make the state secular and genuinely pluralist, with no sign of bias towards the dominant ethno-religious community, and it may be possible to cut back on the confederal or federal character of any solution. It is also because the Tamil people felt like second-class citizens at the centre that they relocated their struggle and demanded more power at the periphery, where they could rule themselves. Had there been genuine equality, i.e., parity of status for all ethnicities, cultures, religions and languages, then there would be a reduced demand or need for federalism.

The answer therefore is a combination of secularisation and genuine, substantial upgrading of powers to the NE Provincial Council, i.e., 13th Amendment plus. The alternative to this in the medium term is probably a loose federalism or a confederation, or even separation. Looking at our history and current global trends, one can understand better though not yet fully agree, with Premadasa's stand on District Development Councils and Provincial Councils during the Jayewardene presidency—though certain subjective factors may have gone into that stand as well. This brings us to yet another problem. Given the severity of the Eelam struggle, it is probably both unavoidable and desirable to have an autonomous unit for the north-east, with enhanced powers. If so, as matters stand, these powers will have to be given to the other Presidential Councils as well. This, however, will obviously weaken the central authority, thus undermining the capacity of that authority to play its vanguard role. So the central authority will be undermined along not just on one axis, but on three i.e. vis-a-vis the Tamıl periphery, the rest of the (Sinhala) areas, and the economy (with the sate divesting itself of its economic assets due to privatisation). If this takes place, the central authority may begin to shrink as did our last kingdoms, on the retreat before the tide of invasion. Anarchy will creep in.

How then to solve this problem? We should not try to cut back too much on the powers of the north-eastern unit, because the Tamil national question must be solved. However, perhaps the basic building block should be the district, provided that the Tamil majority districts of the east could be amalgamated with the north so as to form a smaller, permanently merged unit, excluding the Amparai district.

Furthermore, there is an important psychological factor in operation here. The Tamil people have suffered and struggled for a very long time and as such, feel they deserve something special. If what they have is also what all the other Provincial Councils have, then what's so special about that? They will just keep on demanding more! Certainly, the Tamil problem is a specific one, and requires special arrangements. Why should others, who have not struggled, get the same autonomy as the Tamil people of the north-east? That in fact devalues whatever the Tamils have got in their minds.

As administrative crisis of the state, stemming from the variety of structures—Presidency, Parliament, Provincial Councils and Pradeshiya *sabhas*—could result in multiple dysfunctions and affect its delivery capacity. On the other hand, specially with the electoral distribution of political strengths, this could guarantee a real separation of power and thereby strengthen democracy.

In studying the complex nature of the national question in Sri Lanka, let as remember that there is no theory of the national question in the dependent formations, in Marxism-Leninism to date. This question has been theorised in the three contexts of: pre-capitalist autocracy (Tsarist Russia) which was also a metropolitan (i.e., imperialist) formation; semi-peripheral formations (Central and Eastern Europe); straightforward colonial situations (India, China). Hence the formulation, the national—colonial question, i.e., the question of national liberation.

The Moros of Mindanao, various struggles in India, Pakistan, Eritrea and the Kurds have produced some literature but they are all descriptive, informative and often propagandist. Nothing conceptual or theoretical has been done. No one has addressed the following problems beginning with the problem of the national question in post/neo-colonial formations, i.e., the question of independent struggle within politically independent societies, which unlike Britain/ Ireland or Spain, still have to struggle against dependency and thus have a 'national/patriotic' or 'independentist' aspect to their revolution. These social formations are themselves dominated while they dominate other national groups within.

Secondly, there is the problem of linking this struggle for regional autonomy/devolution/federalism/confederalism with the overall problem of democratising the state structure. A complicating factor for Marxists is that federalism was an anarchist slogan rejected by Marx, but we have things to learn from Bakunin and Kropotkin. Third and fourth are the problems of linking these struggles for democracy with the struggle for socialism, i.e., the connections between the anti-authoritarian and the anti-capitalist struggles; and the problem of linking these three struggles—devolution/ autonomy, overall democracy, and socialism with the anti-dependency, anti-imperialistic struggle.

Fifth, one needs to articulate these with the struggle against fascist movements 'from below' and the ideological struggles against all forms of obscurantism (e.g., BJP-RSS); and finally linking these with the strategic, tactical, organisational, social (displacement, uprooting, refugees), economic (the destruction of productive forces) and human (brutalisation) problems of armed struggle/revolution. We must bear in mind that revolutions hitherto have taken place in contexts that were pre-capitalist (Russia, Ethiopia); colonial, semi-colonial, early neo-colonial (Vietnam, China, Cuba); oligarchic (Cuba, Nicaragua); and fascist (Albania, Yugoslavia and of course Eastern Europe where the revolution was courtesy the Red Army). We have to situate our problem in the very different context of a post-colonial/ politically independent yet neo-colonial/economically dependent, modern capitalist and authoritarian formation. This is an entirely new problematique and conceptual challenge. Sri Lanka won a reputation for being a stable and competitive democracy during its first thirty years of independence from British rule. This remarkable record was tarnished by increasing ethnic violence which plagued the island after the general elections of 1977 and allegations of fraud in the national referendum of 1982.

During this period of political success and then of ethnic crisis, two critical themes emerged in the political system. The first was the renationalisation of the institutions of government as Sri Lankans tried to transform the political institutions which they had inherited from the British into ones which were culturally more suited to their country. The second was the political system's inability to resolve the serious problems facing Sri Lanka, primarily the economic problems facing the people, and the integration of diverse ethnic groups into one political entity.

From 1947 to 1977, Sri Lanka held eight general elections. From the third general elections in 1956, the governing party has always failed to be re-elected. The highly competitive party system emerged with two major blocks of parties centred around the two largest political parties the United National Party and the Sri Lanka Freedom Party. These two parties have directed the post-independence governments of Sri Lanka and have been the primary architects of the changes which have been made in the country.

One of the last legacies of the British rule in Sri Lanka was Soulbury Constitution of 1947 which established a political system modelled on the British system of government. Sri Lankan governments have attempted to adapt the political institutions left by British to the cultural and social characteristics of their society. This re-nationalisation has been a gradual process. Rather than make radical changeover to a Lankan system of government the leadership has gradually adapted the system by trial and error. These changes have met the goal of re-nationlising the political system but they have also created new problems.

By the 1980s, these new problems threatened the stability of the country's democratic institutions which since independence in 1948 had survived serious economic problems, the assassination of one Prime Minister, and the emergence of severe ethnic conflict.

Re-nationalisation meant the imposition of traditional Sri Lankan culture. Unfortunately in this multi-ethnic society there was no one Sri Lankan culture.

The majoritarian system of government established by the British, however, ensured that the Sinhalese Buddhist majority in the country would succeed in asserting itself as the dominant culture.

One of the first actions of Sri Lanka's Westminster-style government after independence was to deny citizenship to an ethnic minority, the Tamils of Indian origin. These were the children or the grandchildren of Tamil-speaking immigrants who had been brought to Sri Lanka by the British in the late nineteenth and early twentieth century to work on tea plantations. They are not to be confused with the Sri Lankan Tamils who trace their history on the island back as far as the Sinhalese do. The Indian Tamils existence in the society was seen by many Sri Lankans as a vestige of colonial rule. Through the Citizenship Act of 1948, approximately 800,000 Indian Tamils were denied citizenship and the government attempted to return them to the nation of their ancestors, either India or, in a few cases, Pakistan. As was to be expected the Indian and Pakistani governments were not receptive to the repatriation of people who, in most cases, had been born in Sri Lanka. The process to determine the citizenship of the Indian Tamils went forward very slowly, and by 1964 the status of very few had been determined. In that year, Prime Minister Sirimavo Bhandaranaike and Indian Prime Minister Lal Bahadur Shastri agreed to repatriate 525,000 out of the 975,000 Indian Tamils who then lived in Sri Lanka. Of the remaining 450,000, two-thirds were to be given Sri Lankan citizenship and the status of the rest was to be determined later. In the 1970s, India and Sri Lanka agreed to repatriate one-half of the remaining and grant citizenship to the other half. However, this agreement was never implemented and the final status of the Indian Tamils was not determined until 1986, when the Sri Lankan government agreed to grant citizenship to the last 100,000 of them. Nevertheless, a significant number of Indian Tamils remained in the country with no status—they were supposed to have been repatriated to India, but had refused to leave.

Following the denial of citizenship to the Indian Tamils the first two Sri Lankan governments elected in 1947 and 1952, did not try to make other fundamental changes to society or the political system.

In 1956, however, a populist coalition of leftist parties led by the SLFP was able to soundly defeat the UNP which had ruled since independence. Their first action after victory was the establishment of Sinhala as the language of government replacing English which had existed as a link language between the Tamil and Sinhala speakers on the island. The action was very popular among the overwhelming majority of the population which spoke Sinhala, but Tamil speakers who comprised about 29 per cent of the population at that time were disturbed. The role of the Tamils in Sri Lanka was debated, but unable to command majority the Tamils could not change the decision; Sri Lankan Tamils who comprised about 11 per cent of the population, were the most vocal.

Although Bandaranaike's Sri Lanka Freedom party was perceived as the anti-Tamil party, the UNP did not try to reinstate English as the language of government when they returned to power in 1965. In fact, while in power they helped to institutionalise the Sinhala-only policy.

In the 1960s re-nationalisation continued on a new front. A new SLFP government, led by Bandaranaike's widow, Sirimavo, sought in 1960 and 1961 to take over Christian-run schools. These schools had been at the forefront of the development of education on the island and were considered to be the best in Sri Lanka. The takeover effectively weakened the role of the Christian churches at a time when the Christian minority comprised an economic and political elite in the country. The intent was not to harm the Christians but to improve the quality of Buddhist education.

Until 1970, there was no attempt to change the fundamental structure of government. In this year the SLFP came together with the Communist Party and a Trotskyite Party, the Lanka Sama Samaja Party, to form a United Front coalition government.

In 1972, this government promulgated a new constitution which tried to remove alien British elements from the country's institutions. The official name of the country was changed from the English name of Ceylon to the Sinhala name of Sri Lanka.

The upper house of the National State Assembly the Senate, was abolished. It had been loosely modelled on the British House of Lords and was seen to be unnecessary. A number of other institutions borrowed from the British political system were also abolished.

Buddhism and Sinhala were given special constitutional status in the new government. The state was to remain secular but the Constitution stated that it was the duty of the state to protect and foster Buddhism while assuring to all religions the rights granted by the Constitution. These changes were not popular with the Tamils; their feelings of alienation and anger with the government were intensified. Although the Constitution promised to protect the ethnic minorities of the country it offered them no legally enforceable protection. An element of economic re-nationalisation was added in 1975 when tea, coconut and rubber estates were nationalised. Most of the tea estates were owned by British corporations or individual foreigners. Tea was the main foreign currency exchange earner and an important sector of the economy. Thus, Sri Lanka took back control of part of the economy from the foreign forces that the United Front leadership believed were dominating it.

In 1977 the UNP returned to power in an overwhelming electoral victory. In 1978, the party promulgated a new constitution. This Constitution, which differed sharply from its earlier predecessors, was structured around the ideas of the man who was to become the first President under it, Junius Richard Jayawardene. It was modelled on the French system of government and discarded those British trappings which survived in the Constitution of 1972. Sinhala was still treated as the official language of the government but Tamil was given special status as a national language. This did not satisfy Tamil-speakers as national language status did not appear to carry any special benefits and Sinhala continued to be the official language. The constituencies were replaced with a system of proportional representation It also created a provision for holding referendums. Since the Constitution's promulgation, no national elections have been held using proportional representation, although on several occasions it has been used in local elections.

In 1982, two national elections were held under the provisions of the Constitution. Jayawardene was re-elected to the presidency for a six-year term in December 1982, a referendum was held on whether parliamentary election should be held in the following year as required by the Constitution or whether the legislature should be given an additional six-year term. Over 54 per cent of the voters supported the extension of the term of parliament to 1989. The referendum, however, was marred by widespread allegations of ballot rigging which left many dissatisfied with the outcome.

Throughout the period following the Sinhala-only legislation in 1956. English was gradually diminishing in importance as a language in the educational system and in government. The onward march of Sinhala, however, was not straightforward; many government officials preferred to carry on business in English and many school subjects continued to be taught in English because of the lack of textbooks in Sinhala or Tamil. In addition, the hostility of the Tamil speakers was growing. They felt discriminated against in the competition for government jobs which carried the highest status in society. They also felt that as the law employment and all important economic transactions increasingly required Sinhala, they were steadily becoming second-class citizens.

As a result of this dissatisfaction, in the early 1970s Tamil youths began to rebel. At first, they launched occasional amateurish attacks against government installations or personnel. But by the 1980s, these youths, now called Tigers, had developed into several well-trained and equipped armies of liberation.

Some observers have estimated that there are over 30 Tiger groups of which the largest and most powerful is that of the Liberation Tigers of Tamil Eelam (LTTE) led by Velupillai Prabhakaran. By 1986 the Liberation Tigers had gained control of much of the northern Jaffna Peninsula. The main demand of the tigers has been the creation of Eelam, an independent Tamil state, comprising the Northern and Eastern Provinces of Sri Lanka.

The 1983 riots were the severest the country has seen and were accompanied by charges that government troops and police stood by and watched as rioters attacked Tamil homes and businesses. After the riots the fighting between the government and the Tigers escalated into open warfare in the Northern and Eastern Provinces of the country. The government's response to the riots and the increasing violence was to improve the fighting capacity of the army by hiring mercenaries, obtaining arms from western countries and taking a harder line towards the Tamil leadership. The non-violent and legal Tamil United Liberation. Front, the main Tamil political party, was expelled from parliament after the anti-Tamil rioting of 1983. Serious negotiations between the Tamils and the government did not occur until 1985, and only then under pressure from the Indian government which was drawn into the conflict because the Tigers has established training and staging bases in the southern Indian state of Tamil Nadu. The main area of disagreement in the negotiations has been over the Tamil demand for autonomy in the Northern and Eastern Provinces. The government has been willing to grant these regions a degree of local autonomy but will not permit to be combined as one province as most of the Tamil leaders demand.

While the nationalisation of the political system progressed, the Sri Lankan economy failed to grow as rapidly as had been expected The high levels of education and the high value placed upon it by Sri Lankans led many social scientists in the 1950s to expect Sri Lanka to develop very rapidly. Admittedly there were some impressive developments in state and society.

The country developed a very effective social welfare system which has elevated health standards and improved the quality of life for most Sri Lankans. Life expectancy at 69 years and other health standards are high when compared to Third World countries. In addition an extensive social welfare system from independence to 1979 provided every Sri Lankan with a free measure of rice as well as other social welfare benefits. Accompanying these was a drastic drop in the birth rate.

At the same time, however, growth was slow, achieving a per capita income of only 330 USA dollars by the mid-1980s. Moreover the country remained reliant on fluctuating international prices in tea, coconut and rubber for generating foreign currency. It was also unable to establish an industrial base.

The UNP government elected in 1977 established a Free Trade Zone but it attracted only a moderate number of multinational corporations. In addition, many of the jobs that were created required low skills levels and offered few hopes of long-term employment. The sluggish economy combined with the high population growth rates of the 1950s created a more serious problem, that of high levels of youth unemployment.

As Sri Lanka heads towards another attempt to solve its ethnic conflict and usher in peace, the signals are mixed and the imponderables have come to the fore. The talks between the government and the opposition on the proposed constitutional changes started on a positive note, but two events—one internal and the other external—struck a jarring note. On March 10, 2000, a day after the ground-breaking parleys began between the government and the opposition, the Liberation Tigers of Tamil Eelam (LTTE) carried out a commando-style operation in Colombo, as a reminder of the secessionist organisation's destructive reach and potential. The same day, the government in Norway, which had taken the challenge of initiating direct talks between the Sri Lankan government and the LTTE, fell, casting doubts about the future of the external effort. However, apprehensions were set at rest with the new government in Oslo assuring Sri Lanka continuity in the process. The incidents in Colombo started in the form of an explosion on a road leading to parliament, which was then debating the routine monthly extension of the island-wide imposition of emergency provisions.

Matters soon developed into a full-fledged commando-style operation, involving LTTE cadres who had infiltrated the well-guarded promenade and taken vantage positions to strike effectively. Thirty people, including eight LTTE cadres, were killed in 12 hours which witnessed pitched street battles and the siege of a residential complex. At the blast site lay the mangled head of the suicide bomber and the body of another LTTE cadre killed in firing, while on the road there was a row of bull et-ridden cars with their window-panes shattered. No VIP was injured, but the suspicion is that the LTTE targeted a prominent politician as parliament was in session.

A carnage of unimaginable proportions was averted by an alert passerby who drew the attention of armed policemen to suspicious movements in an overgrowth. Gunfire between the security forces and the Tigers continued for nearly an hour.

Yet another eyewitness said that when the suicide-bomber exploded, several gun-toting militants descended on the scene and opened fire. "When the armed policemen retaliated, they took cover." This suicide-blast, which failed to take its intended VIP target, came in the backdrop of a failed attempt to assassinate President Chandrika Kumaratunga on December 18. On January 5, a suicide-bomber exploded herself opposite the Prime Minister's office when she was being searched by security forces personnel.

At the site of the blast, four light anti-tank weapons and lengths of wire used by the rebels were found. Taking advantage of the presence of greenery, they had placed claymore bombs on treetops and carried out this edition of urban 'bush-fighting'. "At least seven claymore bombs were fixed to trees by the Tigers on the road leading to parliament," an investigator said. The presence of both Black Tigers and "a heavy count of ammunition" at the site implied the rebel's preparation to wreak maximum damage.

The exact number of LTTE cadres who participated in the operation was unknown, but the police believed that there were at least 10 of them. Eyewitness estimates pointed to a larger number. The shoot-out lasted until the crack of dawn, with Army personnel laying siege to a residential apartment complex a couple of kilometres from the blast site. The 12-hour drama came to an end with four suspected suicide-bombers blasting themselves to death to evade capture, while another was shot dead by Army personnel. The third floor bore ample evidence of the fiery end. On the ground below lay the decapitated body of a guerilla, with the head a few feet away. Analysts say that had the attack been successful, it would have strengthened the position of the Tigers at the talks with the government.

Undeterred by the attack, the peace initiatives rolled on. Three meetings have been held between Chandrika

Kumaratunga and Opposition leader Rand Wickremasinghe. There has been a positive sign in the form of a visible flexibility on the part of Kumaratunga on the contentious issue of transitionary provisions, which the government proposed to introduce in order to enable the President to complete her six-year term in office after the island switched over to the parliamentary mode of governance.

In effect, the present system of executive presidency and titular premiership would continue during the transition phase. The UNP opposed this provision and threatened an agitation. Taking a flexible approach, Kumaratunga told a press conference that "when the Constitution changes from the present one to the proposed one, there would be a certain transitional phase, a period of maybe some years, a couple of years and that's that and then I shall have the pleasure of going to parliament." Emphasising that she would be willing to part with her powers for the sake of consensual politics, Kumaratunga added, "Legally, I have got the mandate for the full second term. So whatever we negotiate will be a give-away for the sake of achieving a consensual agreement and peace in the country." On the negotiation process, she said, "We will give ourselves a limited timeframe for the process with the UNP, with the LTTE. If it succeeds we shall be very happy. Even if it does not, we will bring in the new Constitution."

If the first three months of the new millennium are any indication, the mood is one of cautious optimism, with the onus of conflict resolution shifting to several players, including an external player. An apparent softening of positions by the two main political parties—the ruling People's Alliance (P.A.) and the Opposition UNP—marked the initial rounds of the talks.

Elected for a second term of office, President Kumaratunga set the tone in her first address to the nation, in which she called upon the UNP to join in the efforts to bring peace. In the same breath she exhorted the LTTE and its supporters to eschew violence.

The government intends to complete the process by August, when parliamentary polls are due. The months ahead are to be watched for the positions adopted by the island's political players. Also to be reckoned with are the postures adopted by the right-wing Sinhala hardliners and the left-radical Janatha Vimukthi Peramuna (JVP), who have opposed the externalisation of the conflict. Though they have been for the moment only passive voices of protest, these can ignite public passion.

For the war-weary people of the north and east, the latest peace initiatives come at a time when there has been a lull in the fighting. However, not much hope is being pinned on the latest round of peace talks. Initial hopes surrounding the Norwegian initiative seem to have been relegated to the background as the two major political parties continue with their parleys. An earlier offensive by the Tigers on the crucial Elephant Pass camp has, for the moment, receded. But other operations continue. Even as the confrontation between the government and the Tigers continues in the northern Jaffna and the eastern Batticaloa districts the people await tangible signals of hope.

The Tamil rebels have kept up their pressure on government troops and are gaining ground daily. The question is no longer whether Jaffna would fall but rather when and how it will happen. "The government seems to have no idea about how they will pull out over 30,000 troops from Jaffna if the need arises. They seem to be hoping for foreign intervention to help them do it." Colombo has announced that it will fight to the last man in Jaffna and has thrown in millions of dollars worth of new military hardware into the battle. "Hopefully this infusion will stop the rebel advance. But to safeguard Jaffna, we have to recapture lost ground. There's no way Jaffna can be held without pushing the rebels all the way back to the mainland." That task, considering the demoralisation of the army, is quite a tall order.

The rebels have also targeted military supply fines by directing mortar-fire at the military airport and the only harbour in the peninsula. "The biggest worry here is that they will make it impossible to use the port and the airport. That would effectively cut off the troops." A massive military setback like that would have serious repercussions on the peace front as well.

"The only positive outcome of the current fighting is that it could turn out to be a catalyst for the peace process. There's a view that the LTTE will not enter into any serious negotiations until they are in control of Jaffna. Were this to be the outcome of the current fighting, international pressure too could be brought to bear on the LTTE to enter into talks. As for the government, the argument may well be made that in territorial terms, the situation has reverted to what it was in 1994. But it is clear that for both sides, any decisive result on the ground will be temporary unless it is followed by progress on the political front." "The LTTE has never been seriously interested in anything other than Eelam. For them talks are a tactical move to regroup and re- arm."

Indeed, the four previous attempts at a settlement lasted less than three months. And when fighting resumed each time, it was with a renewed ferocity. But as Sidharthan points out, "The crucial difference between the current fighting in Jaffna and other battles in the past is that now, after the fall of the Elephant Pass, the Tamils feel a separate state is achievable by military means." On the talks front, the LTTE seems to be indicating that it is serious about reaching a peaceful settlement. "The LTTE is supposed to have told the Norwegians that they are realists and understand that a separate state is not achievable and that they could settle for less," says a senior government source.

However, the Norwegian team has been cautious about immediate progress and is awaiting a response from the Sri Lankan government. While Colombo's first priority is to try and hold on to Jaffna, many observers feel that the government is fast heading towards a no-win situation. A grim reminder that not everyone supports peace talks or foreign involvement came in the form of a grenade hurled at the Norwegian embassy in Colombo just 24 hours after their delegation had left the country.

However, despite the military setbacks, the government and the main opposition United National Party (UNP) are going ahead with their discussions. These talks are aimed at reaching a consensus on a new constitution that would be the basis for negotiations with the rebels. But even on this front, progress is unlikely. "The consensus reached so far on a number of key issues—such as devolution of power to provinces and the division of power—is far less than what the LTTE might find acceptable as an alternative to a separate state."

7

LTTE Offensive

The separatist Liberation Tigers of Tamil Eelam (LTTE) has redrawn the military map of the northern territory of Sri Lanka by recapturing within the first two weeks of November areas that were taken by the Sri Lankan Army through various military operations over the past two years. Before Operation Oyatha Alaigal III started, the military map was a matter of satisfaction for the troops. But within days, Army camps fell like nine-pins. Areas that had been captured by the Army, some of them in difficult battles, during its military campaigns, were retaken by the militants with remarkable ease. Oddusuddan, Nedunkeny, Olumadu and Mankulam, important military camps that the Army had established after beating back the Tigers, fell in rapid succession. Puliyankulam and Kanakarayankulam, among the strongest and best-fortified Army outposts along the Jaffna-Kandy highway, were among those that were captured. For over a year since May 1998, this road had witnessed the troops inching forward, fighting to open a main supply route to the northern Jaffna peninsula, which it had regained from the Tigers.

Embarking on their latest thrust along the main highway, LTTE cadres swept vast tracts of land to the east and west of the A-9 highway and took control of several strategic towns. For all practical purposes, the government's military gains, built up over the years, were lost. The island, especially the southern region, was preparing for the presidential election when the LTTE launched its offensive. For well over a year, the Tigers had been at the receiving end.

Some military observers feel that the timing of the operation had nothing to do with the Presidential election. "The main and the only motive was military." The LTTE wanted to make the maximum haul of war equipment. It would have anticipated a further thrust towards Mullaitivu ahead of the election.

Military officers are of the view that the LTTE would have conceived a smaller operation but enlarged it after seeing the effectiveness of the attack. "They have got more than what they would have expected." Although the fighting capability of the Tigers is considered formidable, such a sudden loss of territory by the Army, apparently without even putting up a fight, has caused concern. While opposition leaders have alleged that the government's strategy of gaining more territory was the reason for the "thinly spread out" nature of the Army's presence, sections of the government see a possible political conspiracy behind the military debacle.

The Defence Ministry promptly appointed a court of inquiry comprising senior officers of the Army, the Navy and the Air Force to investigate the reasons for the debacle. Even as this professional exercise was under way, damage-control measures were initiated. Censorship on military news was further tightened. Sections of the national media were accused of providing grossly exaggerated and misleading casualty figures. The concern was more on keeping down the reported number of soldiers killed in action.

War casualties were contained by resorting to what has been described as "tactical withdrawals". This is now an artillery-based aggression by the Tigers. There is less of man-to-man combat and that would explain the relatively lower numbers of casualties. Initial estimates placed the number of soldiers killed at 101 and those missing in action at 743 in the five-day offensive. Military commentators were also quick on the draw. In their analysis, it was the strategy of massing military personnel in the north for a push against the Tigers that led to the debacle.

As the Tigers moved out without offering resistance, it was reasoned, "They were able to keep their fighting units intact." "As the Army had to hold the territory it had gained, it was bound to spread its forces thin. Moreover, the Army had not won major victories by inflicting losses on the Tigers. This meant that the LTTE could strike back with full force."

The Army's fighting units in the north also came in for a restructuring in the command, the most significant step being the replacing of the Commander of the Security Forces in the Wanni, Maj. Gen. Wasantha Perera, by Maj. Gen. Neil Dias. Senior military leaders in Colombo, including Lt.Gen. Sirilal Weerasooriya, the Army Commander, and Major General Lionel Balagalle, the Chief of Staff and until recently the Commander of the Security Forces in the Wanni, reached Vavuniya to oversee the operations. By the turn of the week, the LTTE had reached Mankulam on the Jaffna-Kandy highway. Mankulam was won by the Army last year, when the Tigers overran Kilinochchi during Oyatha Alaigal II, inflicting heavy casualties on the Army. With the retaking of Mankulam, the LTTE consolidated its presence on the Jaffna-Kandy highway and pushed its territorial gains further south.

Then came the threat to Vavuniya, the island's northern garrison town and the headquarters of the Army's Wanni operations. Through announcements, the Tigers asked the civilians to leave the town in view of an impending attack. Although this was dismissed by the government as part of the "psychological operations" of the Tigers, civilians started leaving the town. By November 12, practically the entire town had emptied itself, with only those who could not afford to travel or those who did not have identity passes to move out staying behind. A few days later, the Tigers said that the civilians could return but asked them to stay away from areas situated near the Army camps. Life in the south, however, was largely unaffected by the northern casualties. Colombo continued in its normal self. There was a clear distancing from the battlefield, not only in geographical terms but also in mental terms. But for political leaders, academicians, peace activists and activists of non-governmental organisations involved in relief operations, the northern casualties largely seemed to involve "somebody else's war". But a similar situation existed during last year's Kilinochchi defeat.

One interpretation is that this also has its "positive" implications in that there is "no backlash on the minorities". This, analysts observed, was in stark contrast to the 1983 situation when the killing of 13 soldiers sparked anti-Tamil riots throughout the island. Sunil Bastian of the International Centre of Ethnic Studies, Colombo, attributes the larger 'ambivalence' of the country's population to war as a reason. "People just want to get on with their lives," he said.

Making the point that extreme Sinhala opinion is now divided, Bastian also observed that any "instability in the south as the consequence of an event in the north is always organised." As in the past, some "sections in the parties that held power were behind it." The present southern reaction to the northern debacle, he said, made it "quite clear that now those groups do not exist in the main parties. There is no space for hardliners in these parties."

Moreover, incidents directly involving the southern people, such as those related to the insurrections by the Janatha Vimukthi Peramuna (JVP) during the 1980s and early 1990s, had a more direct bearing on the people in the south. The most telling implication of the Tiger offensive, however, would be on the living conditions of Wanni residents. The displacement of the people, providing food and other essentials to them, and averting chaos will have to engage the attention of the government, non-governmental organisations (NGOs) and international organisations. Some former Tamil militant groups, such as the People's Liberation Organisation of Tamil Eelam (PLOTE) and the Tamil Eelam Liberation Organisation (TELO), have started supplementing the relief efforts of the government and aid agencies. "They were organising blood-donation camps and providing other relief materials for the displaced". If Operation Unceasing Waves III brought more territory to the Tigers, it remains to be seen how they will be able to spread further. Military officials, putting the larger picture in perspective, feel that if the Tigers spread their terrain too far, they would be faced with the same constraints as the Army faced—too much land and too little people to man it.

While recent northern military campaigns have clearly redrawn government, and rebel-held territories, they have also sent across the signal that more than military gains and losses it is in addressing the separatist conflict from the political perspective that would result in the cessation of hostilities. Until then, unfortunately, the wounds of the war will fester.

Facts are invariably the first casualty of a war. Objectivity comes next. Then those killed in combat are reduced to mere numbers, and the ones missing in action are lost in a procedural maze. When the Sri Lankan government in June 1998 clamped censorship on all news relating to military activity in the country, it did what many countries of the world have done during an escalation of armed conflict. Censorship was in place for a brief period in 1995, during the Army operations in northern Jaffna.

If restrictions on access to the conflict zones and a military censorship of all war-related news ensured that the state had defined in clear terms the limits to the people's "right to know", a ban on the Liberation Tigers of Tamil Eelam (LTTE) completed the picture. Effectively, the ban made access to the Tigers, in any manner, illegal. In fairness to the People's Alliance (PA) government, its record on the human rights front—specifically that pertaining to the unhindered working of journalists—is a vast improvement over previous regimes. Reports of the disappearance of journalists critical of the establishment are now a thing of the past. During its early days, the PA government permitted private radio and television stations to present news and current affairs programmes—an area that was until then restricted to the state-run media. A relatively free atmosphere prevailed until the LTTE turned its heat on the government. In a situation where access to the war zone and areas held by the LTTE was restricted, the statements issued daily by the Defence Ministry formed the key source of information. The LTTE's press releases, normally faxed to newspaper offices, gave the rebel version.

In such a restricted atmosphere came the added limitation of the news censorship. Initially, a military officer was made the Competent Authority to judge the suitability of the news. Later a civilian authority was vested with the responsibility.

The government was concerned mainly about reports on casualties. Needless to say, sordid media reports of soldiers dying in large numbers would have had a significant political impact. The stated reasons for the imposition of censorship, however, are "strategic" factors: it is claimed that in the absence of restrictions the media would, through their reports of the war, provide leads to the "enemy" on the moves of government troops. The clamping of censorship has often come in tandem with setbacks suffered by the security forces. For instance, the censorship apparatus was activated when the Tigers overran the northern town of Kilinochchi and during the Operation Watershed III battles. In stark contrast, when Sinhalese civilians were reportedly hacked to death by Tamil militants in the eastern town of Amparai in September, the national media, including the state-run media, went to town with gruesome pictures of the victims, in violation of the censorship regulations. The government ferried a group of journalists from Colombo to Amparai.

Censorship was last imposed in June 1998 and its vigorous implementation happened in two phases: between June and December, when Operation Jayasikurui was in progress, and around the time Operation Oyatha Alaigal III commenced. The government is, however, in a fix: the British Broadcasting Corporation (BBC) has a contract with the state-run Sri Lanka Broadcasting Corporation (SLBC), under which the BBC has acquired air-time on SLBC on the condition that its programme will be broadcast as presented. In contrast, when telecasts of overseas news organisations, mostly Indian and British, are repeated by the island's private media, matters relating to Sri Lanka are often blurred out. There have been knee-jerk reactions as well.

The blacking out of an overseas television story on the positive aspects of the Sri Lankan economy is a case in point.

In yet another instance, the Sri Lankan Customs held back Indian publications when people evacuated from Vavuniya after being asked to do so by the LTTE. Customs officials refused to clear the newspapers and asked their distributors to obtain the permission of the Competent Authority.

The censor, however, maintained that clearance would be given if the Customs sought clarifications on specific reports. The matter, however, was sorted out when the Ministry in charge of the media wrote to the Customs asking it to release the publications. For the residents of northern Jaffna, the areas held by the LTTE, as well as places close to the rebel-held areas, the clandestine radio station of the Tigers, Voice of Tigers (VoT), is a key source of information. Taking the propaganda offensive into the government's turf, the LTTE last year commenced services in Sinhala, aimed apparently at "demoralising the security forces". Of late, according to displaced residents in the north, the LTTE's broadcasts are electronically jammed.

Curbing war-related, news is but a manifestation of the thinking that column-centimetres and sound bytes can defeat into victory. However, a disturbing result of keeping the northern conflict zone and the rebel-held areas out of bounds for the media as well as independent non-governmental organisations has been a consistent deterioration of the living conditions and the people's thinking in those regions. An underlying, perhaps unintended, consequence has been the furthering of the 'us' and 'them' syndrome in an already ethnically divided country.

Revered by people of all religious faiths, the Roman Catholic Madhu Church, in the battle zone, has been a nest of peace through the island's bloodiest conflicts. The Dutch-period shrine was shelled on November 21, leaving 38 civilians dead. The Sacred Heart chapel and a section of the main shrine were damaged. During periods of turmoil, the shrine and its precincts, an enclave of tranquillity, have offered refuge to thousands of displaced persons, almost entirely Tamil. Priests had persuaded both the Sri Lankan Army and the Liberation Tigers of Tamil Eelam (LTTE) not to take their battle to the pilgrimage centre. The situation, however, changed gradually since March.

Once the Sri Lankan security forces gained control over the shrine, the LTTE left the area. A minimal presence of government commandos was maintained there. The priests protested against the militarisation of the pilgrimage centre.

The government took over Madhu in March just ahead of the Provincial Council elections in the south and interpreted this as a "military gain". The town was soon given power supply. Simultaneously, thousands of refugees who had lived there for years were evacuated and "rehabilitated" either in their villages or in government-held areas. In mid-November, the shrine was back in focus. As the LTTE moved westwards with its Operation Unceasing Waves III, some 3,500 persons from Mannar district moved into the church as refugees. The Tigers had earlier taken towns and villages to the north, and civilians had flocked to Madhu.

According to the priests, "The Army came in with its armoured cars into the pilgrimage centre". The peace of the church was shattered by artillery fire the same night. The Lankan Defence Ministry, which had maintained silence on the loss of Madhu, blamed the LTTE: it said that "after the security forces consolidated the area," the LTTE "launched a heavy-artillery-and-mortar attack indiscriminately on the Madhu Church premises." Church authorities said that 13 of those killed were children. At least 56 people including 25 children were injured.

Rev. Dr. Rayappu Joseph, the Bishop of Mannar and the secretary of the Catholic Bishops' Conference of Sri Lanka, said: "Such a desecration has never happened in the church's 450-year history." Church leaders appealed to "both the state forces and the LTTE to immediately withdraw from the sacred area of the shrine of Madhu... to strictly refrain from using Madhu for any strategic or political advantage... and leave Madhu completely free for the pilgrims to visit the shrine without any restriction for their spiritual purposes."

Sri Lanka is at a crucial political juncture. An estimated 11.8 million voters approach the presidential election scheduled for December 21, 1990. The two main contestants are President Chandrika Kumaratunga and opposition leader Ranil Wickremasinghe. Given the country's sensitive voting structure, the minority vote will determine the outcome. Support for the two main contestants, fielded by the ruling People's Alliance (P.A.) and the opposition United National Party (UNP), is evenly balanced.

In the 1994 elections, Chandrika Kumaratunga, contesting on a promise of bringing peace to the northern area, won a landslide victory with the support of the Tamil vote. This time around, she is determined that there will be no cessation of hostilities until the Liberation Tigers of Tamil Eelam (LTTE) is militarily weakened and brought to the negotiating table on the government's terms.

The ruling formation is further handicapped by the current military setbacks in the Wanni region. Wickremasinghe, who had remained silent on the government's peace package for the last four years, approaches the elections with a "pact with the people" agenda, which includes, among other things, talks with the Tigers and a promise of "rehabilitating the militant cadres" after finding a solution to the conflict.

While Chandrika Kumaratunga presents the "peace package" that she was unable to push through in parliament owing to the absence of a two-thirds majority, Wickremasinghe pins his hopes on the "pact".

For his part, V. Prabhakaran, the LTTE supremo, has placed the militarisation issue clearly on the agenda by launching the third phase of Operation Oyatha Alaigal soon after the election dates were announced. Scoring victory after victory in the eastern parts of the Wanni, the LTTE moved to the western flank, thereby maintaining pressure on the government, and consequently, on the southern polity.

The LTTE offensive also ties up the resolution of the ethnic conflict with military action and comes as a challenge to the island's liberal-thinking peace constituency.

Perhaps the most interesting aspect of the electioneering will be the manner in which the majority vote will be sought. The Tamil voters, for all practical purposes, have distanced themselves from Chandrika, who was elected last time on the promise of bringing about an "honourable peace". The experience of the past four years has, however, made it impossible for even moderate Tamil politicians to tell voters to back her this time. "We do not have anything to show the Tamils that concrete gains have been made," a Tamil politician said. Another said that he was likely to be dismissed by the Tamil electorate if he sought their vote for the President.

Wickremasinghe's position is no better. Even those Tamil voters who are opposed to the candidature of Chandrika Kumaratunga are reluctant to espouse the cause of the UNP. Anxious to distance themselves from the mainstream parties, overall a large section of the Tamils seem to show a lack of interest in the elections.

The eastern Batticaloa district overwhelmingly voted for Chandrika Kumaratunga last time. This time the situation has changed. "We gave her the largest number of votes, but we are disappointed," a Tamil leader from the area said.

This sets the stage for the ruling coalition to succumb to pressures from majoritarian sentiments. The recent crossing over of some known Sinhala hardliners from the UNP—Nanda Mathews, Wijepala Mendis and Susil Moonasinghe—points to this possibility. Significantly, Moonasinghe stated in clear terms after his cross-over that he was opposed to the peace package which alters the unitary status of the Constitution. He added that he was, prior to his defection, proposed by the island's Buddhist clergy as a presidential candidate.

The continued impasse on the conflict-resolution front, and the military actions in the north, could also mean a reduction in the number of Tamils who will cast their votes. With the LTTE capturing more territory, there is a possibility of the elections turning out to be predominantly southern.

With 13 candidates in the fray, the largest number in any presidential election in the country, the coming weeks promise to throw up a cacophony of voices. The Janatha Vimukthi Peramuna (JVP) has fielded a politburo member, Nandana Gunathilaka, who espouses a single-point agenda of the abolition of the Executive Presidency.

During the previous election, the JVP had withdrawn its candidate in favour of Chandrika Kumaratunga as she had promised to do away with the Executive Presidency. Given the nature of its left-wing constituency, the JVP could eat into the votes of the PA. This is an added disadvantage for the PA, as already the incumbency factor is working against it. The UNP, on the other hand, is yet to be seen as a party which could provide an alternative. Vasudeva Nanayakkara of the left Democratic Alliance has the backing of non-governmental organisations. He hopes that the Tamil vote would come his way. He has promised to stop the war and end the difficulties faced by Tamils.

The LTTE recommenced its operations on November 18, 1999 by conducting assaults simultaneously on military positions in the north-western sector of the Wanni region, which comprises the districts of Mullaitivu, Mannar, Kilinochchi and Vavuniya.

The Tigers captured several Army camps in these areas; they also took control of the famous Holy Rosary Church at Maruthamadhu, popularly known as Madhu. However, the Army recaptured it within 48 hours. In the process, 38 civilians who had taken refuge in the Catholic church were killed and 60 injured.

The Army and the LTTE have blamed each other for the tragedy. The LTTE has also started attacking military positions on the island off Mannar on the north-western coast. As of November 22, the fighting continued without any signs of abating. The first phase of Operation Oyatha Alaigal was conducted in July 1996 in Mullaitivu. The third phase of the campaign has proved to be the most successful military offensive recorded by the LTTE in the entire history of the armed conflict. If one were to adapt Winston Churchill's famous line after the aerial battle of Britain in

1940 to the LTTE attack, it could be said that "never in the history of the Eelam conflict has so much territory been regained in so few days with so little losses by such small groups of Tigers."

After dislodging the Tigers from the Jaffna peninsula in 1995-96, the Sri Lankan forces had made several attempts to undermine their presence in the Wanni. The idea was to establish a land-linked route between Vavuniya, the southern point of the Northern Province, and the Jaffna peninsula through the conquest of the 77-km stretch of road between Vavuniya and Kilinochchi on the Jaffna-Kandy road, known as the A-9 highway.

After various operations which saw mixed results, the Army succeeded in taking a 44-km stretch of road between Vavuniya and Mankulam. Some of the key areas along this road that were under Army control were Omanthai, Puliyankulam and Kanakarayankulam.

The Army had also made deep inroads into the north-eastern sector of the Wanni, lying to the east of A-9 highway. Government troops had consolidated their positions in areas extending to the north-eastern village of Oddusuddan along the A-34 highway linking Mankulam and Mullaitivu on the eastern coast. Another series of operations saw the Army establish control over substantial areas in the north-western sector of the Wanni too. The place it took control included the Our Lady of Madhu Church. One puzzling aspect of these operations was the lack of resistance by the LTTE in the early stages. But when the Army tried to take over the coastal Mannar-Pooneryn road and establish another land route, the Tigers offered resistance. Significantly, the LTTE's record in the past year was marked by the conspicuous absence of military operations from November 1998. Its spokespersons abroad would maintain that the militants refrained from putting up any resistance for fear of endangering the peace initiatives. But the reality was that the LTTE, in typical guerilla fashion, was trading space to buy time. Ceding land made the Army overextend itself, by spreading thin over too much land, thereby increasing its vulnerability.

The LTTE was quietly recruiting and training cadres, assembling weapons and arsenals and drawing up plans for a counter-attack. The fact that the LTTE had allowed the Army to seize much territory without resistance had demoralised its supporters. In order to regain public support, the Tigers had to complete a military mission successfully.

The onset of the monsoon made the forest terrain sodden. The climate was not conducive to major military activity. Nevertheless, the Tigers had to launch a counter-offensive for politico-military reasons. The LTTE had originally planned its operation for November 11.

Apart from being War Remembrance Day, November 11 also marked the sixth anniversary of Operation Frogleap, the amphibian attack that demolished the complex in 1993. By conducting a successful operation, the LTTE could create the ambience of victory that was necessary for Maaveerar Thinam, its annual Great Heroes' Day.

After a military success, LTTE supremo Velupillai Prabhakaran could deliver his traditional address from a position of perceived strength. The LTTE, however, advanced its operations in order to pre-empt any moves by the Army. The LTTE's military operation was preceded by an unusual manoeuvre by the Army. Starting in mid-October, the Sri Lankan security forces advanced along the old Kandy road from Karippattaimurippu on the Mankulam-Mullaitivu road and established a permanent presence at Ambakamam.

Subsequently, troops advanced from Oddusuddan on the east of Karippattaimurippu on the Mankulam-Mullaitivu road, known also as the A-34 highway. These troops established forward defence lines that were linked to positions at Ambakamam in a somewhat rectangular shape. On October 30 and 31, troops used this rectangular formation to push upwards in the direction of Muthaiyankaddu. After meeting stiff resistance from the militants, they returned to Ambakamam and Oddusuddan on November 1.

The Army operations in the Oddusuddan-Ambakamam sector were described as "Operation Watershed". The nomenclature itself was a give-away of the underlying compulsions for the operation. A presidential election was in the offing. The Chandrika Kumaratunga government was constrained to demonstrate through contemporary military successes on the ground that the Tigers were being defeated. Projecting such an image would have contributed immensely to an electoral success for Kumaratunga, it was felt. The People's Alliance (PA) government has on several occasions been criticised for setting up military deadlines to suit political timetables. Now the government needed a war victory during the election campaign. So, in spite of the adverse weather conditions, the Army was politically pressured to deliver militarily. Calling the operation a "watershed" suggested that the ultimate objective of the manoeuvres may be overrunning LTTE strongholds, including Prabhakaran's "One Four Base". What was hopefully a politico-military watershed paved the way for the Waterloo that followed.

Once the LTTE anticipated Army expeditions, pre-emptive strikes became imperative. So the D-Day of Unceasing Waves-Ill had to be advanced. On November 1, the LTTE held a top-level conference in the historically significant Katsilaimadhu located north of Oddusuddan and south of Puthukkudiyiruppu. Pandara Wanniyan, the legendary Wanni chieftain of Adankapattu who ruled in Panankamam, was defeated by British troops led by Major Drieberg at Katsilaimadhu.

A stone inscription as well as a statue erected about 20 years ago bear testimony to the heroic image of the last feudal ruler, who defied the imperialist aggressor. Katsilaimadhu witnessed another historic occasion on November 1.

Prabhakaran, along with his senior deputies, was there to finalise plans to launch Oyatha Alaigal. Several Tiger commanders, such as Balraj, Karuna, Sornam, Jeyam, Bhanu, Theepan, Rabat, Nagesh, Anton, Selvarajah, Asha, Durga and Malathie, were present at the conclave. Even as the meeting was on, thousands of male and female cadres secretly converged on Muthaiyankaddu, Sammalankulam,

Mulliyawalai, Thanneerootru, Katpoorappulveli, Kodalikkal, Indimadhu and Thanduvan. They were drawn from different fighting formations, such as the Charles Anthony and Jeyanthan infantry divisions, the Sothiya Women Corps, the Kittu Artillery Brigade, the Victor Armoured Corps, the Leopards Commando Unit, the Black Tiger suicide squads and the anti-aircraft unit. There were also members from auxiliary civilian units.

Prabhakaran was both the architect and the chief executive of the operation. Tiger literature claims that the entire operation was guided, inspired and masterminded by the leader who is also the supreme commander of LTTE forces. The LTTE's deputy military commander-in-chief, Balraj, a son of the Wanni soil, was in charge of coordinating the operational headquarters. Karuna, a senior Commander from Batticaloa, was the overall Field Commander. Once Prabhakaran gave the go-ahead, the Tigers started their operations.

The first target was Oddusuddan, which was seized by the Army last December in Operation Revibalaya (Solar Power). Oddusuddan was guarded by the Second Gajaba Regiment on the west and the Walagambaya division of the Navy on the east. Incidentally, three Naval divisions were deployed on land duty in the eastern sector of the Wanni. Likewise, Air Force divisions were on duty in the western sector. Both services were being used as supplementary ground troops to assist the Army. The western and eastern Wanni sectors were demarcated by the A-9 highway, which bisects Wanni. An LTTE commando unit infiltrated the Army lines on Manavalanpattaimurippu on the Mullaitivu road, west of Oddusuddan. Around midnight, the unit attacked the Gajaba troopers from behind. A little later, three formations of LTTE fighters attacked the camp from all three sides. After nine hours of fighting, the LTTE overran the Oddusuddan camp. The Gajaba soldiers and the Walagampaya naval personnel were virtually annihilated. A fresh column of LTTE cadres, along with the civilian militia, came in a motorcade from Mulliyawalai and hoisted the Tiger flag. It is said that Karuna performed the honours. Thereafter, the Tigers and their civilian militia began transporting by road to Mullaitivu the vehicles, arms, ammunition and equipment seized.

The Tigers then proceeded in three directions: to the north-west towards Ambakamam, westwards to Karippattaimurippu and Olumadhu, and to the south-west to Nedunkeny. Nedunkeny was taken in the preliminary stages of Operation Jeyasikurui in May 1997. It is situated on the Puliyankulam-Mullaitivu road and is the interface of Vavuniya and Mullaitivu districts. It is very much the gateway to Mullaitivu, or the Tiger heartland. The access route between Oddusuddan and Nedunkeny had the 3rd battalion of the Sinhala Regiment at Samanankulam and the 8th battalion of the Vijaybahu Regiment at Pandarikulam. After some fierce fighting, Nedunkeny also fell to the LTTE.

In the meantime, the other two Tiger columns were confronting two naval divisions stationed on the western flank of the Mullaitivu-Mankulam road on the one hand, and the 55th division personnel on the Ambakamam rectangle, on the other. After heavy fighting, Karippattai-murippu fell. Then the Tigers proceeded along the old Kandy road towards Ambakamam while other formations kept pounding Olumadhu adjacent to Karippattaimurippu on the road between Mankulam and Mullaitivu. Reinforcements sent from Mankulam were prevented from reaching Olumadhu as Tiger commandos blew up a bridge over a tributary of the Kanagarayankulam.

Soon Ambakamam fell, and it was followed by Olumadhu. Thereafter, advancing LTTE personnel began pounding Kanagarayankulam and Mankulam, both on the A-9 highway. Shortly thereafter, Mankulam fell. The Tigers then started proceeding southwards by vehicles along the Jaffna-Vavuniya road. Government troops had captured the stretch of roadway between Vavuniya and Mankulam in Operation Jeyasikurui after 19 months of fighting.

Finally, on November 7, the LTTE reached Panickan-eeraavi on the outskirts of Omanthai, 15 km south of Vavuniya. Omanthai too had been captured by the Army in May 1997. The rapidly retreating troops finally dug in at Omanthai. Reinforced by troops from Vavuniya and artillery field guns, the Army began defending Omanthai. Other places where some resistance was displayed were Madhiyamadhu and Nainamadhu on the Puliyankulam-Nedunkeny stretch; Othiyamalai and Pattikkudiyiruppu in the Nedunkeny area; Karappukuthi and Katkidanku near Kanakarayankulam; and Semamadhu near Omanthai.

The LTTE has also seized some points on the western sector or areas to the west of the A-9 highway. Moondrumurippu near Mankulam, Mannakulam near Kanakarayankulam and Puthoor near Puliyankulam have been seized. Some Air Force personnel and soldiers were killed or injured.

The LTTE has also begun artillery attacks on Pallamadhu and Palampitty in Mannar. Both these places are of strategic importance in the context of an attempt to take the Mannar-Poonervn road. After Operation Jeyasikurui aimed at securing the A-9 highway was aborted, the Army had launched a series of operations, named Ranaghosha, or battle cry, and seized a lot of territory and vast stretches of the Poonervan road.

The government began its manoeuvres in the Wanni with the launching of Operation Jeyasikurui, but called them off in December 1998. The operation had seen the Army sustain tremendous losses, with the LTTE taking to positional warfare by defending entrenched positions. Now, after the first stage of Oyatha Alaigal-III, the Army has lost 30 km of the 44-km stretch it had seized on the A-9 highway and, according to preliminary estimates, 1,269 sq. km of territory on the eastern Wanni front. Massive amounts of arms, ammunition, equipment, tanks and armoured cars and other vehicles were seized by the Tigers. So too were large amounts of dry rations.

The more significant aspect of the fighting was the fact that the LTTE adopted conventional techniques to chase the Army out. Thousands of troops literally ran away instead of fighting. There have been reports of rebellion, in some places of which officers and military policemen were shot. Large-scale desertions have occurred. There has been a breakdown in discipline. In short, the Army, despite its numerical and logistical superiority, has been decisively routed.

The LTTE used newly acquired anti-aircraft weapons to bring down two helicopters and damage a plane. The Air Force panicked, thinking that the Tigers possessed the ability to blast planes in the skies.

The Air Force suspended all active engagement in the conflict for more than a week. Thus the beleaguered ground troops on different fronts in the eastern Wanni sector could not receive assistance from the Air Force for quite a while. Secondly, the officials in Oddusuddan hastily loaded a South African "Buffel" tank with all communication codes and signal crypts and tried to send it to the 56 Division headquarters at Kanakarayankulam after their camp came under attack. The tank got bogged down in the slush. As the troops abandoned it, the Tigers seized it. Using the codes, the LTTE began penetrating the radio communications system of the Army. As a knee-jerk reaction, the Army stopped all internal communications. The communications equipment within the combat zone went dead for several days. As a result, panic and confusion set in among the troops.

The primary cause for the debacle was the suspension of aerial contact and radio communications. Without a proper leadership issuing directives or morale-boosting reassurances, the individual Army detachments began withdrawing. Several officers had begun retreating, instead of urging the soldiers to stand and fight. The government's refusal to accept the bodies of soldiers from the LTTE in the conflict zone also fuelled troop resentment. A collapse of logistical support hampering transport, food supplies and medical treatment also created a demoralising impact. After fighting at Oddusuddan and a few other places, the soldiers preferred "flight" to "fight".

In its anxiety to find scapegoats, the government has transferred all senior commanding officers. But there is criticism of the political leadership itself. Many intelligence warnings went unheeded because the government wanted a quick military victory to boost its chances in the presidential election. Monsoon rain had made the terrain in the Wanni region difficult for military operations, but Deputy Minister of Defence Anuruddha Ratwatte wanted a military drive. Hence Operation Watershed was launched to take Ambakamam first, and follow it up with further incursions. The stationing of troops on the outer perimeter endangered other points, which the Tigers exploited.

Another reason for demoralisation among the troops was the realisation that they were being cynically expended in a war that had the ruling party's electoral victory as its ultimate motive. According to Lasantha Wickrematunge, editor of the pro-UNP newspaper *Sunday Leader*, "The Government has to face the fact that the defeat was a result of bad military planning. The soldiers deserted because they realised they were not fighting a war to save the country but to further the interests of a particular political party."

Three salient points that contributed to the LTTE successes were tremendous artillery barrages, the rapid mobility of personnel and vehicles, and expert tactics. After the initial stages, the element of surprise was no longer there: thereafter it was only superior mobility, better tactics and the precise use of artillery that mattered. The very same weather conditions that affected military movement did not hinder the Tigers.

Another area where the LTTE made an impact was Weli Oya or Manal Aaru. This strategic region was carved out by the UNP, with the objective of ending the territorial contiguity of the Northern and Eastern Provinces. The PA government, after the initial successes of Jeyasikurui, embarked on implementing the scheme of colonising armed settlers and establishing a network of camps. It must be remembered that Tamil inhabitants were driven away earlier in a systematic form of ethnic cleansing. The LTTE has succeeded in destroying several camps in Weli Oya and continues to put pressure on the region. More than 7,000 Sinhala settlers have fled the area. Vavuniya, the southernmost town of the Northern Province, too is under threat. The LTTE announced that it was going to shell the town and asked residents to move away. This led to about 9,000 people abandoning the town. Fearing a major assault, the armed forces gathered in large numbers in Vavuniya, transforming it into a garrison town. Instead of organising a swift counter-attack, the Army focused its energy on protecting Vavuniya.

The objectives of the LTTE in triggering such an exodus are yet to be revealed. It is, however, assumed that by threatening to invade Vavuniya, the Tigers succeeded in stalling government efforts to mobilise a swift counter-attack in the areas that were lost. Instead, it has concentrated personnel in Vavuniya.

Given the prevailing low morale and poor fighting spirit among the armed forces, the LTTE decided to strike again. After a brief period of "rest" between November 9 and 17, the Tigers recommenced operations, in the north-western sector this time.

A number of military positions were attacked simultaneously. Most of these camps had been established on interior roads after different stages of Operation Ranaghosha. They were extremely vulnerable, being mere "islets" of troops in a surrounding "ocean" of LTTE-infested jungle terrain. They served very little strategic value. But to a government wanting to impress Sinhala voters with the extent of "real estate" acquired from the LTTE, it became a necessity to retain these camps. In the process, the Army spread itself thin and played into Tiger hands. The LTTE took over a number of camps in a matter of days with comparatively little bloodshed. A repetition of the earlier pattern of soldiers deserting positions on their being pounded by artillery was quite evident. Areas such as Palampitty, Thatchanamaruthamadhu, Palamottai, Vaari-kkuttiyoor, Navvi, Perlyathambanai, Periyapandivirichan, Sinnapandivirichan and Periyamadhu were overrun with comparative ease. One area where the LTTE met with stiff resistance was Iranailuppaikulam. The large base there proved to be formidable. With Army reinforcements having been sent to Iranailuppaikulam, fighting continues in the area.

On the Mannar-Pooneryn road, the strategic junction of Pallamadhu was taken, along with Pappamottai and Naayaaruveli. Although the LTTE is yet to gain a permanent presence on the Vavuniya-Mannar road, it has succeeded in driving the Army back from most areas to the north of this road. The Army now retains positions only on this road and has forbidden civilian movement on it.

Emboldened by these successes, the LTTE began an artillery attack against the main camp at Thallady in Mannar district.

The Tigers also shipped field guns to Erukkalampitty on the island and began attacking the Army camp at the Mannar Fort premises. Later, Sea Tiger boats from the Nachikkudah base tried to invade the island at the Pallimunai coast. Another controversial and sad event was the attack on Madhu. On November 18, the LTTE surrounded the outlying areas of the church. The Army left the church premises. The Tigers did not stay in the church, in deference to the wishes of the priests. On November 20, a commando unit stormed their way into the church. About 3,500 refugees were asked to sleep inside the church and the adjoining Sacred Heart Chapel. At about 10.15 p.m. there was some shelling. The Army says that the LTTE fired the shells. The Tigers say that the Army had tried to move on to Palampitty and were repulsed by them. They maintain that the retreating soldiers had trained their tanks on the chapel.

Since fighting continues in the north-western sector and positions are fluctuating, it is not possible to assess the total situation. But the LTTE does seem to have retaken 800 to 900 sq. km of territory at least in this second stage of its operation.

Three major camps at Periyamadhu, Periyathambanai and Palampitty, along with a number of smaller ones, have fallen. Neither the rate of casualties nor the nature of the military tactics adopted by the LTTE is known. But the important question is why the military debacle was in such colossal proportions. In the first stage, of course, there was the element of surprise. But after the fighting started, the other camps should have been vigilant and prepared. The major consequence of this military campaign is that the LTTE has demonstrated its military resilience once again.

The avowed objective of Chandrika Kumaratunga's war for peace stands exposed as a non-workable exercise.

Even if the Tigers are compelled to relinquish the newly taken territory, they have very effectively made the point that the organisation simply cannot be undermined gradually. Also, no strategy based on the ephemeral conquest of territory is workable. As such, bold and creative alternatives for a resolution of the conflict will have to be found in the long term. In the short term, the fighting will continue. The Army's reversals have encouraged the opposition leader Ranil Wickremasinghe, who is the chief opponent of Chandrika Kumaratunga in the presidential election. The UNP chief hopes to hold talks with the Tigers, if elected. He says that there is no military solution to the ethnic conflict and that the Tigers cannot be wished away. The LTTE has to be politically accommodated. The military reversals have considerably diminished Kumaratunga's expectations and increased Wickremasinghe's. The boundaries are now back to where the Wanni hostilities began, and all the gains by the government have been negated. But excessive victories by the LTTE may provoke a Sinhala backlash, which may result in Kumaratunga doing well. The Sri Lankan Tamil diaspora too is elated. Being hopelessly unrealistic and uncompromisingly intransigent, these sections now feel that Eelam is just around the corner.

Now it is Chandrika Kumaratunga's turn. With the Presidential election just around the corner, she would be constrained to launch some dramatic counter-attacks, if possible. This is a risky—and from a humanitarian perspective unacceptable—option, but there does not seem to be any other way out for her. So the cycle of violence will continue. It remains to be seen when the Sri Lankan forces will start their operations and how the Tigers will react.

Vanuniya's woes started in early November when the Liberation Tigers of Tamil Eelam embarked on its offensive in the Wanni region. When Operation Oyatha Alaigal began along the eastern flank of the Kandy-Jaffna road (A-9 highway), the residents were cautiously optimistic that their town would not be affected. However, in just over a week, they found themselves packing their belongings and proceeding to areas specified by the LTTE. The LTTE, in broadcasts on the Voice of Tigers (VoT), asked them to shift from Vavuniya town, Pandarikkulam, Katkuli, Thonikkal, Vairavapuliyankulam, Pattanippuram, Veppankulam, Nelukkulam, Thandikkulam and Pathinarmagilamkulam, as the Army camps there could be shelled. The safer places it suggested included Aasikkulam and Rajendrakulam.

A few days after most of the town's residents, estimated at around 80,000, had evacuated, another LTTE broadcast asked them to shift back to their homes but warned them to keep off the Army camps. (No correct estimate of the population figures of Vavuniya is available, and this confirms the distancing of the northern districts from the rest of the island. As no census was taken in the northern and eastern areas since 1981, actual population estimates vary, from the figure provided by the government, which is 50,000, to that mentioned by relief agencies, 1,00,000.) The confusion over numbers notwithstanding, it was a matter of grave humanitarian concern.

The majority of people who fled Vavuniya during the current offensive were those who had sought refuge in the town after their lives were disrupted in an earlier offensive elsewhere in the north. Thousands of people—students and traders, landlords and the landless, professionals and casual workers, government employees and shopkeepers—who were uprooted from the battle-scarred northern districts had only started life anew in Vavuniya. On November 11, when the LTTE asked them to move out, they were confused.

In Rajendrakulam near Vavuniya, a new settlement had come up overnight. Several families were living under extreme odds—under trees or bullock carts, in makeshift huts, in semi-finished houses and in thatched-roof schools.

Along the dirt track that runs across Bharatipuram, another location near Vavuniya, families live in tents, children play in makeshift swings and men huddle around a tea-stall. Whether they have money or not, what they need are passes. In the militarised zone, only civilians holding a pass issued by the police can move about freely. People without passes could be taken for militants.

Voluntary organisations gave priority to providing shelter. But those who wanted tents were required to produce their passes and register themselves with government officials.

Dharmalingam, a leftist now in his sixties, is in a tearing hurry. "I have a list of 70 people. I want to ensure that everybody gets some kind of shelter. Let us go fast, the officials may go away," he says as he gathers a group of people. At the makeshift office, an empty desk awaits him. "They have gone," a 50-year-old widow tells him. "I have to come back. I hope it does not rain (for the people have no roof over their heads)", he says. He added: "Some of the former militant groups have helped us. The houses, which are yet to be completed, were built at the initiative of the members of Parliament belonging to the People's Liberation Organisation for Tamil Eelam (PLOTE)."

At Bharatipuram, cadres of the Tamil Eelam Liberation Organisation (TELO) were overseeing mass cooking for the displaced.

The situation in Vavuniya changed rapidly when the Tigers asked the displaced people to return to the town on November 17. The residents returned to their moorings, to begin the process of normalcy. But this was shattered by incessant shelling of Army positions north of Vavuniya.

Rather than the threat of a Tiger advance, it is the refugee influx that is a matter of concern for the people living in the vicinity of Vavuniya. In Anuradhapura, further south, Sinhalese residents of Vavuniya had sought refuge with their friends and relatives. The Army maintains a nervous vigil, checking all those who enter or leave the town. At a checkpoint outside the town, students wait for some mode of transport to take them to safety.

8

Suicide Terrorism

The Liberation Tigers of Tamil Eelam (LTTE), which is waging a separatist war against the Sri Lankan state, has staged many deadly suicide-attacks, on the battlefield and off it. It has staged about 180 suicide operations since July 1987. All these have been within Sri Lanka, with the exception of the assassination of former Prime Minister Rajiv Gandhi by Thenmuli Rajaratnam alias Dhanu on May 21, 1991. With a few exceptions, the LTTE has claimed responsibility only for the suicide-attack operations it has conducted against military targets in Sri Lanka's north-eastern region.

The organisation refrains from claiming responsibility, for operations against VIP targets as also non-military infrastructure targets. The LTTE has demonstrated that its suicide-attack capabilities can be effectively used both in battlefield guerilla situations and off the-battlefield terrorist situations. In the spectrum of possible suicide attack operations, the easiest ones for a terrorist group to undertake are those against civilians; and the second easiest are infrastructure targets. In reality, a bomber who targets civilians looks for a target of opportunity. If a bomber on a mission to destroy civilian life comes across an easy military or political VIP target, he or she is likely to try and attack that target rather than the civilian target. Usually VIP targets are on the move and protected and therefore they call for considerable preparation before an attack. Such preparation ranges from the penetration of a target society or a target government to mount surveillance of the target;

planning and rehearsing in a safe zone; organising a safe-house; transporting the bomber and weapons to the target location; and ensuring that the bomber gains access to a protected target. The LTTE has employed suicide-attack operations both tactically and strategically. Although their tactical importance is apparent, the use of a suicide bomber as a strategic weapon has not been adequately analysed by the security and intelligence community.

The strategic implications of the suicide-attack threat have not been adequately understood either by the Sri Lankan political and military leaderships or the public. As such, no counter-measures to deter suicide terrorism in the short term or to mitigate its effects in the long term have been conceptualised, developed or implemented. The most obvious and immediate threat stems from the mere presence of suicide bombers who could strike almost at will. Its consequence is that almost all Sri Lankan politicians refrain from publicly criticising the LTTE. Some leaders have even made pro-LTTE pronouncements thinking that it would enable them to survive longer.

Similarly, military leaders seek to maintain a low profile operationally and within their services refrain from mobilising support to destroy the LTTE. Even political and military leaders, protected round the clock, refrain from calling V. Prabhakaran a "terrorist" or the LTTE a "terrorist organisation". The suicide bomb syndrome, a fear psychosis that a bomber could strike anywhere, anytime and against any target irrespective of the level of protection, has affected both the target government a well as the target society. The suicide-attack threat softened the stand of the toughest of leaders; compromised the position even of hard-line organisations; and debilitated the public will that had all along and firmly argued that the LTTE must be fought to the end. While eroding the nation's political fabric, the suicide-attack threat sapped the courage of the political and military elite. In turn, it degraded the moral strength of the pubic to unite, rally, stand up and fight against an enemy organisation seeking to destroy the Sri Lankan state.

By dividing the target groups into different categories, the long-range implications of the threat can be understood clearly. The off-the-battlefield suicide bomber has destroyed or aimed to destroy human or infrastructure targets.

While the human targets can be categorised into political and military ones, the infrastructure targets can be categorised into those of utility value and those with symbolic value. National political figures and figures among the military leadership form the principal human targets. They include symbolic or able political leaders in government or the opposition; Tamil political leaders who provided an alternative to the LTTE; military chiefs, potential military chiefs, able functional and area commanders; and functionaries, mostly service personnel, who are effective in anti-terrorist operations or public relations skills.

National infrastructure targets include those symbolic value and those of utility value. In order to deprive the nation of a strong leadership, the LTTE aims to eliminate national leaders, including those from political opposition. When it came to the parliamentary opposition, the decision was driven by the potential threat to the LTTE in the event of select opposition leaders assuming office.

As most political targets came into contact with the public during the run-up to an election, election-eve presented the most opportune moment for an assassination. The Sri Lankan case demonstrated that a potential target could become a priority under certain circumstances. First, when a target had either become or was likely to become the centre of resistance against the LTTE, second, when a target had forged relations with India especially with the potential to shift the LTTE-Colombo government balance of power in favour of the government; or third, when the destruction of the target was likely to erode the public will and demoralise the security forces.

The LTTE has not yet targeted leaders in the economic sector, but it is a likely and an obvious target in the years ahead. The military, political, economic or cultural infrastructure targets which the LTTE aimed to destroy were either of symbolic value or were critical to the functioning of the state.

Any infrastructure target can become salient depending on its symbolic or utilitarian value during a certain period. A week before the World Trade Centre was to be inaugurated by the President, the LTTE attacked the infrastructure target.

Likewise, a week before Sri Lanka's 50th anniversary of independence was to be celebrated at the precincts of the Sacred Temple of the Tooth Relic, the LTTE struck there. As fuel was critical to support logistics, the oil storage complex in Kolonnawa, Colombo, was attacked on the eve of the government's operation to recapture the Jaffna peninsula. The LTTE employed off-the-battlefield suicide bombers with the aim of weakening the national political leadership to break the will of the public, the quality of the military leadership at all levels, and the national economic infrastructure in order to make the war against the LTTE unsustainable.

In contrast, the LTTE employed battlefield suicide bombers to destroy military and paramilitary targets. They were either strategic targets or logistics targets. Among the strategic targets are Army camps (for example, Nelliadi, Mankulam, Silvathural); Navy camps (Nagathevanthural); Air Force camps (China Bay, Ratmalana, Palaly) and Special Task Force camps (Puthukudiviripрu). The logistics targets include air vehicles at airports (Palaly, Ratmalana); seaborne craft in seaports (mostly when anchored) or when mobile (Trincomalee, Karainagar, Kankesanthurai or the north-eastern waters, and once in the Colombo port). As the battlefield suicide-attacks were remote and not visible, neither the government nor the public suffered from it.

The public had no inkling of the suicide-attack threat to battlefield targets. Colombo, where the elites lived and governed and public opinion was formed and shaped, was remote from the north-east. As such, there was less attention paid and less thinking and resources invested to disrupt battlefield suicide-attack operations.

In order to protect the national leadership from the off-the-battlefield suicide bombers, the government reactively allocated considerable resources. But the government did not allocate comparable resources to protect the military assets in the north-east to brave the battlefield suicide bombers. Numerically, more LTTE suicide cadres operating in self- contained units or integrated into its battlefield units have died attacking battlefield targets. The battlefield targets were as vulnerable to LTTE suicide bombers as the off-the-battlefield targets. The government's battlefield losses have been high as compared to the LTTE's. Both at the tactical and strategic levels, there were key advantages in using battlefield suicide bombers. The LTTE employed battlefield suicide bombers with the aim of (a) reducing fatalities and casualties of regular cadres, numerically preserving and building the LTTE's fighting strength; (b) destroying Sri Lankan naval logistics capability and strategic targets, thus reducing sea control capability, tactical and strategic mobility, and the strategic depth of the Sri Lankan security forces; and (c) enhancing the overall operational efficiency of the LTTE's land and sea fighting units, thereby demoralising the Sri Lankan security forces and eroding the public confidence in the security forces.

Sri Lanka has had a finite intellectual resource pool. Unlike the infrastructure targets, which could be restored or constructed, the human losses cannot be replaced, especially within a short period.

The quality of the off-the-battlefield targets, especially human targets, destroyed by the LTTE has been extraordinarily high. For the terrorist group, suicide bombing has been a highly cost-effective way of eliminating the core and the penultimate leadership of the nation. An examination of off-the-battlefield operations reveals that the LTTE exploited the relaxation of security during the 1989-90 and 1994-95 peace processes to infiltrate the south of Sri Lanka, especially the capital. LTTE national intelligence cadres as well as Black Tigers penetrated the hostile area and gained access to their human and infrastructure targets.

Such intelligence cadres had two tasks. First, they were to mount surveillance on targets and infiltrate the political, military, police and intelligence establishment. Second, they were to cultivate agents resident in the hostile area and task them to mount similar surveillances.

The surveillance data was dispatched to the LTTE intelligence headquarters to plan operations. With this data, models were built and cadres trained to gain stealth and speed. At times, additional data was requested. At times the data was verified through another source or sources. The success of the assassinations in Colombo was dependent on the intelligence network that was operational in Colombo.

The network was cellular and coordinated from the LTTE-controlled area. Whenever the police or the army apprehended an LTTE cadre alive, there was the likelihood of the security forces breaking up his or her operational cell. As his or her principal agent handler lived in the LTTE-controlled area, the principal agent handler was protected. Parallel to the national intelligence network, the LTTE ran a military intelligence network. This network did not have cadres on the ground in the hostile area but it had agents in the Sri Lankan security forces. The presence of a second intelligence organisation gave the LTTE the advantage of cross-checking and verifying, both raw data and assessments.

The Black Tigers who infiltrated the hostile areas assassinated VIPs or sabotaged infrastructure on their own or acting on intelligence provided by intelligence cadres and/or agents. The Black Tigers infiltrated the offices or the homes of VIPs, gathered intelligence and transmitted them to LTTE headquarters before targeting the VIPs. Similarly, the Black Tigers who mounted reconnaissance on infrastructure transmitted data to the LTTE headquarters before attacking the target. The Black Tigers who infiltrated or mounted reconnaissance were better than others in operational terms. They performed the roles both of the intelligence cadre and the Black Tiger. The Black Tiger who depended on the intelligence cadre for intelligence on a VIP or on infrastructure facility was merely a suicide-attack cadre. In the latter case, the intelligence cadre often accompanied the suicide-attack cadre to the target. Every Black Tiger needed a support cell to provide him or her the weaponry, transport to and from the target, communication to the headquarters, and so on. Gradually the LTTE realised the vulnerability of its large operational cells and made them smaller. Unless a number of Black Tigers were needed for a mission, the cell remained small; at times it comprised just a single resourceful intelligence cadre. This cadre, designated the controller, looked after the needs of the Black Tiger, in respect of everything from logistics to communication, until the mission was completed.

At times the controller escorted the Black Tiger to the target, provided security or guided him or her to reach the target with the least resistance.

As a consequence of stepped-up counter-terrorist measures, including operations ranging from round-ups to checkpoint monitoring, the original networks established by the LTTE during the peace process have been disrupted or have disintegrated.

In order to maintain an uninterrupted flow of intelligence data, the LTTE has built layers of fresh networks. These networks have been structured or strengthened on the basis of the identified flaws of the previous networks. The September 11, 1999 bomb-blast at the Jaffna Municipal Council premises in the high-security area of Nallur within Jaffna municipality is the latest manifestation of the destructive capability of the Liberation Tigers of Tamil Eelam (LTTE). The bomb had been concealed between the false ceiling and the roof the previous night and was activated by a remote control mechanism.

The explosive device was of the arc-shaped anti-personnel claymore mine variety that was used by the LTTE in previous attacks on mobile and pedestrian army patrols. This is the first known instance of the LTTE planting one at an elevation inside a room in order to set off a rain of shrapnel that causes death. Twelve people, including Tamil United Liberation Front (TULF) leader and Jaffna Mayor Ponnuthurai Sivapalan, Jaffna town commandant Brigadier Susantha Mendis, several senior police officers and high-ranking officials of the Municipal Council were killed, and 20 people were injured in the blast.

As serious as the loss of lives and damage to property was the damage done to the process of the return of normalcy in Jaffna. Whatever progress was made in re-establishing representative democracy in the Peninsula has been undone. Even more serious is the fact that the LTTE has demonstrated that it continues to be active in the Jaffna area. Taken with some other developments, it indicates that the LTTE, which had been pushed back militarily, is seeking to occupy centre stage in Tamil politics again. The Jaffna Municipal Council, run by the moderate TULF, has been the target of LTTE hostility in the past. The Tigers saw the council as a symbol of the yearning of the Tamil people of Jaffna for the return of peace and democracy. On May 17, Jaffna Mayor Sarojini Yogeswaran, who had refused to have bodyguards because of her commitment to remain accessible to the people, was gunned down at her residence. Following that killing, many TULF councillors and the Deputy Mayor resigned in fear.

However, the party's legal secretary Ponnuthurai Sivapalan and a young lawyer named Nadarajah Raviraj took up the challenge and became Mayor and Deputy Mayor respectively. New councillors were appointed and work began in earnest. The LTTE saw this as defiance and planned an attack. Its intention in placing the bomb was to kill all Council members at one stroke: the bomb was intended to explode when the Municipal Council was in session. The meeting, however, was postponed at short notice to make room for a conference of officials of the Army, the police and the Municipal Council. Nevertheless, the LTTE went ahead with its plan.

The execution of the blast indicates the extent to which the LTTE is capable of infiltrating high-security areas in Jaffna. The job could not have been carried out without help from persons connected with the Municipal Council. These are dangerous indicators that the LTTE is capable of coaxing—or coercing—Jaffna residents into going along with its terrorist activities.

The blast raised doubts about the future of the Jaffna Municipal Council. An LTTE front organisation, named "Friends of Tamil National Liberation", has sent letters to all councillors directing them to resign their posts immediately or face death. This is likely to cause the TULF to undertake a painful reappraisal of its options. TULF parliamentarians, Joseph Pararajasingharn and Neelan Tiruchelvam, have been quoted in the newspapers as saying that the party would not try to run the Council any longer.

When the People's Alliance government launched Operation Riviresa in three stages during 1995 and 1996, the LTTE, after putting up some resistance, withdrew from Jaffna Peninsula to the Vanni area with most of its military assets intact. Later it began infiltrating the Peninsula in small numbers. A suicide bombing in July 1996 killed the Jaffna town commandant, Brig. Ananda Hammangoda. A few weeks later the Mullaitivu camp of the Army was overrun and more than a thousand soldiers were killed. After this, the mood in the North turned against the Army and the rapport the Army had established with the people suffered. Hundreds of Tamil youth, who were taken away by the Army, were later declared "missing". In 1997, the Sri Lankan government started Operation Jayasikuru aimed at capturing and consolidating the military's hold on the stretch of road between Vavuniya and Kilinochchi on the Jaffna-Kandy highway.

Large contingents of military personnel, who were stationed in the Eastern Province and in the Peninsula, were redeployed for this purpose. This resulted in a security vacuum in certain areas in the east which the LTTE was quick to exploit. Today a substantial portion of territory to the west of the Batticaloa lagoon is under LTTE control. In the Peninsula too the level of LTTE reinduction increased. Although the LTTE's presence in the Peninsula is not strikingly high, the LTTE has certainly spread its tentacles wide. It has established "tax collection" centres at Punkudutheevu, Vallipuram, Kodikamam and Ponnalai in the Peninsula. Clandestine notices demanding "donations" are sent to rich people and traders. These are by and large "respected". The LTTE also has an overt presence in the coastal strip of Vadamarachchi East, between Nagar Kovil and Thalaiady. It also has clandestine camps in the interior areas of the southern regions of the Peninsula.

In the area between Kachchai, Eluthumattuval, Sarasalai and Varani, LTTE cadres move about freely. But when Army patrols scour the area, they take flight. The same is the case in the coastal area of Vadamarachchi East. This kind of presence helps the Tigers maintain contact with their cadres in Chundikulam and Mullaitivu by sea. The 250 to 300 LTTE cadres stationed in the Peninsula continue to receive supplies and reinforcements this way. The LTTE, however, has not been able to re-establish itself in the densely populated parts of the Peninsula; it has conducted ambushes and assassinations in these areas, but these were the work of cadres who came in from elsewhere. These areas are under tight control of the armed forces. Until recently, the armed forces received tip-offs from the people about movement of LTTE cadres. Elections to the local bodies in January, in which nearly 50 per cent of the eligible voters in the peninsula cast their votes, and the consequent formation of the Jaffna Municipal Council were symbols of the Chandrika Kumaratunga government's success in reintroducing representative democracy and ushering in normalcy. However, the LTTE has struck back decisively.

In May, a suicide bomber killed Vadamarachchi Army Commander, Brig. Larry Wijeratne; days later, Sarojini Yogeswaran was gunned down. The September 11 blast, taken with the previous killings, has shocked the people of Jaffna. There is growing resentment over the government's inability to ensure security and to safeguard the area from LTTE attacks. The people are concerned that the armed forces may not be able to prevent an escalation in LTTE activity. If such feelings gather momentum, the government may lose the war for the hearts and minds of the people. The LTTE has been quick to capitalise on this perceptible mindshift. LTTE leaflets distributed in Jaffna have called upon government officials to stop cooperating or associating with the Army. While expressing regret for the deaths of civilian municipal officials in the bomb attack, the LTTE claims that they were died because they were collaborating with the Army. Given the shock waves caused by the recent blast, most government officials are likely to avoid contact with the armed forces in the future. This in turn will strain the civil administration set-up further. The LTTE has also put up handwritten posters in various areas in Jaffna city, listing the names of Tamil civilians who, it alleges, have contacts with and divulge information to the Army. It has served an ultimatum on these persons to sever all links with the Army immediately. This measure too is likely to affect the relations between the Army and the public.

The five courts in the Peninsula have not been functioning for months owing to LTTE threats to the court staff, and it seems likely that most structures of civil administration will be under similar strain following the LTTE's threats. Incidentally, the private airline that operates services between Jaffna and Colombo has been warned by the LTTE to stop its air service.

The situation in Jaffna today is in one way similar to the situation that prevailed during the early 1980s. At that time, the militants presence in Jaffna was covert; only about a few hundred were active. Yet a series of strikes effectively undermined the civil government structures.

Gradually, all vestiges of government control began to decay. Given the current military balance, the threat of the LTTE driving out the Army and capturing territory in the Peninsula may not come true immediately.

The danger now is that the groundwork is being done to thwart all efforts at re-establishing democracy in Jaffna. In the early 1980s, the situation was such that the then prevailing democratic structures were undermined in order to create a vacuum that was filled by militant groups. Today, attempts to revive and promote democratic structures are resisted by the LTTE in order to blunt the efforts to restore normalcy.

Although the setback in the realm of civil administration in Jaffna is largely the result of LTTE violence and the element of fear, the Sri Lankan government would be making a grave error if it assumes that is the sole reason for the current situation. Colombo must take note of the Tamil people's growing disappointment with and their lack of confidence in the government's record.

Although President Chandrika Kumaratunga was elected with a mandate to secure peace and held out much hope to the Tamil minority, her performance in office has not won her many admirers in the North.

It is, of course, true that she has not been able to deliver on her promise to settle the ethnic crisis largely because the LTTE and the opposition United National Party (UNP) have not been cooperative. But public memory can be fickle. The reality is that in spite of Chandrika Kumaratunga's efforts, the ethnic problem remains unsolved. The current "war for peace" has brought no end to the misery of ordinary Tamils. They continued to endure the hardship in the hope that a political settlement would follow. But now the Tamil people feel that they are in a no-win situation.

On the one hand, the UNP's non-cooperation, coupled with hawkish Sinhala opposition, has cast doubts on whether the devolution package will be implemented.

On the other, the LTTE has been able to hold its own against the Army in positional warfare for nearly one and a half years, which makes people wonder whether the war will ever be over. All this has led to frustration and a sense of pessimism in the Tamil people. This attitude is fertile ground for the growth of the LTTE's influence. Sensing this, the LTTE seems to be driving home the advantage gained by its recent attacks in Jaffna.

If the government is not able to deliver quickly on its promises to the Tamil people, it seems inevitable that the LTTE will gain in strength in the near future. Sri Lanka's presidential election campaign ended on December 18, 1999 with two explosions, one in Colombo and the other in suburban Ja-Ela. The first one was targeted against President Chandrika Kumaratunga and the second against the former Chief of the Army Staff Maj. Gen. (retd) Lucky Alagama, Kumaratunga, who was campaigning for a second term as President, survived the attack, carried out by a suicide bomber.

The two explosions have come as another grim reminder to the government and people of the island nation that the deployment of terror continues to be a potent political strategy in the Sri Lankan context. It is dearly a strike by the Liberation Tigers of Tamil Eelam (LTTE). The suicide bombing bears its signature. The attempt on Kumaratunga came as she finished addressing her final rally before the December 21 election. A stunned nation termed her escape a "miracle". It was a combination of planned and unplanned factors that helped save her life.

A sterile zone with metal barricades between the audience and the speaker was the first line of protection. The suicide bomber, seated in one of the first two rows of the moderate-size audience, was stopped by the police while attempting to cross the barricade. At the same time, Kumaratunga's driver of over three decades had reversed the car to where the President paused to answer questions from an Indian television crew. When the bomb went off, the car stood between the assassin and the President. Twenty-one persons were killed in the explosion, four of them police personnel, including Colombo's Deputy Inspector-General T.N. De Silva. Kumaratunga's driver was also killed. The police estimate that the distance between the bomber and the President was about five metres, but others present at the spot claim that it was more. The type of the bomb and the number of persons involved in the attack remained unknown. No arrests were immediately made. The police denied reports that a person with a cyanide capsule had been apprehended at the site.

As a direct consequence of the bomb attacks, dealing with terrorism may once again appear on top of the island's political agenda. In view of the international reaction to the incidents, there has to be a reiteration of the posturing on containing terrorism. Nationally, condemnation came from all political parties including those representing minority Tamils and Muslims, the media, and society at large.

International condemnation came in the form of messages from India, Pakistan, the United States, France, Nepal and Japan. The world media reported the assassination bid as the top news story. Sri Lanka is relieved not only that the President survived the attack but also that the nation responded to the incident in a generally correct manner. If the perpetrators of the attempt had hoped to trigger reprisal attacks, they were disappointed. Soon after she was admitted to a private hospital, Kumaratunga told her media adviser that her main concern was the maintenance of peace and inter-ethnic harmony. Curfew was clamped on Colombo on the night of December 18, 1999. It was withdrawn the next morning. Political leaders remained calm and urged restraint on the part of the people.

The next day, in a radiobroadcast from her hospital bed, the President appealed to the nation to remain calm and said that it was the bounden duty of all citizens "to protect all Tamil citizens of this country". She said: "Let not the terrorists of the LTTE destroy the last chance we have in transforming this country of ours into one of decency, ethnic harmony and humanism and modernism."

In one of its most challenging moments in two decades, the ethnically polarised nation responded positively to the appeal. Any reprisal attacks by the Sinhala majority had the potential to damage the pluralistic character of the nation. Through its reaction and its resilience, Sri Lanka has shown to the world that it has come a long way from July 1983, when the killing of 13 soldiers who were carrying out counter-insurgency operations sparked one of the worst ethnic riots in the island.

9

Security of Sri Lanka

Sri Lanka, which has experienced severe security crisis in the mid-eighties, a CCS framework can deliver several benefits at a lower cost. First, the core 'India factor' in Sri Lanka's strategic thinking and security policy will gradually lose its hardened effect when structures of fear and threat perceptions are replaced by a sense of shared interests and destiny. Secondly, Sri Lanka's security apparatus and institutions will gain strength to deal with extreme forces of internal political disorder in the wake of cessation of external negative responses. Thirdly, a tension-free relationship between India and Pakistan will resolve Sri Lanka's regional policy dilemmas. Fourthly, a regional CCS environment will enhance the island's autonomy in foreign policy decision making and assertion of independence *vis-a-vis* extra-regional powers and influences. Thus, the principal utility of CCS framework lies in maximising Sri Lanka's security and independence by removing the sources of threat and concerns.

Since the nature and magnitude of threats underline the specificity of national concerns, which, in turn, determine the state's security policy and its cooperative relations, it is essential to address a wide array of questions relating to the security problems of Sri Lanka: What are the bases and sources of threat to its security? What are its specific security concerns? What are the core principles of its security policy? How does it manage its security problems? How can CCS be evolved to the benefit of Sri Lanka? Sri Lanka's insecurity stems from both internal and external sources and the linkages between the two often led to a security crisis that the country could barely manage.

At a closer look one finds that threats generated by internal sources are real, whereas external sources have merely created its fear of threat, except in the mid-eighties when the linkages between the two sources became well pronounced in strategic terms.

The consensus among the policy makers and academic analysts is that India is by far the most dominant factor in Sri Lanka's security. It singularly occupies the larger consciousness of the Sri Lankan strategic community, which relates the country's survival to India's fairplay and sensitivity to the interests of small states in the region. No one in the island escapes from the unending 'India fear', cultivated so systematically in every mind and reflected so vividly in almost all security policy decisions of the successive regimes. It stems from both built-in factors—location, size, culture, and power—and India's approach to regional security. The strategic reality is that the tiny island state, located in what D. S. Senanayake described as the 'strategic highway' of the world, is juxtaposed with India, whose overbearing size (fifty times more than that of Sri Lanka), population and economic-military strength have a definite intimidating effect on Sri Lanka.

A long continuum of cultural contacts and spread of Indian influence in the island have caused serious security implications in the present century when intense cross-boundary ethnic interactions (between the Tamils across the Palk Straits) carried the task of countering the central authority's approach to nation building. If the country's open coastal belt in the north-east region provided the gateway for the successive invasions from the South Indian kingdoms in the ancient period, the outbreak of ethnic conflict in the eighties has once again activated the 20 miles long Indo-Lanka maritime route for the movement of militants and refugees. Much of Sri Lanka's fear of India arises from its proximity to Tamil Nadu, a state which articulated its ethnic demand for a separate Dravidastan in the fifties and provided the necessary ideological strength and political support for the competing Sri Lankan Tamil nationalism.

In the post-colonial period, India's attempt at defining its strategic goals and approach to regional security has operationalised the built-in factors such as asymmetrical power relations, historical memories about South Indian invasions and locational proximity to cause fear and heighten the threat perception in the minds of Sri Lanka. While trying to evolve a strategic doctrine on the eve of decolonisation of South Asia, Indian leaders and strategic thinkers sought to explore all possible ways to develop a vibrant policy of Indian defence. The idea of 'strategic unity' was thought out to be an option, but soon it became clear to its protagonists that it was not only undesirable but also unrealistic. Although the idea remained only at a conceptual level, without getting any consideration for its inclusion in independent India's strategic doctrine, it formed a powerful factor in Sri Lanka's strategic thinking and behaviour.

Successive Sri Lankan leadership continued to harp on it to add a greater dimension to the country's security concerns and, in the process of evolving a structure of defence against a vaguely formulated and perceived threat from India, Sri Lanka became a strategic ally of the West. This, in a way, constituted a formidable challenge to India's strategic interests, which are coterminous with that of the region, and the envisioned-security framework for South Asia. Conceived within this framework are India's concerns that arise from any threat to the security of its neighbours or strategic postures and alignment of any South Asian country with extra-regional power(s) aimed at tilting the balance of power in the region. As this policy came to be strongly articulated only in the post-Nehruvian era and Nehru himself was cautious about dealing with the small neighbours so that its security sensitivities were not offended, Sri Lanka's strategic alignment with Britain until 1957 was not an irritant in Indo-Lanka relations. Even then, there was no scope for greater amelioration in Sri Lanka's fear of India, as leaders like John Kotelawala became more vocal in articulating the 'India factor' in the island's security and survival. They suspected that Nehru's ambition to make India a strong power would lead to its domination over the smaller countries of the region and his continuing interest in Sri Lanka was "solely on account of its strategic importance" arising out of its natural harbour in Trincomalee. As a corollary, fears were also expressed in some quarters that India would make covert attempts to occupy the Trincomalee harbour to the advantage and expansion of its regional strategic interests, and Sri Lanka would lose its newly gained independence if it were left alone to tackle its security problems.

Although SWRD Bandaranaike and later, his wife Sirimavo Bandaranaike, repudiated Sri Lanka's fear of Indian aggression and considered India a friendly power, they were not prepared to completely ignore the 'India factor' in the island's security. Mr. Bandaranaike trusted Nehru's India but was not sure about the intentions and attitude of its future leaders. It was probably on the unexpressed premise of the danger, that is India, that he, as a pragmatic security policy, opted against abrogation of the 1947 Defence Agreement while negotiating for the withdrawal of British bases from the island in 1957. Britain was still considered as a source of military support under the agreement, whose clauses could be evoked with mutual consent in the event of any threat to the country's security.

Similarly, while appearing to be sensitive to India's strategic interests and aspirations and refraining from contributing in any direct way to vitiate the strategic environment in the region, Sirimavo Bandaranaike revealed her government's desire and efforts to maximise the island's manoeuvrability *vis-a-vis* India by cultivating China and Pakistan. Thus, the 'India factor' as an independent variable in Sri Lanka's security policy and a source of its insecurity continued to maintain its operational relevance, even though there were changes in the successive regimes perception of India. The difference was that, whereas the United National Party (UNP) regime under D. S. Senanayake and John Kotelawala suffered from an acute sense of fear, the Sri Lanka Freedom Party (SLFP) Prime Ministers—SWRD Bandaranaike and Sirimavo Bandaranaike—did neither overplay nor ignore the 'India factor'. This indicates the varied level of threat that the Sri Lankan leaders and their regimes perceived from India. By any standard, the SLFP government nurtured a low level of mutual suspicion and threat perception as compared to the UNP regime's high level in the dyadic relationship. Until the seventies, India had been deliberately made out to be or misperceived as a potential source of threat to Sri Lanka's security by the successive ruling elite because of their strong desire to assert their country's identity and achieve a status for themselves vis-a-vis the Indian leaders.

Later, in the wake of the outbreak of ethnic conflict in the eighties, some policy postures and responses of India, as is analysed below, might have contributed to the island's fear and threatened its security. If India has come to be the core factor in Sri Lanka's security, it does not mean that it is the sole source of the island's insecurity and threat perception.

In varying degrees, and at different points of time, the country felt threatened by forces that were operating in the confrontationist cold war framework of international politics. One of the less articulated and short-lived concerns of the UNP Prime Ministers (1948-56) was the threat that Communism perceivably posed to Sri Lanka's security. D. S. Senanayake openly declared his fear of Soviet intrusion into the island through leftist forces and saw the 1947 Defence Agreement as a bulwark against Moscow's covert designs of destabilisation.

Similarly, John Kotelawala had equated "Soviet colonialism" with "Western imperialism" and resolved to oppose both by all means. It was also feared that China would spread Communism in Asia, leading to its confrontation with the United States, as had happened in the Korean Peninsula, and small states like Sri Lanka would not be able to counter the expansion of Communist influence. John Kotelawala was more explicit in articulating this view. Later, Dudley Senanayake (1965-70) saw the free flow of Maoist literature and badges for distribution among the leftist cadres in the island as a part of Chinese covert operations to bring about internal subversion.

Although China refuted such allegations and tried to allay the Sri Lankan government's fear of Communism, the UNP leaders, until the seventies, remained as suspicious as ever without much objective basis. On the contrary, the SLFP leaders did not perceive threat from international Communism; they focused on developing good relations with China and the former Soviet Union as a meaningful strategy to protect its security. An important pitfall of Sri Lanka's strategic partnership with Britain was its identification with Western military strategy. Although the island did not join any military engagement led by the Western bloc, it was still perceived as an indirect participant in cold war politics. This is best evident from the continued Soviet veto, until December 1955, on Sri Lanka's application for the UN membership.

Another source of Sri Lanka's insecurity since the sixties has been militarisation of the Indian Ocean as a part of abrasive cold war politics. A centrally located state, Sri Lanka feared that control and domination of the Indian Ocean by extra-regional powers would erode the freedom and sovereignty of the littoral and hinterland states of the region. And Sri Lanka itself would inevitably be drawn into power politics because of its locational factor, buttressed by the strategically important Trincomalee harbour. Noticeably, the end of the cold war has changed the strategic situation in the Indian Ocean region and, as such, the US Naval presence is not perceived any more as a serious challenge to security of the littoral states like Sri Lanka.

Sri Lanka's dependent economic structure marked by a vibrant import-export sector, heavy reliance on foreign capital and growing debt burden makes it vulnerable to changes in global market and supply conditions. This peculiar built-in economic feature has intrinsic security implications, which the Sri Lankan leaders can hardly ignore in any strategic decision making.

Much of the country's vulnerability arises from its heavy thrust on export-import market as a crucial factor in its economic survival. If foreign exchange earnings, through export of agricultural and industrial products, form the core component of the island's economic development programme, large-scale import of primary commodities imposes severe strains on its resources. Although the country's export has registered a phenomenal growth over the years, both in terms of volume and value due to diversification of products and markets, the real economic benefits are offset by growing cost and volume of imports. This is clearly evident in the deteriorating trade deficit which accounted for Rs. 72,731 million (9.5 per cent of GDP) in 1996.

A drastic decline in Sri Lanka's exports as a result of any downward trend in the world market prices or fall in external demand for its commodities and, at the same time, hike in import prices will tend to affect its ability to pay the larger import bill, leading to serious economic and social problems in the country.

Sri Lanka's constraints in raising adequate revenue from national sources to meet the growing recurrent and capital expenditure have increased the importance of foreign sources of finance, including remittances from emigrants and development assistance, in sustaining its economic development.

Until 1977, when the UNP government introduced the policy of economic liberalisation, foreign aid played an insignificant role in financing budget deficits. This means that the country could enjoy greater flexibility and dependence in formulating economic policies.

The structural adjustment programme, since 1977, has brought to the country a large quantum of foreign assistance, but various conditionalities—such as removal of restrictions on external transfer of finance and reduction of social welfare expenditures—imposed by the donors have sufficiently eroded its autonomy in economic decision making. Some of the conditions are based on blanket ideologies, which Sri Lanka accepted out of economic compulsions. The situation now is that any drastic reduction in external resource flows will substantially affect Sri Lanka's economic development programme and, at the same time, growing foreign debt is a matter of serious national concern. In recent years, the island's economic insecurity has attained a serious dimension because the protracted ethnic war has weakened the economic fabric of the society. The cost of protecting the state and ensuring the country's territorial integrity is steeply increasing with every passing year.

We have stated earlier that the real threat to Sri Lanka's security has arisen from within, in two dominant forms, viz., insurrection and ethnic conflict. In both, the state has figured as a dominant adversary—against the Janata Vimukti Peramuna (JVP) and the Sri Lankan Tamils respectively. The external linkages of these potentially destabilising events, operationalised either as a background and ideological stimuli for the internal forces or in a more functional way of direct external involvement in support of them, are the dependent sources of Sri Lanka's insecurity. Incidentally, the insurrection, especially in the eighties, was largely triggered off by the direct involvement of India in the ethnic conflict as a part of the process of its greater externalisation. This, in turn, aggravated the problem of security and survival of the island.

The abortive JVP insurrection to capture state power, by force of arms, was launched in two phases—in 1971 and during 1987-89. The second phase was better organised and more deep-rooted than the first and, as such, security implications were correspondingly greater. Born largely as 'a rural youth movement in the late sixties, it grew, in the eighties, to become a powerful force in many urban and quasi-urban areas.

The JVP insurrection was a demonstration of the dissatisfaction and alienation of educated-unemployed Sinhalese youth, who got attracted to the group's localised revolutionary ideology based on a thoroughly diluted socialist doctrine, a highly popularised claim to nativism and a strong articulation of Sinhalese chauvinism.

In exploiting the reservoirs of political alienation in the society and due to its long commitment to revolution, the highly ambitious JVP leadership nurtured the hope of achieving state power. Thus, the JVP insurrection was an exercise in "political entrepreneurship" by military means. Although the internal socio-economic and political conditions provided the base for its growth and revolutionary adventurism, the external factor, i.e., Indian hegemony, was invoked to facilitate the process of the mobilisation of support. Opposition to India's domination over Sri Lanka was one of the fundamental objectives of the JVP.

The presence of a large contingent of the Indian Peacekeeping Force (IPKF) in the island under the July 1987 Agreement had vindicated its position. Incidentally, the 1987-89 insurrection was solely triggered off by the 'India factor' in the ethnic conflict, because of which the JVP could gain the support and sympathy of a large section of the anti-Agreement forces belonging to the Sinhalese Buddhist constituency and some of the political parties.

The JVP's strategy in April 1971 was extremely limited and ill prepared. It merely carried out attacks on police stations in different localities until the entire movement was crushed within a week, with prompt military assistance from several countries including India.

The tactics of the JVP during 1987-89 were far more organised and ruthless. The chosen targets were wide-ranging. Apart from attacking military installations, government offices and visible infrastructure (television stations, electricity stations, and bridges), it organised demonstrations in provincial towns against the government and the IPKF, campaigned the boycott of Indian products, periodically enforced limited work stoppages, carried out various kinds of attacks on the official media, exploited labour discontent to call major strikes and, above all, carried out assassinations of prominent figures including some politicians and businessmen.

The entire campaign was so vigorously launched that the Premadasa regime appeared to have headed towards an irretrievable collapse. However, it finally managed to survive the frontal attack of the JVP because of the indiscriminate use of the coercive state power against the group's cadres and a large number of suspects, including many innocent youth. The cumulative effect of the JVP movement was that the integrity and cohesion of the Sri Lankan polity came under severe threat. Apart from the fact that the insurrection had a crippling effect on the economy, what raised the country's security concern was the sympathetic attitude of a section of the Sri Lankan security forces towards the movement.

Evidence revealed that the JVP had infiltrated the police and army through the opportunity provided by the major expansion of their ranks since 1983, in the wake of the intensification of the internal war. It was feared that a section of the army would revolt against the state, thereby causing a serious security crisis.

The curtailment of the interpenetrative ability of the democratic institutions and the demoralising effect it had on the society led to a clear breakdown of relations between the state and civil society. Most Sri Lankans lived under constant fear of threat, which the state could not remove, and its inability to protect them resulted in the erosion of their faith in state institutions. This became more intensified when the state itself, through its indiscriminate, ruthless measures and coercive tactics to combat the JVP movement, turned to pose a serious threat to the civil society. The fear which the state instilled in the minds of people was as acute as the JVP's campaign itself. As a long-term implication, it was feared that the spread of revolutionary ideology in the country would threaten established democratic norms and ways of governance.

Unlike the JVP insurrection, the ethnic conflict since 1983 has a larger enduring effect on the island's security. A clear operational linkage between internal and external sources of threat became evident in the mid-eighties as a result of the internationalisation of the ethnic conflict, with India figuring as the dominant factor in Sri Lanka's security considerations and calculations. From the island's standpoint, India's threat was not merely perceived, but real in the sense that its response to ethnic violence had completely ignored the security sensitivities of its small neighbour, which had no adequate military means to counter the over-imposing behaviour of a dominant power in the region.

Many incidents during 1983-87 led to the creation of such a fear complex: First, Tamil Nadu's demand for a Bangladesh-type action in Sri Lanka. When large-scale killing of Tamils in the July 1983 riots and the subsequent military operations in the north-east evoked a spontaneous indignation of the people of Tamil Nadu, pressure was exerted on the Indian government to intervene militarily in the island to create a separate Eelam. Although the Indian central leadership—Mrs. Gandhi and Rajiv Gandhi—resisted such pressure and pledged to honour Sri Lanka's sovereignty and territorial integrity, Colombo did not rule out the possibility of India's military intervention out of political compulsions, if not for regional strategic considerations. Secondly, India's tough policy postures—illustrated by its strong condemnation of violence against the Sri Lankan Tamils, mobilisation of international sympathy and support for the beleaguered minority by highlighting the human rights violations in the island, constant pressure on the Sri Lankan leadership to halt the Sri Lankan Army's military operations in the north-east and accept the legitimate Tamil aspirations and, above all, strong opposition to Sri Lanka's search for international security assistance and guarantees—all these, made the Sri Lankan government feel that the country's independence was under serious threat from its powerful neighbour.

Thirdly, India's clandestine military support to the Tamil militants provided the most authentic evidence of its threat to the island. As a part of its strategy of empowering the weaker party so as to create a structure of near-parity of relations in political negotiations, India supplied arms and extended sanctuary facilities to the militants in Tamil Nadu.

The entire Palk Straits became a major conduit for arms and militants. For the Sri Lankan government, India's support to the militants amounted to waging a proxy war, with the ultimate aim of disintegrating the country. Fourthly, Operation Eagle—para-dropping of food and medicine—undertaken by the Indian Air Force, on 4 June 1987, as a protest against the military moves of the Jayewardene regime, was a clear demonstration of India's open threat to Sri Lanka's security. The military action, in violation of Sri Lanka's air space, had badly jolted the country and brought to reality its worst fears of India. It also revealed the limits of external military support to the island in times of crisis, as none of its strategic allies extended or promised any assistance to counter India's threat. The real threat that Sri Lanka faced from India, probably for the first time in the post-independence period, was short-lived. It diminished considerably in the months following July 1987, when both the countries signed a bilateral agreement to restore peace on the island, and completely ceased to exist since the early nineties as a result of the perceptible changes that have occurred in India's policy towards Sri Lanka. This, however, has not improved the island's security, as the ethnic conflict remains as much a source of threat as ever. Apart from the rising cost of the war and proliferation of small arms, the country's security concerns arise out of the pro-active support extended by the Tamil diaspora to militancy in the north-east of the island.

Diaspora can be an asset as well as a threat to their country of origin. In recent years, their role as a transnational factor in national security is underlined in many studies.

The active involvement of the Sri Lankan Tamil diaspora in the ethnic war between the government forces and the Liberation Tigers of Tamil Eelam (LTTE) demonstrates that India is not the only external source of threat to the island but also, more importantly, its own expatriate population. Ever since India's support to the Tamil militants ceased in the late eighties, it is the Tamil diaspora in the UK, Canada, the US, Germany, France, Switzerland, Norway, Denmark, the Netherlands and Australia that has emerged as the most important source of support to the LTTE. A huge amount of money is collected, either through extortion or voluntary contribution, from the Sri Lankan Tamil refugees living in these countries and used for acquisition of weapons, explosives, telecommunication equipment, etc. It is estimated that about 40 per cent of the LTTE's resources in 1995 were generated from abroad; it rose to 60 per cent in 1996 when internal resource-mobilisation capacity of the organisation was affected by the loss of its control over the Jaffna Peninsula in the war. The group has developed a highly efficient international network through which external support and sympathy for the Tamil cause are mobilised.

The rising cost of the war since 1983 and its debilitating impact on the country's economy have definite security implications. Many studies have made various assessment of the overall economic loss suffered by Sri Lanka on account of destruction of property and infrastructure, rising military expenditure, rehabilitation of displaced people and refugees, and reduction in income and economic growth.

A recent study puts the total cost of the war at about Rs. 4,100 billion and the cost of repairing the damage in the main sectors is expected to be more than Rs. 50,000 billion. Even if one thinks that the amount is slightly inflated, the cost of the war is quite undoubtedly substantial in real terms. For a country like Sri Lanka this is highly an undesirable and unbearable cost, escalating as it is, with every passing year, in view of the war continuing without any end in sight. The country's external debt has increased over the years partly because of the growing military expenditure. Defence spending constituted about 1.5 per cent of the GDP in 1983 (4 per cent of the total government spending). It rose to over 5 per cent of the GDP in 1987-88 (almost 18 per cent of total government spending). During 1985-95, the expenditure increased by 4.9 per cent of the GDP. The actual amount of increase was from Rs. one billion in 1981 to Rs. 5.6 billion in 1985, Rs. 11.3 billion in 1987, Rs. 35 billion in 1995, and Rs. 46 billion in 1996. As a result, there has been a general fall in social expenditure and investment. Military expenditure was equivalent, on average, to 7.2 per cent of new debt incurred in 1980-82, although the proportion rose to 36.3 per cent in 1990. Both debt service and military spending constitute "unproductive" expendi-tures proportion averaged 9.4 per cent in 1980-82 and rose to 25 per cent in 1990-91.

The proliferation of small arms, as a result of the protracted ethnic war, is also a matter of concern to Sri Lanka. Mines have been laid by the LTTE in many areas in the north. The task of clearing these mines is difficult. The north-east Tamil society is highly militarised and there has been a phenomenal increase in the induction of arms into the society, both by the government and the militants. This shows the growing intensity of war, resulting in large-scale loss of lives.

It is clear from the foregoing analysis that the fundamental concern of Sri Lanka has been the protection of its independence, sovereignty, and territorial integrity. The security crisis, which the island had experienced in the eighties, was unprecedented in its history and its survival, as a single political entity, is a matter of great relief to the Sinhalese ruling elite. Although India can never cease to be a factor in Sri Lanka's security, a formidable challenge in recent years emerged from the forces within the country. The extent to which Sri Lanka has developed its military capabilities to defend its security is analysed in the section below.

Sustained efforts to develop the defence capability began only in the eighties, when the ethnic conflict led to deterioration in the security situation in the country. Until then, defence received a low priority in the successive government's policy and military remained a token force which discharged largely ceremonial functions, like providing guard of honour for state visits, and peripheral security duties, such as controlling illegal immigration and smuggling and assistance to the police in maintaining law and order. Unlike in India, there is no genuine military tradition that evolved under the British rule in Sri Lanka; nor did the Army gain experience in conducting military operations against any external aggression. Being a force without any combat experience and lack of training and sophisticated weaponry, it was therefore not surprising that the Army was not able to tackle a small-scale insurrection like the one the JVP launched in 1971.

Given such a background, building up a viable defence structure in response to growing internal insecurity has been a tremendous task. There is a need to mobilise additional resources to increase the army's strength by raising new columns, imparting hardened training to soldiers in anti-insurgency operations, procuring sophisticated weaponry, and strengthening the command and control system, the steep escalation in Sri Lanka's defence spending over the years and, as a result, the growing economic vulnerability of the country.

Since 1983, the government has embarked on an aggressive recruitment campaign to augment the strength of the military. It has grown up by about 600 per cent in the last 15 years, from a mere 16,000 men in 1983 to about 1.15 lakh in 1997. The Army has a total estimated strength of about 95,000 troops (including 42,000 recalled reservists and 1,000 women). Its crack unit, the special commando force, consists of about 1,500 men; the strength of the infantry, the basic unit of organisation in field operations, is about 23 brigades. Also, there are three reconnaissance regiments, four field artillery regiments (regular and reserve), one anti-aircraft regiment, four field engineering regiments, one engineering plant regiment, one signals battalion, a medical corps and a variety of logistics units which provide support to the infantry.

In 1988, a structural change in the Army led to the creation of several high-level posts and reorganisation of the command system. The Sri Lankan Navy is relatively small, with a total strength of 10,300 men, including active reservists based in Colombo (West, HQ), Trincomalee (East) and Karainagar (North), Tangalle (South), Kalpitiya (West), Galle (South) and Weligama (South). Much attention was paid to modernise the Navy whose role in fighting the insurgency has assumed a critical importance because of the Tigers' destructive capability to conduct sea warfare. The 10,000-strong Sri Lankan Air Force is divided into four squadrons with a variety of support units; its bases are located at Anuradhapura (Northern Command), China Bay (East), Katunayake (West) and Ratmalana (South),

Kankesanturai, Minneriya, Koggla and Sigiriya, besides the Palali air base in Jaffna and the Batticaola airport also provide operational facilities to the Air Force. As a part of the measure to increase the operational efficiency of the forces, the government created a Joint Command in 1985 to coordinate anti-insurgency operations of all three services and the Police Special Task Force (numbering about 3,000 men).

Under-staffing was not the only glaring deficiency that plagued the Sri Lankan military; an equally serious problem was the lack of sophisticated weaponry. Until 1971, when the JVP fired its first shot, the Army used the British Lee Enfield rifles and 4.2 inch heavy mortars of Second World War vintage. But there has been a steady expansion in the range of weapons acquired by the armed forces since the mid-seventies.

An upward trend in the mobilisation of sophisticated weaponry is witnessed since the mid-eighties. New weapons and equipment include T-54/55 tanks, T-85 Chinese-built armoured personnel carriers, surveillance command ships, inshore patrol craft, Israeli Dvora attack Naval craft, Korean fast attack Naval craft, Chinese gun boats and a wide variety of combat jets and ground attack Naval aircraft—SIAI-Marchetti, SF-260 turboprop trainers from Italy, Bell 212 and 412 helicopters from the US to serve as gunships and transport vehicles for commando assault operations, Chinese Yun-12 turboprop transport aircraft, a variety of Cessna aircraft for transport, training and surveying functions, Russian and Ukranian helicopters, and Israeli fighter/ground attack aircraft. Besides, in the mid-eighties, Belgium and Pakistan supplied a large number of rifles, field guns, and mortars.

As a part of the military expansion programme, training facilities have been enhanced at various centres. The Army Training Centre in Diyatalawa, Badulla district, and the Sir John Kotelawala Defence Academy in Ratmalana impart training to the army personnel. General training for Naval officers and ratings is provided at the Naval and Maritime Academy in Trincomalee, while the Air Force Academy at the China Bay Air Base offers flight training.

With the intensification of the war and the resultant demand for more sophisticated tactics on the battlefield, the government has sought foreign training assistance from Britain, Pakistan, Australia, Malaysia, and the US.

The Israeli security agency, Shin Bet, was invited to Sri Lanka under a deal worked out in 1984 to train Army officers in counterinsurgency strategies. At the height of the war during 1985-87, a number of foreign military advisers from the UK, Pakistan and South Africa seemed to have taken part in combat operations against the insurgents. Since the defence build-up is entirely necessitated by the ethnic war, the military strategy and capabilities appeared to be designed to counter the internal threat to the island's security. This is also evident from the nature of weaponry and training, the size of the armoury, the strength of the Army and the weak command and combat system. The point is that the Sri Lankan Army is not equipped to defend the country's security from any external threat and the absence of any security doctrine indicates the government's realisation that the preparation for an external defence is not affordable.

External defence arrangement necessitates a complete transformation of the existing structure—from a brown water (patrolling and surveillance) to a blue water Navy; from a counter-insurgency force to a highly trained conventional force, and from an auxiliary Air Force to actual fighting force. It is also necessary to have an indigenous industry to cater to the needs of the defence forces. All these are not possible to achieve even in the distant future. Now, the question arises, how far is the Army capable of safeguarding the country's internal security? Although the army has been successful enough in protecting Sri Lanka's territorial integrity, it is not able to completely marginalise, if not defeat, the internal forces of threat—the Tamil militants—so as to remove the real sources of the island's insecurity. For the Army, the battlefield experience is nothing splendid, as the overall result of war has so far been mixed—some success and many setbacks. If it killed a large number of Tamil militants in the war, it could do so at a very heavy cost—thousands of soldiers and officers have lost their lives or suffered serious injuries.

Some of its successful operations to recapture territories, including Jaffna, from the LTTE are not accompanied by a greater demonstration of their capability to hold on to them.

This is further revealed by the ongoing Operation Jaya Sikuru, launched in May 1997, with the specific aim of restoring a land route to Jaffna. Incidentally, this remains the longest operation, which the army has ever undertaken. It must be stated that the army's failure to defeat the LTTE does not mean that the latter is able to register victory. What we see today in the battlefield is a hurting stalemate. This raises the question regarding the specific weakness of the army in ensuring the country's internal security. First, defence build-up and preparedness seem inadequate or incommensurate with the extent and magnitude of threat posed by the Tamil militants.

Sri Lanka faces severe resource constraints in developing its military beyond a certain level and, at the same time, the LTTE's fire-power has not diminished despite the several military reverses it suffered in the past. The Tigers (conflictingly estimated at 5,000-10,000) are not larger in number than the Army and their weapons are, by any standard, matchless to the Army's arsenal. Yet, they are strong enough to harass the Army, which has nothing even remotely comparable to the Tiger's supreme power of self-sacrifice and martyrdom—often demonstrated by the Black Tigers. Secondly, the government has not been able to ensure adequate manpower in the Army. Despite a heavy hike in salary, perks, retirement benefits and other allowances, military service is no more an attractive profession for the youth. Many calls for recruitment (based on walk-in-interview) have drawn a blank, as the Sinhalese youth do not want to go to the war-front after a brief training that lasts a few weeks. Their aversion to the service stems from the heavy casualty being suffered by the army in its no-win war against the LTTE. This also explains the large-scale desertions in the Army: out of about 22,000 deserters in 1996, only a few responded to the government's offer of amnesty and rejoined the service. Under these circumstances, in 1995, the Kumaratunga government was even contemplating to introduce a policy of conscription in the country. Thirdly, despite the creation of the Joint Operations Command, the coordination of operations and intelligence system remain poor.

The army suffered a number of reverses because of intelligence failure and improper coordination between all the three services. There were reports in the recent past that fearing the LTTE's missile attack, pilots refused to fly crucial supplies to the camps in the north. On some occasions, air cover to ground forces was not readily extended.

The absence of adequate defence to deal with external threats does not mean that the Sri Lankan leaders have completely neglected or ignored their country's security. From 1947 onwards, i.e., even before the island attained independence, successive governments have seriously addressed the question of evolving a viable defence system through a bilateral arrangement or multilateral diplomacy.

Sri Lanka's security policy has been in a constant change owing to the changing perception and orientation of its regimes and the ideological proclivities of leaders who play a key role in security decision making. Thus, the UNP government's security policy, as is discussed below, is distinct from the SLFP government's; so is the differing level of their success in managing the island's security. Of course, the country witnessed a security crisis only during the UNP rule (1983-87, to be specific), partly due to Jayewardene's ill-conceived regional security policy and partly due to his government's political failure to manage ethnic tensions. Evidently, the Sri Lankan leaders have tried varied options for the island's security and, apparently, none of them appears to have totally satisfied the country's needs.

During the first decade of Sri Lanka's independence, the UNP government's security policy was based on the pragmatic consideration of the country's absolute weakness in defending its sovereignty and freedom. It was D. S. Senanayake, the first Prime Minister and elder statesman, who realised the island's defence needs against a vaguely formulated threat from India, and strongly articulated the option of seeking external military assistance under an institutionalised bilateral framework.

As early as in 1945—almost three years before the country became free—Senanayake declared his choice for the UK in the matter of strategic cooperation and committed to conclude a defence pact as a part of the entire process of decolonisation. Thus, when the 1947 Defence Agreement was concluded, Sri Lanka's security policy for the next ten years came to be framed along the lines of D. S. Senanayake's strategic thinking. Although the 1947 Defence Agreement was based on the principle of mutual reciprocity, it was Britain's commitment to defend Sri Lanka against any "external aggression" that formed the core objective of the entire spectrum of security relations.

The extension of Air and Naval base facilities, in Katunayake and Trincomalee respectively, to Britain was seen, from the UNP leaders stand point, in conjunction with its commitment to Sri Lanka's security and not as an actual demonstration of the island's reciprocity. The argument was that the British troops needed to be stationed in Sri Lanka essentially to discharge their security obligations under the Agreement and Sri Lanka's reciprocal commitment was only to the extent of giving military assistance to Britain in the event of any external aggression—a help on which, in practice, Britain did not count much. As a long-term measure, Britain also undertook to assist Sri Lanka in training and developing its armed forces. The defence requirements of both countries were to be determined by a coordinating machinery. Thus, Britain assumed total responsibility for Sri Lanka's external defence, at a seemingly lower cost as far as the UNP leadership was concerned. But, there was hardly any national consensus on the Agreement.

The Opposition—the Left parties and the SLFP—stood against the security arrangement, suspecting a secret understanding between the two countries. Their suspicion grew out of an ambiguity in the Agreement—there was no specification of the actual period of validity of the Agreement; nor were the specific conditions for the use of base facilities by the British spelt out in categorical terms. If Sri Lanka's firm faith in the Commonwealth arose out of its security interests, it was mainly to strengthen its defence cooperation with Britain. Its connection with both the Commonwealth and the UK was viewed in a common framework of interests—counter and redress the balance against India, with each impinging on the other as a dynamic aspect of the island's security policy having got tied-up with the UK under a defence agreement, Sri Lanka could not totally ignore the Western strategic framework for Asia.

Since 1950, its pro-American tilt manifested itself in the country's foreign and security policy considerations. Thus, when the membership in the SEATO was made open for countries in Asia, John Kotelawala felt quite tempted to avail of the opportunity. He even unsuccessfully attempted to convene a meeting of the Colombo powers in September 1954 to ascertain their views on the SEATO membership, but totally gave up his desire when India, Burma (Myanmar) and Indonesia indicated their opposition to the US-sponsored treaty. Additionally, fear of domestic political repercussions and opposition from some UNP leaders had also dissuaded him from seeking membership. Along with its search for a solution to its defence problem, Sri Lanka's foreign policy approach during the first decade of its independence was also oriented towards removing some of the external sources of threat to its security. The specific efforts of the UNP Prime Ministers to express and demonstrate Sri Lanka's commitment to Asian solidarity should be viewed as a broad diplomatic strategy to evolve peace and friendship among Asian countries, including those that perceivably posed a threat to its security.

With the change of government in 1956, Sri Lanka's security policy underwent a drastic change. The SLFP government under SWRD Bandaranaike did not approve of the strategic thinking and security perception of UNP leaders and sought to replace the policy of defence cooperation by a policy of complete neutrality in world politics as a viable security option for Sri Lanka.

The idea of neutrality, as underlined by Bandaranaike on various occasions, implied the country's refusal to align with power blocs and, as a corollary, a policy of friendship with all countries irrespective of their political ideologies.

The aim was to develop Sri Lanka as the Switzerland of Asia. Thus, the defence agreement with Britain was no longer seen as a source of Sri Lanka's security but a threat because it faced the risk of getting involved in bloc politics. As an implication of this policy, the 1947 Defence, Agreement and Sri Lanka's membership in the Commonwealth came under a critical review by the SLFP government.

Bandaranaike strongly felt that in the island continuation of British base would militate against his government's foreign policy principles and conception of the island's security. Even the country's 'complete independence' was linked to the vacation of bases by Britain. A determined leader, who believed in what he thought and advocated, he successfully negotiated a deal with the British government for the withdrawal of bases in 1957. The entire deal cost Sri Lanka Rs. 22 million on account of compensation to the UK. Thus, when the British government's guarantee to Sri Lanka's security was dispensed with, its reliance on a policy of neutrality became complete.

As regards the Commonwealth, Bandaranaike opted to retain Sri Lanka's membership in view of the fact that there was no immediate prospect for a regional security pact, which he preferred with India, Pakistan, Burma, Indonesia and Malaysia. Also, India's continued membership in the Commonwealth had dispelled the SLFP government's doubts about pursuing an independent foreign policy while being a member of the Commonwealth. The point is that by 1957 Sri Lanka lost the external security guarantee that Britain was providing under the Defence Agreement for the past ten years. However, there was no change in the strategic situation in the region, but the security perception of the Sri Lankan leadership became completely different. India was no more considered a potential threat, but a friendly neighbour.

Although the policy of neutrality appeared to have lacked a visible plan of action and there was a total security vacuum as a result of withdrawal of British bases,

Bandaranaike's approach was not completely guided by political idealism alone. That he advocated a pragmatic security policy was evident from the way he dealt with the future legal status of the 1947 Agreement. While negotiating for the withdrawal of British bases from the island, the Sri Lankan Prime Minister did not ask for abrogation of the Agreement *per se*. Instead, he wanted to keep the Agreement valid for future use against any external threat.

Continuing essentially her husband's foreign and security policy, Sirimavo Bandaranaike activated the policy of neutralism. Non-alignment became the first line of Sri Lanka's defence and its national security got linked with global security. Thus, the emphasis was largely on international peace in which Sri Lanka had to find its security.

The Non-aligned Movement and the UN General Assembly provided the forum for mobilising international opinion on world peace. Military pacts and alliances were disapproved; militarisation of peaceful regions was viewed with concern. Friendship with all countries—in the neighbourhood as well as afar—formed the considered objective of Sri Lankan diplomacy. And the interests of the Third World countries, with which Sri Lanka identified the most, had a significant place in its diplomatic initiatives.

Thus, Sri Lanka's global initiatives at the United Nations to de-nuclearise the world and demilitarise the Indian Ocean had the profound national objective of protecting its security. It was not only the SLFP government but also the UNP government of Dudley Senanayake (1965-70) which sought to forge a link between national and global security. However, Senanayake's non-aligned policy lacked dynamism; the previous government's efforts for world peace were hardly sustained.

Sri Lanka's search for security, through global peace and order, appeared to be a viable option only because of the changed strategic situation in South Asia. Here, the 'India factor' was extremely important. Both the countries, especially during 1960-65 and 1970-77, enjoyed cordial relations and shared common strategic interests. As mentioned earlier, India was not perceived as a threat to the island's security, but a great help in times of crisis, as in 1971 in the wake of the JVP insurrection. This incident raised the question regarding Sri Lanka's self-defence. The government realised the need for, at least, a minimum level of defence preparedness to tackle internal subversion and measures that would supplement its dominant approach based on active international diplomacy.

Sri Lanka's faith in neutralism, non-alignment and multilateral diplomacy as a guiding force of its security policy lasted amazingly for about ten years, i.e., until 1977 when the UNP government under J.R. Jayewardene reverted to the pre-1956 approach with some modifications. The core element of the new policy was friendship with the US and the UK, as spelt out by the UNP's pro-Western foreign policy, and cultivation of anti-Indian forces, as warranted by the security perception of its leadership. For Jayewardene, a peace zone in the Indian Ocean or active diplomatic campaign for peace would not be sufficient security guarantee for small states like Sri Lanka located in an asymmetrical power-region. As early as in 1974, he questioned the SLFP government's approach towards security. While disapproving Sirimavo Bandaranaike's approach to security and demonstrating its pro-Western foreign policy tilt, the UNP government's pronouncement of its security policy was not followed by concrete actions until 1983.

The outbreak of ethnic violence, however, led to greater activation of the 'India factor' in the island's security, which, in turn, strengthened its desire to join the Western strategic framework for the Indian Ocean. The steps in this direction were: extension of refuelling and recreation facilities to US Naval ships; granting a contract for the operation of the oil tank farm in Trincomalee to a US company; and permission to set up a powerful Voice of America (VOA) station on the island.

China and Pakistan were also approached for military assistance. While offering military supplies and arranging intelligence support, none of these countries was prepared to become Sri Lanka's strategic partner or commit itself to the latter's security. To that extent Jayewardene's security policy was not successful. Contrary to his desire and expectations, the Western powers did not buy Colombo's argument of characterising India as potential aggressor; their advice to the Sri Lankan government to seek India's help in resolving the ethnic conflict indicated their limits of extending military support to the island. Along with its search for direct external security assistance, Sri Lanka has embarked upon a massive military development programme. Suffice to say that the most significant aspect of the UNP government's security policy was the development of military capabilities to tackle the internal threat to the country's security.

In the late eighties, significant changes had taken place in the UNP government's approach towards security, in the wake of the failure of its earlier efforts to obtain a definite security commitment from the West.

The Jayewardene administration opted, as a pragmatic approach, to deal directly with India, the country that impinged on the security sensitivities of Sri Lanka. As part of the long drawn out process of regulating the ethnic conflict under the bilateral agreement of 1987, both the governments undertook to accommodate each other's security concerns. While agreeing to consult India on the relevance and employment of external military and intelligence agencies and seeking its involvement in the restoration of the oil tank farm, Sri Lanka promised to renew its agreement with foreign broadcasting organisations to ensure their use solely for public broadcasting and forbid the military use of Trincomalee harbour by "any country in a manner prejudicial to India's interests".

These simple commitments were made to extract assurances from India that it would deport all Sri Lankans with terrorist or secessionist connection and extend training facilities and military supplies to the Sri Lankan Army. India also undertook to ensure that its territory was not used for activities "prejudicial to the unity integrity and security of Sri Lanka", it offered the cooperation of the Indian Navy/Coast Guard with the Sri Lankan Navy in preventing Tamil militants' activities, and declared to provide military assistance as and when requested to implement the peace agreement.

These assurances, made in the spirit of reciprocity and mutual accommodation, constituted a significant step towards strategic harmony between the two countries. Of course, the general impression in Sri Lanka was that India, a regional power, coerced a strife-torn small country to make extensive unilateral security concessions and offered its military help with a view to restricting the country's external defence contacts. The entire arrangement was, therefore, seen as a demonstration of India's desire for regional hegemony, subjecting Sri Lanka to be its dependent neighbour. For the Jayewardene administration however, this appeared to be the only viable option available at that time. And its conscious decision to accommodate India's security concerns was based on a realistic assessment of the strategic situation in the region.

A dramatic development, with far-reaching implications for Sri Lanka's security, took place in 1989. Guided by its desire to rectify its position as the weaker contracting party in the security arrangement and to evolve a long-term strategic cooperation with India on an equal basis, Sri Lanka proposed a friendship treaty. It was to supersede the understanding reached through the letters exchanged between Rajiv Gandhi and Jayewardene on 29 July 1987. This was evidently to remove the 'India factor' from Sri Lanka's ethnic conflict and security at large.

As the provisions of the draft treaty point out, Premadasa's strategic initiative constituted a drift from the UNP leader's traditional policy of 'strategic partnership' with the West, avowedly pursued until 1956, and a step forward from the SUP leader's policy of friendship with India. The Sri Lankan draft of the treaty insisted on mutual commitments by both countries to respect each other's independence, unity, sovereignty and territorial integrity; to consolidate their mutual trust, confidence and cooperation; to resolve their bilateral problems through political negotiations on the basis of their sovereign equality, and to non-interference in internal affairs.

The Indian draft sought to include, apart from the earlier commitments contained in the letters of 29 July 1987, provisions for mutual consultations in the event of any external aggression or other forms of threat to each other's security, and non-aggression and non-participation in any alliance directed against each other. Importantly, Sri Lanka wanted to make the treaty valid for an indefinite period. At the same time, India stipulated a period of 20 years at the first instance, and automatic extension for subsequent periods of five years at a time (unless either party wanted to give the other a notice of one year for its termination).

The UNP government's desire to change its security policy by proposing a friendship treaty with India was based on a careful cost-benefit analysis. Sri Lanka could not think of forging such a relationship with India in the late forties (when it concluded the Defence Agreement with Britain). And, the very fact that it finally came around the idea of seeking India's strategic cooperation indicated the latter's growing importance in the island's security and the failure of security policies of the successive governments. Incidentally, the present security initiative also failed, even before a serious discussion on the draft treaty began, presumably because of Sri Lanka's refusal to uphold its earlier security commitments (made in the letters of 29 July 1987), about which India was very particular.

Having exhausted various security options by the end of the eighties, the Sri Lankan government was left with the choice of using its foreign policy channels to strengthen the country's defence. Premadasa did not take fresh initiatives for security cooperation with any country. At the same time, his pro American foreign policy, in line with the UNP government's tradition, seemed to have created some sort of an artificial assurance for security assistance. A change in India's stance on the ethnic conflict has benefited Sri Lanka in a significant way, so that it could merely concentrate on its internal defence preparedness, without continuing its pro-active search for external defence cooperation and security assurances.

Unlike the Premadasa regime, the People's Alliance (PA) government (1994) under Chandrika Kumaratunga has adopted a broad-based approach towards security. An effective use of foreign policy channels has brought about incredible results. As a pragmatic approach and the foremost foreign policy task, Kumaratunga has made concerted efforts to cultivate India by recognising its "uniquely central and pivotal position" in the region. Foreign Affairs Minister Lakshman Kadirgamar articulated Sri Lanka's new approach towards India, when he appreciated the latter's desire for a better understanding of its security needs and sensitivities by its neighbours, and acknowledged the benefits which the region can accrue from its economic preponderance and centrality.

India's special concern, whenever expressed, about Tamil interests and welfare in Sri Lanka is not to be considered as an interference; its legitimate desire for a political settlement of the ethnic conflict is not viewed anymore with concern in Colombo. Seeking military cooperation with extra-regional powers is considered futile. There is also a growing realisation that a carefully designed regional policy, with due considerations to India's security sensitivities, will be in the interest of Sri Lanka. India has been well appreciative of Sri Lanka's approach towards regional security, and Colombo is pleased with New Delhi's present stand on the ethnic conflict. It is in the context of growing bilateral understanding and cordiality that Sri Lanka's prompt endorsement of India's decision to conduct nuclear tests in May 1998 should be viewed. By this stand, the PA government has sought to ensure India's continued support to its war against the LTTE and non-involvement, in the spirit of the Gujral Doctrine, in the ethnic conflict. Not only these, the growing economic interaction between the two countries and their undeclared naval cooperation in containing Tamil militant activities have a definite and positive impact on the island's security.

Kadirgamar's active diplomatic campaign in the US led to listing of LTTE as one of the terrorist groups in the world. Many other countries have also responded to Colombo's diplomatic pressure by imposing restrictions on the activities of the LTTE. The growing international image of the country, brought about by the government's systematic publicity of protection of human rights and commitment to political settlement of the ethnic conflict, is being made use of by Colombo to promote the country's interests.

A variety of approaches, which Sri Lanka tried at various points of time, show the difficulties in evolving a composite and consistent security policy. Inevitably, this is the result of the changing national security perception of regimes and their foreign policy orientations.

The real threat to Sri Lanka emerges from within. The internal sources of threat are more serious than external sources, and their linkages create crisis, it is essential to analyse the prospects of evolving a CCS framework in two different contexts. From the point of external security, India still remains a key factor even though the security perception of both countries have tremendously changed in recent years. The experience of the past shows that the fundamental cause for strategic divergence, leading to the insecurity of the island in Indo-Lanka relations was mutual mistrust and misperception rooted in a variety of socio- historical settings and circumstances. Hence, any serious attempt at evolving a CCS framework should address these psychological issues which govern bilateral interactions.

Development of mutual trust will promote a constructive bilateral engagement between the two countries, to the mutual benefit of both. Of course, Sri Lanka will stand to gain more than India in view of the higher level of its security needs, arising out of its limited capability to counter threats through 'indigenous' means of defence. A readily suggestible framework for building 'trust' between countries, harbouring mutually adversarial images, is a bilateral friendship treaty incorporating guarantees to security of the contracting parties and well-defined mechanisms to develop a modicum of strategic harmony. While this approach has, by and large, been adopted to forge a CCS system in many cases, it may not bring about the desired result in Indo-Sri Lanka relations.

There is a deep-rooted fear of India in the minds of a majority of the Sinhalese, which cannot be removed by a mere friendship treaty concluded at the governmental level. Understanding between governments does not necessarily mean that mutual trust and confidence between their peoples is restored. Then, there is the question of autonomy and independence.

In a relationship forged under a treaty between two unequal countries, there may arise a situation where the weaker contracting party (Sri Lanka) will perceive domination by the big power (India). This may give rise, in the minds of the former, to a feeling of dependence and fear of losing autonomy and independence in foreign policy decision making. The first step towards a CCS framework, involving India and Sri Lanka, should be one of mobilising and tuning the peoples of both countries for a harmonious relationship without fear and prejudice. And, an institutionalised arrangement like a friendship treaty should figure as the last step.

There has, so far, been no systematic effort to develop a healthy interaction between peoples of India and Sri Lanka, even though the scope and opportunities are plenty. As a precondition for better bilateral relations, the image of India as a destabilising and hostile force should be replaced with an image of a friendly power which believes in peaceful coexistence.

The 'enemy image' given to India is rooted in the Mahavamsa tradition and cultivated for mobilisation by post-colonial political entrepreneurs. At the same time, Sri Lanka's image of an intolerant society dominated by the Sinhalese chauvinistic forces, has to be changed with the government demonstrating its faith in a truly pluralistic framework of governance.

The point is that the better positive images of both countries should be presented to each other's population through institutionalised agencies like friendship societies, which are at the moment lying dormant, and an accelerated exchange programme should be initiated by both governments. The missing point in any discussion on

Indo-Sri Lanka relations is the Tamil Nadu factor. As events of the past indicate, the political forces in Tamil Nadu have always sought to influence India's policy towards Sri Lanka. No government in Delhi can afford to be indifferent to the opinion of Tamil Nadu on various bilateral issues in which the state's interests are involved. It is not that successive governments in Colombo have been unaware of this domestic factor in India's relations with Sri Lanka. Being geographically closer to Tamil Nadu, and given the ethnic linkages between the Tamils across the Palk Straits, Sri Lanka's main source of security concern has been this South Indian state itself. Such a concern is deep-rooted in historical antecedents. Any attempt at building trust, and confidence between the two countries, therefore, should take the Tamil Nadu factor into serious account. We argue that an understanding between Sri Lanka and Tamil Nadu is vital for Indo-Sri Lanka friendship and cordiality. Any steps in this direction should include intense and broad-based people-to-people contacts and economic interaction within the framework of sub-regional cooperation mooted by India.

At the governmental level, there should be an institutionalised framework for larger bilateral engagement. It need not be under a bilateral treaty arrangement but within the normal structure of foreign policy institutions.

Trade and economic cooperation, both under the bilateral and the SAARC frameworks, provides an important area for engagement. The scope for greater economic interaction arises from Sri Lanka's dependent economic structure and India's growing industrial and commercial sector.

There is also scope for bilateral maritime cooperation. Apart from policing the border along the Palk Straits, both countries can jointly exploit marine resources. As regards security matters, frequent consultations at a higher political and official level and a permanent regulatory mechanism to deal with issues of mutual concerns and misperceptions will contribute to bilateral trust and understanding.

For Sri Lanka, the cost of seeking cooperation with an extra-regional power will tend to be more than what is required for its friendship with India. As the island's past experience indicates, extra-regional powers will be reluctant to forge security cooperation with a strife-torn country and involve themselves in problems between India and Sri Lanka. If at all a country is willing to provide security to Sri Lanka, it is bound to extract greater concessions by making use of the island's vulnerability and compulsions. In addition to its bilateral approach to CCS, Sri Lanka should embark on multilateral diplomacy to create a security regime for small states under the auspices of the SAARC. The SAARC structure and processes have so far been narrowly based on socio-economic goals. Every attempt to expand its role by incorporating in its agenda the task of creating a regional security framework has been resisted by India. While it is true that meaningful economic cooperation will provide greater impetus to regional security, it cannot be fully realised so long as the military aspect is completely ignored. Of course, the difficulties in converting the SAARC into a security community are seemingly insurmountable because of the strategic divergence between India and Pakistan.

As early as in 1985, at the first SAARC Summit in Dhaka, the member countries reaffirmed their commitment to peaceful settlement of disputes, non-interference in internal affairs and non-use or threat of use of force against the territorial integrity and political independence of other states. This was repeated at the subsequent summits.

The Islamabad Summit, in December 1988, condemned the abortive coup attempt in Maldives and expressed its solidarity with the small states. The Fifth Summit, in November 1990, acknowledged the need for special measures to safeguard the "independence and territorial integrity" of small of states. Since then, every Summit has reiterated this collective stand of the association.

The Seventh Summit in Dhaka, in 1993, further said that real protection of small and weaker states should be firmly rooted in the Rule of Law and strict adherence to universally accepted principles and norms relating to the sovereign rights and integrity of all states—big or small. This was further reiterated in all the subsequent Summit declarations. Thus, the SAARC remains committed, in principle, to the security of small states, giving scope for developing an institutionalised mechanism to deal with all possible threats—military and non-military. In this context, the efforts of Sri Lanka should be directed towards formulating a 'regional convention on security of small states', under which its fear of India can be completely obliterated.

For Sri Lanka, it seems to be an easy option as it does not involve any substantive cost. India may be willing to accept this framework of security relation with small states, because their reciprocal security commitments will provide a way to strengthen its own security interests in the region. Possibly, the proposed 'convention on security' and strict adherence to the 'Convention on Suppression of Terrorism' will strengthen Sri Lanka's capability to deal with the threat posed by the Tamil militants. These suggestions, if implemented, will prove to be a viable approach to Sri Lanka's external security. But, the daunting task of the government has been to maintain its internal security, which is contingent upon the resolution of the intractable ethnic conflict. This, however, does not appear to be an easy proposition in view of the intransigent position of the contending parties—the Sinhalese and Sri Lankan Tamil leaders—on certain core issues.

From the internal security point of view, any effort towards restoration of civil order should include the creation of a truly multi-cultural framework, with institutional structures to promote and protect minority interests. Political steps to resolve the conflict should be accompanied by active state policies to strengthen the civil society. Apart from demilitarising the entire Sri Lankan society, it is also essential to evolve institutional mechanisms to prevent and contain violence, as different from a political framework for conflict resolution.

10

Indian Peace-Keeping Force

In his annual Great Heroes' Day message on November 27, 1999, Velupillai Prabhakaran, the leader of the Liberation Tigers of Tamil Eelam (LTTE), declared:

> We have not abandoned the path of peace. We want to resolve the Tamil conflict through peaceful means, through civilised methods, without recourse to a bloodbath and the destruction of life.

Prabhakaran's statement naturally attracted a lot of attention in Sri Lanka and abroad. A careful reading of Prabhakaran's speech brings out the following points:

First and foremost, the LTTE has catapulted itself to centre stage and Prabhakaran is speaking from a position of strength. The military campaign called "Unceasing Waves III" demonstrated not only the resilience of the Tigers but also the weaknesses and vulnerability of the Sri Lankan Army.

To quote Prabhakaran:

> A colossal military structure with multiple military complexes, well-fortified bases and camps suddenly collapsed with the... Tiger offensive... This current offensive has turned the balance of military power in our favour.

Second, Prabhakaran has elaborated on the LTTE's preconditions for peace talks.

> Peace talks should be held in a cordial, peaceful atmosphere of mutual trust and goodwill with... international third-party mediation. By peaceful

> atmosphere we mean a condition of normalcy characterised by cessation of hostilities, withdrawal of troops occupying Tamil lands and the absence of economic blockades.

At the same time, Prabhakaran is of the view that the Sinhala leadership will not agree to "create a peaceful environment". It will not abandon its "long-standing policy of military violence and repression", says Prabhakaran and adds that therefore, the Tamils are left with no alternative "other than to fight, secede and establish an independent Tamil state.. Tamil Eelam is the only and final solution to our national conflict."

Before analysing the implications of Prabhakaran's statement, it would be worthwhile to keep in mind the LTTE's stance during earlier attempts to resolve the ethnic conflict. The first time the LTTE participated in such an exercise, it was (as an integral part of the Eelam National Liberation Front) in the two rounds of Thimphu talks in July and August 1985. Prabhakaran was convinced that these talks, arranged by New Delhi, would not lead to a solution. But he did not want to alienate New Delhi by boycotting them.

In Thimphu, the Tamil groups put forward four cardinal principles, which were deliberately couched in ambiguous terms. These were (1) Recognition of Tamils as a distinct nationality; (2) Recognition of the traditional Tamil homeland and a guarantee of its territorial integrity; (3) Recognition of the right of self-determination of the Tamil nation and (4) Conferment of citizenship to all Tamils. To Colombo, which viewed even federalism as the first step towards separation, these principles were like a red rag before a bull. The Thimphu talks were a fiasco.

The second futile exercise was former Tamil Nadu Chief Minister M.G. Ramachandran's attempt to bring about a meeting between President J.R. Jayewardene and Prabhakaran, the leader of the Liberation Tigers of Tamil Eelam, during the South Asian Association Regional Cooperation (SAARC) summit in Bangalore in November 1986. Although Prabhakaran went to Bangalore, he refused to meet Jayewardene. What is more, he made it clear to the Indian emissaries that he would never give up the demand for Tamil Eelam. Another important phase of LTTE involvement in the peace process began with the India-Sri Lanka Accord, 1987.

Prabhakaran was unhappy with the Accord, but he knew it was a *fait accompli* and, therefore, wanted to use the opportunity to salvage his position as much as possible. Prabhakaran received "financial incentives" from New Delhi; he was also assured of majority representation in the interim administration. Even then, he made only a "symbolic gesture" of surrendering arms. In the famous Sudumalai Amman temple speech, after giving his version of the background to the Accord, Prabhakaran maintained: "But let me make it clear to you here, beyond the shadow of a doubt, that I will continue to fight for the objective of attaining Tamil Eelam."

President Ranasinghe Premadasa's negotiations with the LTTE extended from May 1989 to June 1990. The two hitherto antagonistic forces came together because they found a convergence of interests—get the Indian Peace-Keeping Force (IPKF) out of Sri Lanka. Prabhakaran had no illusions about the bona-fides of the Premadasa government.

Bradman Weerakoon, adviser to President Premadasa, has pointed out that "there is no record of any serious political talks" between the two sides. It is well known that Premadasa provided "secret supply of money and weapons to the LTTE to fight the IPKF". What is more, the vacuum left by the IPKF was filled by the LTTE and it gained complete control of the north and east. Prabhakaran put forward two demands. The dissolution of the North-eastern Provincial Council and the repeal of the Sixth Amendment to the Constitution. The government rejected the two demands, and the Second Eelam War commenced.

The LTTE's negotiations with President Chandrika Kumaratunga during November 1994 and April 1995 revealed that the two parties were speaking on different wave lengths. The peace process, according to the LTTE, should proceed in two stages. The early stages of the negotiations should address the restoration of normalcy and the creation of a peaceful environment. After normalcy is restored, talks can start in order to find a meaningful solution. Colombo, on the other hand, maintained that there should be simultaneous talks relating to the day-to-day problems of the people and with the aim of finding a political solution. Finally, the LTTE accused the government of acting in "bad faith" and started the Third Eelam War in April 1995.

Considering these past realities, the question arises whether Prabhakaran is really interested in finding a peaceful solution to the ethnic conflict in the framework of a united Sri Lanka. The immediate objective of the LTTE is to come out of its growing international isolation.

Prabhakaran's peace offer is a projection of the "soft face" of the LTTE—a liberation organisation that is an "aggrieved party" and a "victim of oppression". The preconditions laid down by the LTTE for talks indicate that negotiations would be extremely difficult. According to the LTTE, negotiations can take place only in an atmosphere of peace and normalcy, free from conditions of war and economic blockade. Such a demand will not find favour with the Sri Lankan Army, for it will amount to its committing hara-kiri. The question of third-party mediation is likely to be another thorny issue. Here again Prabhakaran has made a somersault.

During the earlier negotiations with Premadasa and Chandrika, the LTTE considered the ethnic issue as one that should be settled by the two major players.

In an interview to *The Times* of London, LTTE ideologue Anton Balasingham said: "India has no legal or moral right to talk of security of Tamil people. This has to be worked out between Sinhalese and Tamils. Foreign intervention has failed to bring peace."

As far as Colombo is concerned, Chandrika has made the position clear thus: "We don't want mediation, we are willing to take third party facilitation... foreign."

Above all, the Indian involvement in Sri Lanka (1987-90) is a clear illustration of the inherent limitations of what an external power can do to resolve what is essentially "a domestic conflict". Prabhakaran's message, coming as it did in the midst of the presidential election campaign, widened the chasm between the two major Sinhalese parties, the People's Alliance (PA) and the United National Party (UNP).

While Prabhakaran clubs the UNP and PA together as "chauvinist organisations" which compete with each other in "intensifying the oppression against the Tamil people", Chandrika is singled out for a vitriolic attack. Prabhakaran stated: "We do not trust Chandrika. She does not have the honesty and determination to resolve the Tamil national conflict in a fair and reasonable manner." The UNP naturally wants to exploit Chandrika's predicament to its advantage. Its leader Ranil Wikremasinghe's call for unconditional talks with the LTTE and his suggestion that interim administration in the north-east could be headed by the LTTE should be viewed as part of the UNP's attempts to win back Tamil support. It is obvious that increasing divisions among the Sinhalese will suit the long-term objectives of the LTTE.

Amnesty International, the London-based human rights organisation, issued in August a direct appeal to the Liberation Tigers of Tamil Eelam (LTTE), that has acquired over the years a reputation of being one of the most ruthless guerilla organisations in the world. The appeal was extraordinary in three respects. First, it was unusual for Amnesty to direct such an appeal to an organisation that has no legal basis to be considered a *de jure* entity.

Usually Amnesty's appeals pertain to alleged human rights violations by sovereign states and their duly constituted governments. Basically a guerilla outfit, the LTTE is at best a sort of non-governmental organisation that is entitled to certain "belligerent rights" as a consequence of its protracted military campaign, during the course of which it established territorial control over certain parts of Sri Lanka. Secondly, the appeal was in essence a pre-emptive move against the LTTE. It was not a case of Amnesty merely reacting to a past event; the appeal was based on a prognosis for the future. The Amnesty communique highlighted the civilian status of certain Tamil politicians, mentioning them by name, and of other unnamed persons falling under that category, and appealed to the Tigers not to assassinate them.

Taking into account the record, Amnesty is clearly trying to prevent further such incidents—again an unusual move. Thirdly, Amnesty expanded the scope of its appeal by not restricting it to just the LTTE's international secretariat based in Britain but extending it to several other branch and front offices of the Tigers.

Amnesty issued the appeal as a proactive venture and as a means to exert pressure on the LTTE on as many fronts as possible. This is perhaps the first time that the overseas branches of the LTTE are being subjected to humanitarian pressure inspired by Amnesty. Usually, Tiger propagandists use Amnesty appeals concerning human rights violations by the Sri Lankan state and its organs for their own purposes.

Whenever charged with human rights violations, it has been a routine ruse for the LTTE to condone itself on the grounds that it was a government in the making and that having to conduct a liberation struggle against overwhelming odds, it was not always possible to adhere to human rights tenets. While disclaiming any responsibility to adhere to the principles of human rights on those grounds, the Tigers, on the other hand, insist that they and they alone should be recognised as the sole representatives of Tamils and that Tamil Eelam was already a *de facto* reality.

The killing of perceived opponents and dissidents from the Sri Lankan Tamil community is a brutal manifestation of this objective. The LTTE has for quite some time gotten away with such dual conduct, and the Amnesty appeal in a way attempts to check that.

The LTTE is forced to accept the reality that there are some universal rights it must recognise if it wants the civilised world to accept its bona fides. That the overseas branches of the LTTE are feeling the pressure inspired by the Amnesty seems evident from the reaction of some of its minions. The Amnesty appeal to the LTTE is based on the premise that owing to their civilian status most of the Tamil non LTTE political leaders are entitled to full protection under international human rights laws. Of its own volition, the LTTE had agreed to adhere to the Geneva Convention, which among other things has set down rules regarding the treatment of civilians in troubled situations.

The LTTE finds that in spite of years of fighting and innumerable losses, it is nowhere in sight of its political objective. What is more, it finds itself increasingly alienated from international opinion. The territory controlled by it in Sri Lanka has shrunk considerably. Although by no means a spent force, the LTTE is certain that the process of decline has begun. Furthermore, there is a possibility that the devolution package may be implemented bypassing the Tigers. Under these circumstances, the resulting political frustration seeks to target perceived scapegoats for this state of affairs.

The tradition in Tamil politics has been to blame forces or individuals among the community or the internal enemy as the source of all troubles. Therefore, the LTTE has apparently turned its wrath on Tamils who are a hindrance to their goal. After all, Prabhakaran had his baptism of fire by gunning down former Jaffna Mayor Alfred Duraiappah on July 27, 1975. The LTTE has its own motives for targeting Tamil political parties. According to the Editor of *Lanka Guardian,* Dayan Jayatilleke, "the LTTE's plan is to monopolise the Tamil nationalistic space and present the Colombo-Delhi-Washington axis with a *fait accompli* and force the latter to arrive at a *modus vivendi* with it. The LTTE's goal goes beyond the limited objective of monopolising the Tamil political space ahead of any talks with the Sri Lankan government."

If the prognosis about the LTTE's current hostility is correct then some more killings can be expected. In that context, Amnesty's appeal is a desperate measure enacted under desperate circumstances to mobilise international opinion against the LTTE and prevent a blood-bath of Tamil innocents. What is further needed is for the Amnesty initiative to be supported by other human rights and non-governmental organisations too.

Only a worldwide campaign of great proportions can possibly contain the bloody strategy. Though some would say that the neo-fascist LTTE would not respect even international opinion, it does seem worthwhile to make such an attempt, however quixotic it may appear. There are two other issues in this regard. One, the Sri Lankan government must wake up to the imminent danger most Tamil politicians are in and provide them adequate security. The TULF with its "unarmed democracy" policy is particularly vulnerable. The second issue relates to developments in India, notably Tamil Nadu.

The Tamil Nationalist Movement led by P. Nedumaran, a longtime supporter of the Tamil Eelam and LTTE cause, is currently engaged in a campaign to get the death sentences imposed on four persons convicted in the Rajiv Gandhi assassination stopped. As part of this campaign, Nedumaran and other like-minded persons have been arguing strongly against the concept of capital punishment. In that process, some eloquent and emotional points have been made regarding the sanctity of human life, how no one has the right to deprive a person of life and how killing someone does not deter the cause and so on. Now, the life and death question before these people is whether the same yardstick does not apply to the LTTE. If death sentences imposed after due process are a matter of objection, then what is to be done in the case of Tiger killings that are arbitrarily executed? If the supporters of the LTTE who are clamouring for eradication of capital punishment in India can prevail upon the LTTE too to implement a moratorium on civilian killings, then it would provide a reprieve for many beleaguered persons on the brink of death in Sri Lanka and elsewhere.

Efforts to end the conflict in Jaffna have been stalled for lack of modalities of negotiations. The murderous blast on September 11, 1998 had complicated the situation. Colombo was awash with expectations of a resumption of talks for a negotiated settlement to Sri Lanka's ethnic conflict. Separate statements by three important players—the government, the Liberation Tigers of Tamil Eelam (LTTE) and the Opposition United National Party (UNP), generated these hopes. President Chandrika Kumaratunga made the government's position clear when she ruled out any form of mediation but said that there was scope for the involvement of a facilitator for talks with the LTTE.

The Tiger's point of view was expressed through a letter written by its political committee to South African President Nelson Mandela, seeking his help to work out a negotiated settlement. This was followed by an interview published in a Sunday newspaper from Colombo, in which the leader of the LTTE's political wing, Thamilchelvam, reiterated the need for talks. The UNP, on its part, called for talks but demanded that the negotiations be unconditional, a demand which was rejected by the government. Although the inevitable game of one-upmanship on the correct approach to the question of negotiations followed, with the two major political groups, the ruling People's Alliance and the UNP, trading charges, the people had not given up hope. It was at this stage that a bomb ripped through the Jaffna Municipal Council building on September 11, 1998, killing Mayor P. Sivapalan, Brigadier Susantha Mendis, Senior Superintendent of Police Chandra Perera and nine others.

The bombing caused a rethink on the proposal for talks. Two shades of opinion are emerging now. One is that the blast has only re-emphasised the need for early and unconditional talks. The other is that any negotiation would further strengthen the rebels, who set off the blast in an act of desperation. The blast was a setback to the process of local self-governance that was ushered in early, this year, and the concrete moves that were made towards good governance in the northern Peninsula. It was also an apparent warning to the whole of the island-nation, particularly to sections of the Tamil people, by the Tamil separatists that any attempt by the military to move closer to the people of Jaffna would not be tolerated.

Mendi's predecessor, Larry Wijeratne, who had established a rapport with the people of Jaffna, was killed on May 14, 1998. Perhaps it was this message from the Tamil Tigers that was discernible during a visit by media persons to the northern Peninsula on September 11, 1998.

The residents appeared resigned to the fact that political parties cannot reinforce democracy in the Peninsula if they did not enjoy the confidence of the Tigers.

The councillors, although sincere in their attempts to chalk out a solution to the crisis facing Jaffna, are under the close scrutiny of the Tigers. While all these factors build up a case for involving the Tigers in a meaningful dialogue, observers have not overlooked the futility of such an effort in the light of the earlier experience in this regard: both the parties involved in the process have only played for time or broken their promises.

Right from the Bandaranaike, Chelvanayakam Pact, the history of negotiations as a method to resolve the strife is replete with instances of either side letting down the other. Both the rebels and the government have addressed the problem with incompatible mindsets. Added to this is the not-too-cooperative role played by the opposition parties.

As part of the efforts towards a bipartisan approach to find a solution to the conflict, a workshop was held recently by Professor Fraser who played an active role in bringing the warring political groups in Northern Ireland to the negotiating table. But with the opposition not too willing to play ball with the government to push through the political package it had evolved, the impasse on constitutional reforms continues. Another dimension to the problem emerged when it was reported that the LTTE was considering shifting its base of international operations from the United Kingdom to South Africa. This report, viewed along with the separatist's appeal to Mandela, has given rise to the line of thinking that the rebels would seek inspiration from Mandela's own past as a liberation fighter.

Political observers in Colombo feel that the LTTE could gain the sympathy of at least some native South Africans who led a long struggle against white rule. The plans for a change of base have apparently come in the light of a tough piece of legislation that the UK plans to introduce with regard to terrorist activities. There has been a consensus against an IPKF-type intervention. But no party has opposed sending arms to Chandrika's besieged government.

Though the export destinations have never been revealed, one of the biggest consumers of Indian ammunition (less of arms) has been the one-lakh strong Sri Lankan army. Much of the sales was at lower than market rates, essentially aimed at keeping India's strategic hold on the island state. The exports have reduced to a trickle, and naturally Sri Lanka is desperate. Based on reports of a fresh logistics supply from Southern Lanka, military analysts in Delhi believe that the besieged Lankan army can hold on to their position for a few more weeks. "But Chandrika's concern must be over how much is left in the southern depots."

The fact is that the Sri Lankan Army has been fighting on its stomach for some time. Short of guns and bullets, the Army has been faced with large-scale desertions. Hardly two months ago, seven officers including two Major-Generals and one Brigadier had been court-martialled and compulsorily retired for abandoning their positions in November, leaving 10 bases and about a hundred villages to the LTTE. The generals were not outnumbered by the enemy; they were out-gunned. And Lankan Police have now been instructed to hunt for about 9,000 deserters from the Army.

By the time India said no to the third option of persuading the Tigers to the talks table, it was already out. Apparently Delhi had hoped to become a mediator once again in Lanka, given the goodwill that the Tigers were enjoying from some of the parties and individuals in the Vajpayee government. All the same, Delhi was worried whether Colombo had put forward the third option only to expose Delhi. By the time the dilemma was resolved, events had overtaken it. All along Delhi's actions had been based on a premise that India alone could mediate the situation or at least that Colombo would come round to such a realisation. Apparently, Delhi had underestimated the role others had been planning. If India had lost much of its influence over the LTTE following the assassination of Rajiv Gandhi and the subsequent ban on it, Colombo had slowly been slipping out of its hand in the last couple of years. The warning was very much there when

Chandrika dragged in the Kashmir issue into a SAARC meeting in Colombo last year, much to the discomfiture of India.

All the same, Delhi acted on the premise that Colombo would finally come round to seek its help in bringing the Tigers to the table. This much was evident when External Affairs Minister Jaswant Singh said in the Rajya Sabha that the Norwegian role is not workable. But as days passed, it appeared that both Colombo and the Tigers had more trust in Norway as an honest broker than India. New Delhi bad to accept the *fait accompli* of being a facilitator for Norwegian mediation. "It is simple logic," said a senior Indian Army officer, "Norway enjoys the trust of both sides, because they have been selling arms to both."

One peculiarity of the Sri Lankan situation right from the beginning is that it is a match in which everyone plays for both sides. If Pakistan has supplied arms to Colombo, the LTTE has smuggled heroin to the West for ISI in return for weapons. If China has supplied weapons to the Lankan army, its client state Myanmar's military junta has hobnobbed with LTTE. The UK was selling arms, while hosting LTTE elements to use British territory for their global propaganda. But of late, the British have been perceived by Colombo as more pro-LTTE.

In January, London banned Sri Lanka and 21 other countries from getting arms purchase credit and within weeks, there were demands from Sinhala organisations to declare Britain a 'terrorist state' for allowing LTTE to use its territory for propaganda. The US has hardly any clout over the LTTE, given its record of selling arms to Colombo and declaring LTTE a terrorist organisation.

Military analysts believe that Chandrika's plea for material support could be the "last SOS from the last India-friendly government in Colombo." Clearly, India's counter-offer of getting the troops safely out has hardly enthused the Lankan President. India's counter-offer of "humanitarian intervention" has been with two riders—one there has to be a request from Colombo. Two, there should be "right conditions", a euphemism for ceasefire. In real terms, India has offered to send some planes and ships to evacuate the soldiers, if Colombo asks for them and can guarantee that the Tigers won't fire upon the hired Indian military ferry service.

In effect, as a senior Army officer put it, Indian government is insisting on a guarantee which even civilian lorry drivers did not ask for when carrying supplies to the Kargil heights. Even the politically besieged Chandrika could not help being contemptuous towards the Indian counter-offer. The fact is that the Sri Lankan Air Force, though not much of a fighting force, has the capability to evacuate the troops in the event of a ceasefire. Apart from its depleted transport squadron, the Lankan Air Force has wet-leased a fleet of An-26 military transport aircraft from Ukraine with Russian and Ukrainian crew.

The fact is that there is no way Chandrika can agree to the evacuation of the Jaffna region, which would politically and militarily amount to conceding the territory to the Tigers who would then negotiate from a position of strength. What she wants is to get the Tigers to the table when at least part of Jaffna is under the Lankan Army.

Chandrika's mistake has been that she failed to follow up politically what her military had been able to achieve. After overrunning much of the Peninsula, Colombo did little more than setting up a series of garrisons. There was hardly any development activity, no attempt to woo the Tamils and hardly any concerted attempt to get the Tigers to the negotiations table.

Anyway, having weakened its clout over both Colombo and the Tigers, the only option left for India has been to play second fiddle to the Norwegian negotiators. The fact is that if India does not play along with the Norwegians, who enjoy Colombo's trust, powers which are more unpredictable may get into the act.

A bigger threat is perceived to be from China, though its Navy still does not have the strength to reach out as far as Sri Lanka. All the same, the Chinese Navy has of late been on a world tour of sorts, and did make a low-profile courtesy call on the Lankan Navy two years ago.

But more significant is the Chinese Navy's hidden presence in the waters around India and Sri Lanka. Any Indian Naval movement from the Andamans can be detected by the signal intelligence stations that China has put up on the Coco Island about which Defence Minister George Fernandes has been publicly worried about. Incidentally, much of Indian Navy's operations against gun-running LTTE boats had been conducted from the Andaman base.

The departure of the IPKF from Sri Lanka brought an end to India's longest war, and one in which it had over one thousand soldiers killed with three thousand or more wounded. The presence of the IPKF in the north and east of Sri Lanka, and in such large numbers, had proved to be a self-defeating exercise. The IPKF had failed in one of its principal objectives as a peacekeeping force, to disarm the Tamil separatist groups, and especially the LTTE, even if one disregards the timetable set out in the Indo-Sri Lanka Accord as hopelessly optimistic and therefore unrealistic. Nor did the IPKF succeed in eliminating the LTTE as a fighting force after it was decided to turn its guns on them, thus opening themselves to the charge that they had been incapable of doing that, or that it was never intended to do so. There is considerable evidence that instructions had been issued to the IPKF in 1988 through the Indian High Commission that the leadership of the LTTE should be eliminated.

A concerted attempt was made in May and June 1988 to eliminate the LTTE leader, Velupillai Prabhakaran, and his second in command, Mahendraraja, but the IPKF found it impossible to get to them in their jungle hideouts or elsewhere. The assumption was that, if this had been done, the LTTE would have disintegrated, as indeed the JVP did, when the Sri Lankan army eliminated its leadership in 1990. The LTTE was aware of this threat and took extraordinary precautions to protect its leadership there were concentric circles of armed men, around them all the time, assigned the task of protecting them at all costs.

Despite all this, the LTTE was driven to the bargaining table because of a perceived weakening of its military strength, sapped in the course of a long and debilitating struggle against the IPKF. Had the LTTE not reached an understanding with the Premadasa government after April 1989, the IPKF would have gone on to weaken them further, and may perhaps have even eliminated the LTTE leadership before leaving Sri Lanka. As it was, the rapprochement with the Sri Lankan government permitted the LTTE to escape a crushing final defeat at the hands of the IPKF. Thus the LTTE was doubly fortunate.

In July 1987, the Indian intervention and the Indian army had saved them from further humiliation at the hands of the Sri Lankan Army. By the time the IPKF left, the LTTE, which had been cornered and weakened, had been allowed to re-establish itself as a political and military force. Its leadership was intact and safe; its troops battle hardened and ready for combat; its morale high as a result of its "diplomatic" coup in reaching out to the Sri Lankan government.

The presence of the IPKF in the north and east of the island was not without advantages to the Sri Lankan government. For one thing, the country's defence expenditures dropped noticeably after mid-1987.

The Indian government bore the heavy expenditure involved in the pacification—such as it was—of the north and east. This decline in defence spending on the part of Sri Lanka would have been more substantial if the threat posed by the JVP had not been so serious. More important, the fact that the IPKF kept the LTTE at bay in the north and east of the island greatly helped the Sri Lankan security forces, and in particular the army, to crush the JVP militarily and to eliminate it as a political force. The violence and turmoil in the last few months of President Jayewardene's period of office were, if anything, on a more fearful and more widespread scale than the riots of 27 July to 2 or 3 August 1987 in the wake of the signing of the Indo-Sri Lanka Accord. They were also sustained over a longer period of time and were more difficult to contain. The source of the trouble was the same: Sinhalese intransigents, led and manipulated this time by the Jonatha Vimukthi

Peramuna (JVP) in association with the Sri Lanka Freedom Party (SLFP).

The Sinhalese areas of the country were convulsed by violence directed by the JVP against supporters of the United National Party (UNP), in which hundreds were killed. In the first two weeks of November a series of politically inspired strikes and disturbances organised by the JVP sought to bring the government down. By this time the JVP had made yet another change of policy. After agitating for over a year for presidential and parliamentary elections, they now demanded that the elections be postponed until the Indian Peace-Keeping Force (IPKF) had left the island.

The JVP violence was directed at all political parties (including their new found ally, the SLEP) participating in the elections. It required President Jayewardene's skilful use of the unwavering support the security services and the Police gave him—although he was a lame-duck President—to hold the government and administration together in the face of the JVP's campaign of violence.

The presidential election of December 1988 was perhaps the most violent ever held in a democracy, and most unusual compared to. violent elections elsewhere, such as the national elections in Jamaica in the 1980s, because those who indulged in violence were not the supporters of the three candidates. In fact, those engaged in the campaign became the victim of terror directed by a group who wished to see the elections postponed

The JVP was persisting in its policy of using the presence of the IPKF as in emotionally divisive issue in its national campaign. The Indian government was now on the defensive because both principal candidates in the Sri Lankan presidential election, R. Premadasa of the UNP and Sirimavo Bandaranaike of the SLEP had gone on record as being opposed to the IPKF presence in the island. In an effort at damage control, the Indian High Commissioner J. N. Dixit, was sent to meet the two candidates with a message from New Delhi that the IPKF would he withdrawn soon. Both candidates were given the Indian government's views on the mechanics and timing of the withdrawal. They were urged to tone clown public criticisms of the IPKF, as these would hamper the Indian government's efforts to prepare public opinion in India for the withdrawal. R. Premadasa paid heed to this appeal and his criticisms of the IPKF presence became more subdued. Nevertheless he stuck to his claim that he would persuade the IPKF to leave as soon as he came to office.

The outcome of the election gave the Indians great satisfaction. They had good reason to claim—as some officials of the Indian High Commission did claim at that time—that the IPKF's presence in the north and east, (especially the east) of the island, made the difference between defeat and victory, given the wafer-thin margin Premadasa secured over Mrs. Bandaranaike. Indeed some political observers believed—and they too had good reason to do so—that the IPKF had done more than that on Premadasa's behalf, that they had brought votes to the polling stations with the knowledge that this would help his cause.

Once the election was over and the UNP candidate had won, Dixit met President Premadasa just after he had been sworn in. Apart from the conventional good wishes of his government Dixit conveyed what he thought would be the message the new President really wanted, that is to say, when the withdrawal of the IPKF would begin. The Indian government's message, that the first batch of IPKF soldiers would return to India in January 1989, should have delighted the new President. Instead, Premadasa urged that the process be delayed, that the IPKF should remain in the north and east of the island during the election campaign for seats in parliament so that people there would feel secure enough to go out to vote. This surprising request, from a man who had opposed the entry of the IPKF to Sri Lanka and had pushed for their early return to India, left Dixit more than a little surprised. He returned from the meeting rather bemused but very satisfied at the prospect of what he saw was a more friendly attitude to India from the new President. President Premadasa's narrow victory over Mrs. Bandaranaike did not lead to anything more than a temporary relaxation of the JVP's violence. It was resumed before the end of January 1989—around 20 January, to be more exact—and continued beyond the parliamentary elections of February 1989.

The parliamentary elections, the first under proportional representation in Sri Lanka, saw the UNP winning 125 seats out of 225, while the SLFP, who obtained 30 per cent of the votes, secured 66. The renewal of the UNP's mandate did not ensure a return to political stability. Instead the new President confronted a challenge from the JVP, which continued its career of terror, ruthlessly and relentlessly, and showed no signs of a change of attitude to the government despite the policy of conciliation he initiated and pursued. As part of this policy, he relaxed the state of emergency and released the JVP activists taken into custody on suspicion of involvement in the violence. The decision to release the latter was taken in the face of the reluctance of the police and security services to endorse such a policy. The JVP spurned this attitude of forbearance and continued its attacks on the government supporters. The Indian government's reading of the political situation in Sri Lanka was both sombre and realistic. As they saw it, the government was reeling in the face of the JVP's attacks. The IPKF's continued presence was being used by the JVP as an excuse for its brutal campaign of violence directed against the new government and its supporters.

The new President placed no trust in either Gamini Dissanayake or Lalith Athulathmudali, both of whom had been involved—the latter in particular—in previous negotiations with the Indian government under President Jayewardene. Instead, the new foreign minister, Ranjan Wijeratne, was given charge of the negotiations, such as they were. Since he was also minister of state for defence, the IPKF's "de-induction", the technical term used during these negotiations for the removal of the IPKF's soldiers to India, was assigned to him. Thus his responsibilities were more onerous, particularly because President Premadasa deviated from his predecessor's practice in deciding not to preside at meetings of Sri Lanka's Security Council, the meeting of the defence and police chiefs and senior officials involved in national security matters. Wijeratne carried this responsibility as well.

The first phase of the negotiations commenced in March 1989, when the mechanics of the "de-induction" process were discussed between the Indian and Sri Lankan foreign ministers, P.V. Narasimha Rao and Ranjan Wijeratne.

Under the proposals set before Wijeratne by his Indian counterpart, the departure of the IPKF would begin almost immediately, that is to say, in March or April. The plan envisaged the withdrawal of at least half of the IPKF in June and July 1989, leaving around 25,000 to be withdrawn in batches of fifteen hundred or so a week until all of them were out of the island by the end of December.

The Indian elections expected in early 1990 figured prominently in the calculations of the Indian government. The advantage of this projected timetable for the departure of the IPKF was that, even if the elections were held late in 1989, the great majority of the IPKF troops would have been withdrawn. This would ensure, or so the Congress I leadership believed, that the IPKF's continued presence in Sri Lanka would not become an election issue to be used against them.

In March it was announced that J. N. Dixit would be leaving Sri Lanka to take up duties as the Indian envoy in Pakistan. Thus the virtual co-author of the Indo-Sri Lanka Accord and the man who gave political and administrative leadership to the IPKF operation would be leaving the country before the IPKF itself departed from its shores. Four years earlier, J. N. Dixit had arrived in Colombo from Kabul, leaving one trouble spot for another. He was no run-of-the-mill diplomat; he was one of India's best, and in choosing him for the Colombo post in 1985 Delhi was acknowledging the need for a man of unusual ability to handle matters there for India. Very few people in Sri Lanka were really aware of Dixit's role in the creation of Bangladesh in 1971-72. He was a young man of thirty-seven at that time. Beginning as an important middle-rung officer in New Delhi and later on operating actively in the border between West Bengal and India and troubled East Pakistan, he made an important contribution to the success of the Indian exercise in subversion. Once the new state was created, he was sent to Dhaka as Deputy High Commissioner. In describing him as head of mission, the Indian weekly quoted above was making a mistake of fact but not of substance. Subimal Dutt, the Indian High Commissioner in Dhaka, an elderly Bengali long past the age of retirement, was only a figurehead chosen for his familiarity with the former East Pakistan.

Dixit's task, as the Indian weekly put it, was to "oversee the reconstruction of the country... and the consolidation of Indian interests." Bangladeshis who remembered Dixit during his Dhaka days believe that he paid more attention to the latter role than to the former. He earned the trust and respect of the victorious Indian army in Bangladesh for his political and diplomatic skills, and again in Sri Lanka after the IPKF came in. In yet another parallel, the Indians hailed as liberators in Bangladesh—as the IPKF were in the initial stages in Jaffna—soon became unpopular. There were a number of reasons why India and the Indians became unpopular in Bangladesh so soon, despite the swift return of the Indian Army to their bases in India. Bangladeshis realised very quickly that India was too poor to finance the reconstruction of their country, and that Indian businessmen were seeking to establish a grip on the Bangladeshi economy.

The simmering discontent with the Indians erupted to the surface in June 1974 during the visit of Pakistani Prime Minister Zulfiqar Ali Bhutto, who had been invited to Bangladesh in an obvious gesture of reconciliation. To the amazement of practically everybody in Bangladesh, Bhutto was given a tumultuous welcome in a country that not so long ago had risen in revolt against the Pakistani establishment. Bangladeshi academics remembered this occasion as one on which anti-Indian feeling bubbled to the surface. Bhutto mistakenly thought the jubilant crowds were hailing him as a friend. This was only partly true. The mood of the crowd was more complex than that. Their effusive welcome to Bhutto was more in anti-Indian demonstration than a pro-Pakistani one, as Dixit himself learned to his dismay. His car was caught in a traffic jam as vehicles endeavoured to make their way through the massive crowds returning to their homes after the reception for Bhutto. Trapped in his car, a stunned Dixit watched in pained disconcertment as a section of the crowd, recognising the vehicle as one belonging to the Indian High Commission, began pelting it with shoes and sandals, the ultimate gesture of insult in Bangladesh.

Dixit was one of the few links between India's Bangladeshi and Sri Lankan interventions. In both instances Dixit was closely linked to a military exercise; in both his mission ultimately failed. In Bangladesh that aspect of the Indian venture was a pronounced success, but the equally important political aspects of the enterprise were a dismal failure. The memory of that successful military intervention no doubt encouraged its use in Sri Lanka, although the circumstances were very different. There were very few precedents in international politics for the decision to use an Army in an attempt to resolve an ethnic conflict in a neighbouring state.

The Indian intervention in East Pakistan that led to the creation of Bangladesh was, of course, the classic case in recent years. There was also the Turkish intervention in Cyprus. Both were unilateral decisions of the governments involved. The contrast between these and the use of the Indian army, in the north and east of Sri Lanka, has been referred to earlier, in particular the acquiescence if not support of the Sri Lankan government and of its President at that time, J. R. Jayewardene.

In Sri Lanka as in Bangladesh, the Indian Army was used in a calculated demonstration of military power to impose the will of the Indian government in support of what were seen to be India's national and strategic interests. The difference was that the tactics and strategy were so dissimilar in Bangladesh the aim was to dismember Pakistan and ensure the triumph of Bangladeshi separatism; in Sri Lanka the objective was to prevent the success of separatism but at the same time to ensure a dominant voice for India in the affairs of the island. In the first instance, the Indian army did help achieve that objective; in the second, it did little to resolve the conflict. On the contrary the consequences were nearly disastrous for India's own national interest. Thus Dixit presided over a failed Indian enterprise in Sri Lanka, and while there were no sandals and shoes to dramatise it and to speed him on his way, Dixit must have had a sense of *deja vu* as he left Sri Lanka and remembered his departure from Bangladesh fifteen years earlier.

In a farewell interview he gave the government-controlled *Daily News,* he said he was leaving the island "with a sense of satisfaction of having played the role of a catalyst in preserving the unity and territorial integrity of Sri Lanka and safeguarding India's interests."

Describing his stint in Colombo as the most challenging in his twenty-eight-year diplomatic life, he claimed that the Indo-Sri Lanka Accord had met the aspirations of the Sinhalese, Tamils and India. The Sinhalese wanted the preservation of the unity and territorial integrity of Sri Lanka. That has been served. The Tamils wanted to live in peace and security in the areas they traditionally lived in and an arrangement to manage their own affairs. India wanted a stable, democratic Sri Lanka.

Even the friends he made in Sri Lanka would have agreed that he was putting the best possible gloss on a failed enterprise. On March 10, he gave a more comprehensive and forthright defence of India's intervention in Sri Lanka. The setting was Delhi's elite United Service Institution, where he addressed a gathering of high-ranking bureaucrats and an array of senior and middle-rung representatives of the defence services. At first glance the speech, which was subsequently published in the journal of that institute, seemed unusual for an Indian diplomat—for its candour and for being delivered at all given the sensitive nature of the subject, especially because he was still High Commissioner in Sri Lanka. But a careful reading shows that it was a skilful exposition of the essentials of Indian policy on Sri Lanka as the Indian government and New Delhi's South Block wished the world to see it.

The opening paragraph set the tone for the evening, initially somewhat defensive, but leading to a self-confident defence of Indian policy.

> I am slightly overawed by the audience because I see people whom I viewed from the lower and middle levels of the bureaucracy like General Candeth and I see a number of colleagues with whom I was associated during my assignment in Bangladesh and then Sri Lanka. I have not brought a written text but had I known that it would be such an august audience, I would have been prepared for a more structured presentation.

Our interest in this speech lies in the reasons he gave for the Indian intervention. The exposition was as notable for its mixture of truth with half-truth and, occasionally, downright invention, as it was for the clarity with which realpolitik was identified and defended as the essence of tactfulness. "The first reason why we went into Sri Lanka was the interest to preserve our unity to ensure the success of a very difficult experiment that we have been carrying out ourselves. We claim to be the largest functioning democracy in the world.... Let us not forget that the first voice of secessionism in the Indian Republic was raised in Tamil Nadu in the mid-sixties.... So, in a manner, our interest in the Tamil issue in Sri Lanka, Tamil aspirations in Sri Lanka was based on maintaining our own unity, our own integrity, our own identity in the manner in which we have been trying to build our own society.

"The second reason why we went in was to counter the Sri Lankan government over its reactions to the rising Tamil militancy since 1972.... In the period, between 1978 and 1986 the strength of the Sri Lankan Army was raised from approximately 12,000 to 35,000. The overall strength of the Sri Lankan Armed Forces rose approximately from 15,000 to 17,000 if we include the homeguards and paramilitary units. Sri Lanka signed informal confidential agreements with the governments of United States and United Kingdom to bring their warships into Colombo, Trincomalee and the Gulf. The frequency of visits by the Navies of these countries showed a quantum jump between 1982-83 and 1987.

"Sri Lanka invited British mercenaries into its Intelligence Services. It invited Shin beth and Mossad, the two most effective and influential Intelligence agencies of Israel. It sought assistance from Pakistan to train its Home Guards, and its Navy, and offered broadcasting facilities to the Voice of America, which would have enabled the United States to install highly sophisticated monitoring equipment on Sri Lanka soil. This could have affected our security in terms of their capacity to monitor our sensitive information for their own interests. Sri Lanka bought arms from countries with whom our relations have been difficult. So, the second reason, why we had to be actively involved in Sri Lanka was to counter, to the extent possible, this trend.

"The IPKF has been a catalyst for reviving democratic institutions in Sri Lanka after a gap of eleven years. Very few people remember that the last series of general elections were held in Sri Lanka in 1977. And what triggered off elections, which were held between November 1988 and January 89 was the successful management of the elections to the Eastern Provinces by the IPKF. The credit entirely goes to our armed forces. We have projected our armed forces, therefore, not only in a peacekeeping role, but in a political role. Secondly, we are undoubtedly a factor against insurgency and mayhem in Sri Lanka.

"The worst critic of the IPKF in Jaffna asked if we shall withdraw immediately. And what is interesting now is, that view is shared by the Foreign Minister and the new President of Sri Lanka, which gives us perhaps the capacity to negotiate from the position of strength and detachment because Indian public opinion and our own good sense impels us to say that you must not be in a foreign country for a very long time. We must move out, and it is a good approach. But the fact that despite performing a highly complex and at times unpalatable role, IPKF is being considered a necessity in a foreign country where there are so many complexes against India is a symptom of two things. First, that you are a factor of stability. Second, that whatever tasks have been assigned to us, we have done them with a sense of fair play and detachment regardless of minor criticisms here or there.

Finally, we must remember the special context in which Dixit's speech was delivered on 10 March 1989. It came at a time when he was still High Commissioner in Sri Lanka, and well before all unorthodox political initiative by President Premadasa brought the two countries once more into an acrimonious dispute, on this occasion over the timing of the departure of the IPKF from Sri Lanka.

L. L. Mehrotra arrived in Sri Lanka to replace Dixit as India's new High Commissioner only to face the difficulties that stemmed from a surprisingly new initiative taken by President Premadasa, a rapprochement between the government of Sri Lanka and the Liberation Tigers of Tamil Eelam (LTTE). The expectation that the animosities and hostilities of a decade could be overcome through negotiations conducted against the background of a common opposition to the IPKF was unrealistic except as part of a public relations exercise. Actually the LTTE was responding to appeals, which the government aimed primarily at the JVP for discussions instead of violent confrontation. While the JVP contemptuously rejected this conciliatory gesture, the LTTE seized the opportunity to escape from the noose the IPKF had placed around them.

The initiative now lay with the LTTE rather than the Sri Lankan government, and it made the most of the opportunities that had come so unexpectedly. The major premise of the new president's thinking was that no lasting peace settlement could be made with the Tamil minority if it did not include the LTTE as part of the peace process. He did not share his predecessor's antipathy to and mistrust of the LTTE, nor did he have his experience of dealing with them over a long period of time. Apart from that he was full of admiration for the LTTE leader's military prowess and for his and the LTTE's dogged resistance to the Indian army; besides, he took the view that neither the Indian nor the Sri Lankan army had been able to crush the LTTE. Some of his senior advisers—civilian and military—took an even gloomier view of the situation; they argued that the LTTE would prevail over all other forces in the north and east of the island, and that it was politic therefore to come to terms with it sooner rather than later. In coming to this latter conclusion they ignored two important facts—that it was the Indian government that had prevented the Sri Lankan army from crushing the LTTE in May-July 1987, and that the Indians had weakened the LTTE to the point where they had turned in desperation to negotiations with the Sri Lankan government. He was also impressed by the strong and enthusiastic support the LTTE enjoyed from and among the overseas Tamils, who had evolved in time into a very vocal and politically effective lobby in Western countries.

There was another and more practical reason given for opening talks with the LTTE. Because of the enmity between the Indian government and the LTTE, there seemed to be much less chance than ever before of the triumph of Tamil separatism and the establishment of a Tamil state in the north and east of the island.

Not many people outside the government shared President Premadasa's confidence in the moderation and good sense of the LTTE. Certainly there were individuals, if not groups, in the cabinet and the government parliamentary group who were sceptical given the turmoil and violence generated by the JVP, those critics remained silent lest they be accused of pro-Indian sentiments. President Premadasa deputed Ranjan Wijeratne, the foreign minister and minister of state for defence, to lead the Sri Lankan delegation to the talks with the LTTE, the first of which was held on 12 May. Wijeratne was assisted by A.C.S Hameed, the former foreign minister, a Muslim who had the advantage of being able to speak Tamil fluently. Other cabinet ministers were brought in when it was thought necessary to do so, but the crucially important fact is that none of them had any previous experience of negotiating with the LTTE. The announcement of the commencement of negotiations between the Premadasa government and the LTTE had an immediate impact or informed opinion in India in strengthening the groups who were calling for a withdrawal of IPKF as expeditiously as possible. One by one the major Indian newspapers began urging the government to cut its losses and to bring the troops back. Left of centre weeklies such as *Mainstream,* which had been sceptical about Rajiv Gandhi's Sri Lankan policy from the outset, became more outspoken in their criticisms.

The foreign ministers of the two countries met for the second time in Zimbabwe in the last week of May. This was the highest level of contact between India and Sri Lanka since the new president had assumed office. At this meeting the Indian foreign minister confirmed the Indian government's commitment to the decisions arrived at between him and his Sri Lankan counterpart at their previous meeting in March, on the mechanics and timetable of the IPKF's departure to India.

Ranjan Wijeratne arrived in Colombo from Harare, after his discussions with his Indian counterpart, with what he believed was a mutually acceptable timetable for the withdrawal of the IPKF, only to find the situation changing dramatically when President Premadasa dropped a verbal bombshell in a speech on 1 June, made at a temple at Battaramulla, a suburb of Colombo.

President Premadasa's unorthodox diplomatic intervention can only be understood in the context of his own, and his government's, deteriorating political position. The government was reeling under the relentless pressure of the JVP, who had just announced a campaign to boycott Indian goods, a decision they were intent on enforcing on the people through their usual mixture of bluster, intimidation, and selective violence against random victims among persons who ignored or defied instructions issued by JVP cadres. But there was more to it than a mere wish to preempt the JVP, or to outdo them, in anti-Indian rhetoric. One needs to emphasise President Premadasa's deep-rooted distrust of the Indian leadership and visceral dislike of Rajiv Gandhi. His astonishing diplomatic initiative could be attributed to his strong conviction that, unless some unorthodox measures were adopted to force the issue, the IPKF's departure would be delayed to conform to the political imperatives confronting the Indian government in an election year, while ignoring his own desperate need to stabilise his government against the pressures from the JVP. He placed no trust in the Indian government's assurances or the timetable they had committed themselves to. And this was despite his own initial requests conveyed through Dixit that the departure of the IPKF should be delayed.

Whatever the motive, once the speech was made the IPKFs departure became a major, and very acrimonious, diplomatic issue between the two countries. The result was to delay the process rather than hasten it. President Premadasa followed his speech of 1 June with another on 9 June at Mahiyangana in Uva, the site that year of the annual village reawakening ceremony—the *gam udava*, as it is called. On this latter occasion he not only reiterated his demand for withdrawal of the IPKF by July 29, but suggested in addition that if the Indian government was unable to withdraw all troops from Sri Lanka by that date, those left behind could be "confined to barracks" until the process of bringing them back to India was completed. This was seen as a gratuitous insult to the Indians and was treated as such by Rajiv Gandhi.

To the beleaguered Rajiv Gandhi, already under a cloud because of the Bofors scandal (involving the acceptance of alleged commissions—kickbacks—from the Swedish company, Bofors, which had won a huge contract to supply weapons to the Indian army), and facing a difficult election, President Premadasa's calculated conversion of the IPKF's departure into a divisive political issue, despite India's efforts to withdraw the IPKF on a timetable mutually agreed to, came as a wholly unexpected setback in the course of delicate negotiations for a return of the IPKF to India. To yield to the Sri Lankan president's unilateral demands was to risk a further and, perhaps, precipitous erosion of political support for him as well as for his party in the forthcoming elections. Besides, there was the need to make some arrangements for the protection of the Eelam People's Revolutionary Liberation Front (EPRLF), whose position had now been rendered hopelessly vulnerable by the rapprochement between the Premadasa government and the LTTE.

He described the Sri Lankan president's demand that the IPKF be withdrawn on a timetable set by him as "unrealistic" because it was "unilateral". Thus the Indians were insisting on a mutually agreed upon timetable, which was a continuation of a policy outlined in March 1989, but in linking the phased withdrawal to certain conditions such as an improvement in the security situation in the North-Eastern Province, and an effective devolution of power, they were going well beyond the scope of the obligations assumed by them as signatories of the accord. He made the point that "as the Indo-Sri Lanka agreements get progressively implemented, and as the mischief-making potential of extremist elements opposed to the agreement are reduced, further withdrawals will be made in consultation with the Sri Lankan government." Thus Rajiv Gandhi had introduced a new element into the negotiations on the transfer of the IPKF to India.

The practical effect of this controversy, however, was that the plan to send half the Indian troops back to India by the end of July was shelved. No troops left the island until 29 July. Instead, there followed an exchange of letters between the two heads of government and the unilateral publication of the letters by the Sri Lankan government.

The Indian government sent its foreign secretary to Sri Lanka in an attempt to break the deadlock. The first set of discussions proved to be a failure. As the deadline of 29 July approached and no IPKF soldiers had left the island, the Sri Lankan government faced a dual threat, one a diplomatic impasse with the Indians, who were in no mood to yield to pressure to withdraw their troops by 29 July, or even to begin to do so, and the other a three-day island-wide strike called by the JVP to coincide with the second anniversary of the arrival of the IPKF in Sri Lanka, a strike intended to underline their opposition to the continued presence of the IPKF in Sri Lanka.

The mounting tensions between India and Sri Lanka were abated when the Indian government agreed to receive a delegation from Sri Lanka to discuss the withdrawal of the IPKF. The delegation left the island for Delhi on 28 July. On 29 July, in a deliberate attempt to lessen the dissonance between the two countries, India withdrew six hundred troops. Once the negotiations were completed on 5 August, the departure of the Indian soldiers from Sri Lanka was resumed. Within three days of the completion of negotiations, over 1,500 soldiers departed to India.

The Sri Lankan delegation that left for Delhi on this occasion was led by Ranjan Wijeratne. Considering the acrimony that followed President Premadasa's speeches of 1 and 9 June, and the exchange and publication of the correspondence between the two heads of government, the negotiations in Delhi were surprisingly cordial. It was clear to the Sri Lankans that the Indians were anxious to get the IPKF back, and were not inclined to leave any of their soldiers in the island. What they sought was a face-saving exit for the IPKF, without any semblance of departure under pressure. This was stressed at all levels.

The Indians stated that all troops would be removed from the island before the end of February 1990, that is, at the rate of 1,500 per week beginning in August 1989.

The Sri Lankan delegation wished that this process be completed much earlier, if possible by September 1989, but it was evident that the Indians, their eyes set on the forthcoming general elections, did not want to hasten the withdrawal to a point which could be construed in India, and especially in Tamil Nadu, as a precipitate surrender to Sri Lankan pressure. In his correspondence with President Premadasa, Prime Minister Rajiv Gandhi had sought to link the departure of the IPKF—or at least the speed of its departure—with the effectiveness of the actual devolution of power to the provinces. At the discussions in Delhi, the Indians dropped their insistence on such a linkage.

The Indians expressed great concern about the need to plan ahead for the deployment of Sri Lankan troops to the north and east of the island and to re-establish law enforcement authorities there to take control of the areas evacuated by the IPKF. They were anxious also about the safety (even survival) of the EPRLF ministry in the North-Eastern Province, a concern and anxiety that was both natural and inevitable. Prime Minister Rajiv Gandhi made particular mention of these two points in his discussions with the two Sri Lankan ministers, a discussion that took over six hours and from which all officials, Indian and Sri Lankan, were excluded.

The Indian representatives would not agree to the Sri Lankan government's request that the IPKF stop its offensive operations against the LTTE. Indeed the Indians stressed the need for the LTTE to surrender their arms before the IPKF would consider a ceasefire. The Sri Lankans came away with the impression that the Indians seemed intent on weakening the LTTE further before the IPKF left. An agreement between the two governments was reached on 18 September 1989, based on the discussions held in Delhi in July and August and subsequently through diplomatic channels.

Under the terms of the agreement, India would withdraw between fifteen hundred and sixteen hundred soldiers each week until March 1990, when the "de-induction" process would be completed. There would be no linkage between the withdrawal of the IPKF and the implementation of the devolution proposals in the Indo-Sri Lanka Accord. The agreement incorporated proposals for security in the north and east with the withdrawal of the Indian forces. The two sides agreed that the Sri Lankan army and police would move into the areas evacuated by the IPKF. At the insistence of the Indians, an elaborate security system was devised for the transfer of power in the north and east. These included a coordinating committee consisting of representatives of all the ethnic and political groups in that part of the country; a security coordinating group with an Indian General, a Sri Lankan official of similar rank, and the Chief Minister of the North Eastern Province; and a military observer group led by the head of the IPKF and the Commander of the Sri Lankan Army. Together they would ensure that the transfer of authority would not lead to turmoil.

In early September the rate at which the IPKF's units left Sri Lanka was increased. This acceleration took place against the background of dramatic political events in the two countries, beginning with the destruction of the JVP's leadership by the Sri Lankan Army and the virtual collapse of the JVP as an insurgent and political force, and then the calling of a general election in India.

The agreement reached between the two governments in August and September 1989 did little to alleviate anxieties in India and in the IPKF about the fate of the EPRLF government and the EPRLF cadres once the IPKF left. President Premadasa, if not the Sri Lankan government as a whole, did not share the Indian suspicions about the LTTE; on the contrary, relations between the Premadasa government and the LTTE were now so cordial that the latter was permitted to move into the areas evacuated by the IPKF. This was contrary to the terms and spirit of the understanding reached with India, which assumed that the Sri Lankan Army would take control and that the Sri Lankan police would take over the normal law and order functions of a civilian administration. The anxieties stemming from this drove the Indian government and the IPKF to take a most short-sighted decision, to create an IPKF-sponsored Tamil National Army (TNA) linked to the EPRLF, and to supply it with sophisticated weapons, all in the hope that the TNA could stand up to the LTTE in the inevitable conflict between them. Mistake followed mistake in the pursuit of this disastrous policy. Large quantities of weapons, including light artillery, were supplied to the TNA. The Sri Lankan authorities, civil and military, were aghast at this new development, but their protests against establishing the TNA and arming it were not heeded. The LTTE was the principal beneficiary of the Indian government's short-sighted and hasty attempt to establish the TNA as a military arm of the EPRLF. First, it enabled the LTTE, to coordinate an anti-IPKF policy with the government of Sri Lanka, who, not to be outdone by the Indians in lack of forethought, was persuaded to let the LTTE' bring in arms from abroad, through Colombo, allegedly to meet the threat faced from the TNA.

Second, the TNA eventually succumbed to the LTTE without firing a shot. The LTTE gained access to weapons from two sources: the IPKF and the Sri Lankan government.

The supply from the IPKF via the TNA was not only much larger, it included more and powerful weapons such as light artillery. By the beginning of 1991 the disintegration of the TNA was complete.

The irony of arming the TNA was lost on the Indian government. A peace-keeping force brought in to disarm Tamil separatist groups not only failed to do so but, worse, actually ended its stay in the island by arming a ragtag force linked to its puppet regime.

Rajiv Gandhi's defeat at the general election of November 1989 was greeted by President Premadasa with a sigh of relief. On the morning of 5 December, even before the new Indian cabinet had been sworn in, President Premadasa telephoned the new Indian Prime Minister, V. P. Singh, to offer his congratulations personally. In the course of the conversation he expressed a wish to send a delegation to see him almost immediately—a delegation consisting of the Foreign Minister (Ranjan Wijeratne) the Foreign Secretary (Bernard Tillakaratne), the President's Adviser on foreign affairs (Bradman Weerakoon), and the Defence Secretary. The new Prime Minister agreed to this proposal with some hesitation. The news that a delegation would be in Delhi even before the new Prime Minister had picked his cabinet took the principal Indian officials of the Prime Minister's office and the Ministry of External Affairs by surprise. None of them was very receptive to the idea and S. K. Singh, the Foreign Secretary at the time, actually urged the Sri Lankan High Commissioner, Stanley Kalpage, to persuade the delegation to postpone their visit by forty-eight hours—until the weekend or thereafter. Eventually, however, these officials reluctantly agreed to go along with the idea of receiving the Sri Lankan delegation. But there was still a problem—a Foreign Minister had not been named yet. The official acceptance of the Sri Lankan President's urgent request that the Indian government meet a delegation from Sri Lanka came before the Indian cabinet was announced.

The Sri Lankan President's anxiety to establish contact with the new Prime Minister of India was, naturally enough, the subject of much speculation in New Delhi. Was it done in the hope that the Sri Lankan version of events in the north and east of the island would be given to the new Prime Minister before the Indian officials established their hold on him? If this was indeed so, then it demonstrated the wide difference in the political cultures of the two countries. India had a powerful and highly professional civil service elite who made a major contribution to policy making—in contrast to Sri Lanka—and no Prime Minister could entirely ignore their views or do without their expertise. Unlike in the situation in Sri Lanka, there was an official "memory" on policy matters that a new government would have to take into consideration even if it eventually decided that a fresh initiative was required. Thus a change of government in India would not necessarily lead to any dramatic changes in India's Sri Lankan policy.

By Tuesday 5 December it was known that a Sri Lankan delegation was due to reach Delhi the next day or the next night. The delegation left Colombo that evening. When they got to New Delhi in the early hours of Wednesday, they found to their chagrin that there was no Minister or even Minister of State to receive them. The senior officials who greeted them there explained that, for security reasons, Indian Ministers did not participate in such welcoming ceremonies at night. The real reason, however, was that the process of cabinet making was not complete; and most politicians preferred to concentrate on that rather than on welcoming importunate visitors. The delegation was lodged at the Taj Hotel. They had come equipped with an album of photographs of the arms supplied to the Tamil National Army.

The Sri Lankan delegation expected to meet the Prime Minister and the Foreign Minister in that order. The Indian officials shrewdly arranged for them to meet the new Foreign Minister, I. K. Gujral, before they met the Prime Minister. In this way they would be able to listen to what the Sri Lankans had to say to the Foreign Minister and prepare their answers for the meeting with the Prime Minister, since much the same arguments were likely to be used on the second occasion.

The interview with Gujral went off very well. He was in a very conciliatory mood, and began by apologising for not being able to greet them personally when they arrived. The Sri Lankan delegation's sole spokesman was Ranjan Wijeratne, who dwelt on three themes: the need to adhere to the previous agreement on the departure of the IPKF, with 31 December as a possible new deadline; the IPKF's role in arming the TNA; and a friendship treaty as a substitute for the one-sided concessions made by Sri Lanka in the letters which formed part of the Indo-Sri Lanka Accord of July 1987.

Gujral assured his Sri Lankan counterpart that the IPKF would leave as soon as possible. The Indian government would seek to advance the deadline for the departure of the IPKF to 31 December, but if this proved difficult, the two sides—the Indian and Sri Lankan governments—could reach an understanding on a new timetable. The fact is that there were 25,000 troops still in the north and the east. He did appreciate the significance of the points made about the IPKF and the TNA, but gave no indication of his own response to this difficult situation. The Sri Lankan delegates were very impressed by Gujral's sincerity and moderation. He was very accommodating about the friendship treaty.

Earlier in the year, with Rajiv Gandhi and his Foreign Minister there had been, generally, a rather tense and confrontational atmosphere during discussions. Some of this was blamed on J. N. Dixit, India's envoy in Pakistan, who had participated in the last set of talks (July/August 1989), travelling from Islamabad for that purpose. The Sri Lankans were relieved that Dixit had not been invited to the talks with Gujral. Apart from the meeting with Gujral, Ranjan Wijeratne had a very successful press conference that evening. Indeed the Sri Lankan delegation was quite elated; it had a good day; the Indian officials had remained more or less silent.

The communique that was issued was a very bland one reflecting the influence of the officials in the South Block. There was no firm commitment about expediting the departure of the IPKF so that they would be away from the island by 31 December. Nor was there any great enthusiasm for the friendship treaty. The problem was that the IPKF's departure had been at the rate of fifteen hundred a week up to the end of November. With 25,000 soldiers still left in the island by the end of December, it would take at least three more months for all of them to move out, unless the process were expedited by the provision of more transport facilities by sea, or if air transport were resorted to.

The process was not hastened very much. The last IPKF soldiers left the island on 24 March 1991, a week before the deadline of 31 March. They left, ironically enough, to the strains of "Auld Lang Syne". By the time they left they had seen the collapse of the TNA, and were compelled as a matter of humanitarian assistance to help some of the TNA's "soldiers", and supporters of the EPRLF, to escape to safe havens in Tamil Nadu and Orissa. The V.P. Singh government attempted to persuade its political ally, the new Chief Minister of Tamil Nadu, M. Karunanidhi, to bring the Sri Lankan Tamil factions in Tamil Nadu together, in an attempt to protect them from the vengeance of the LTTE. But all attempts failed. By the time the last IPKF soldiers reached Tamil Nadu, there were already over three thousand Sri Lankan Tamil refugees there belonging to the EPRLF and its allies.

11

The Unending War

As the war rages in Sri Lanka, India finds itself cornered into a no-win strategic situation. The question is the survival of one-third of the Sri Lankan army. Fighting near Jaffna they have simply run out of guns and bullets. What Colombo is asking for is fire-power. What India has offered, "if the request comes", is free transport with packed lunch. To use the classical adage, Chandrika Kumaratunga asked for guns; Vajpayee is offering butter. Perhaps out of its own desperation, Colombo has once again cornered India into a no-win strategic situation. From the public statements of Lankan leaders, including President Kumaratunga, it is apparent that she has asked for any one of three things: one, an armed Indian intervention which she knew India would refuse, given the IPKF experience; two, material support (arms and ammunition) which she was not sure of; three, India's persuasive power over LTTE to bring it to the negotiating table before Jaffna fell. A yes to any of the three would have kept Colombo within the strategic stranglehold of India, whose Navy thinks that all the waters from Yellow Sea to northern Arabian Sea should be one Indian backwater.

The first option was out for India even before the request was made. In the public and parliamentary discussions, there has been a consensus against an IPKF-type intervention. Not only the Tamil parties, even the BJP and the communists do not want the Indian armed forces to be bloodied once again in a conflict abroad. But except for the radical Tamil parties, no political party has opposed sending arms to Chandrika's besieged government. "She asked for military 'assistance', which does not mean troop assistance," said an intelligence analyst.

However, this option was discussed only within the corridors of the South Block which houses the Prime Minister's office, the ministry of external affairs and the defence ministry. Interestingly, the rejection of the second option appears to have much to do with the origin of the present crisis itself and the real clue to it lay buried in the order books of India's 40-odd ordnance factories and half a dozen defence public sector undertakings. Since 1997-98 their exports have declined to a sixth or seventh of what they had been till the previous year; from a claimed Rs. 186.27 crore, it has fallen to Rs 25 crore in 1999-2000. Obviously, they have lost one big customer after the Vajpayee government came to power.

The fall in exports has little to do with the Kargil crisis when the Indian Army needed all the bullets and mortar shells made in India and available abroad. The decline started a year before the Kargil crisis. When the Jaffna Peninsula slipped out of the control of the Liberation Tigers of Tamil Eelam (LTTE), in November 1995, the out-of-power Dravida Munnetra Kazhagham (DMK) leader M. Karunanidhi led a "black shirt" procession in Chennai. At the end of the month he called a 12-hour bandh that was supported by all political parties, including the ruling All-India Anna Dravida Munnetra Kazhagham (AIADMK). Curiously, five years later, when the same LTTE is today poised to regain control of Jaffna, Karunanidhi, once again the Chief Minister, has not only distanced himself from Eelam, but also rubbishes the Tigers as the organisation that has killed more Tamils than served their cause.

LTTE supremo Velupillai Prabhakaran was never close to Karunanidhi. But after years of trying to build bridges with the Tigers, Karunanidhi's unwillingness to associate himself with the outfit that has posted significant military successes has stumped political circles. Political circles in Chennai, however, linked Karunanidhi's new stance to a union government order on May 12, 2000, extending the ban on the LTTE for a further period of two years. Extension of the ban was routine. What was entirely new was the reason cited for such action in the preamble to the government order.

According to the order, the ban on the organisation was being extended because the concept of Eelam—a separate homeland for Tamils—that it was pursuing could pose a threat to India. The ban order has unintentionally come to redefine the parameters of the politics of Dravidian parties in Tamil Nadu. It has effectively capped competitive mobilisation of public opinion on Sri Lankan Tamil interests by the two major regional parties, the DMK and the AIADMK. In the first four days that it came into existence the ban order had the most debilitating effect on Karunanidhi. It forced him not once but twice to revise the statement he made on the floor of the Tamil Nadu Assembly about Eelam and the LTTE.

On May 11, 2000, he said the DMK would be happy if the LTTE got Tamil Eelam. The following day he clarified to the press that his statement in the Assembly did not mean his government would demand creation of Eelam. The DMK, he emphasised, had given up the idea of a Tamil-nation state way back in 1962. The party's founder and legendary leader, C. N. Annadurai, had formally renounced secessionism after the Sino-Indian conflict. On May 15, 2000, Karunanidhi went a step further. In the state Assembly, he rubbished the LTTE for killing Tamils more than furthering their cause.

The ban had a salutary effect on the AIADMK, the main opposition party outside the Assembly, that it refrained from making an issue of the Chief Minister's flip-flop. The *volte-face* was an embarrassment to the DMK allies like the Pattali Makkal Katchi (PMK) and the Marumalarchi Dravida Munnetra Kazhagham (MDMK), which have been advocating a proactive Indian role in helping the Lankan Tamils. According to them, the DMK leader's about-turn was a device to isolate both the MDMK and the PMK. With the opposition in disarray, Karunanidhi feels he has no need for the two allies in the Assembly elections due next year. With

the AIADMK and the Tamil Maanila Congress (TMC) unable to reach an agreement on forming a coalition, the DMK appears poised for a re-election.

The ruling party's indifference to the Eelam issue has not dampened the enthusiasm of Tamil chauvinist fringe groups like the Tamizhar Desiya Iyakkam (TDI). The group has been consistently working towards making the LTTE acceptable to the people of Tamil Nadu soon after Rajiv's assassination. It managed to build some public support for the outlawed organisation in its campaign against the death sentences handed out to the 26 accused in the assassination case. Tamil groups like the TDI and the Dravida Kazhagham (DK) have been trying to organise public meetings and mobilise public opinion.

At this points to the core question of whether the muted interest in the Lankan problem reflects a weakening of the spirit of Tamil subnationalism. "Identity formation is not a static process," explains Suryanarayanan. "It is a dynamic process of social formation.

Linguistic identities came to the fore when linguistic states were formed. Now the emphasis on the language is not important. The DMK Chief Minister himself has now emerged as a champion of English. Former AIADMK Minister S. Ramachandran says, "If the LTTE takes Jaffna, the Lankan Tamil issue would not be a problem. As far as people are concerned it would be a settled affair. However, if the LTTE is beaten back from Jaffna, suspicion against India will arise." For the moment, the projections about the fallout of the developments in Sri Lanka on Tamil Nadu politics may appear exaggerated. All the same, the public mood could change from muted interest to an outcry if thousands of Tamil refugees begin to arrive in the state.

The Sri Lankan army is facing annihilation and a panicky government has appealed for help. If the rebels capture Jaffna Peninsula, over 35,000 troops will be killed or taken prisoners and that will give the Tigers a leverage at future talks. People everywhere in Sri Lanka speak of the impending defeat. A strict government censorship has blacked out all war news except for military propaganda and the government has shut down three independent newspapers.

Tamils living in government-controlled areas fear a backlash against them, especially in Colombo, as in 1983. These fears increased when a local newspaper published that the UN office in Colombo was preparing for such a contingency, including plans to turn its compound into a refugee camp. The UN denied the story. But the government has banned all public meetings and worker's strikes.

President Chandrika Kumaratunga has vowed that she will not retreat from Jaffna, knowing full well that the opposition will make political gains if she does. But if the rebels advance, the question will not be whether she will pull the troops out, but how. The only air base in the Peninsula is being constantly shelled. Troops will have to be evacuated by sea, but again the Lankan Navy is not up to such a huge task. Half a million Tamil civilians in Jaffna, with no way to get out, will add to the confusion. Although the rebels had scored a series of victories last November, many believed that the 17-year civil war was nearing an end, with the Norwegian government involved in negotiations between the two sides.

With general elections due in September, Lankan leaders brushed aside the threat to Jaffna, confident that the rebels will not be able to get past a 17,000-strong garrison at the Elephant Pass base. The government poured its finest troops into the Peninsula. Three divisions of 35,000 soldiers, including the elite 53rd and 54th Divisions, and Special Forces and commandos, backed by Air Force jets and helicopter gunships, faced some 5,000 rebels. A week before Christmas, the rebels trained their guns on Jaffna, which troops controlled since 1995. By January, the 53rd Division was defeated in a series of daring attacks. In March and April, the rebels surrounded the 54th Division at Elephant Pass, and forced the desperate troops to leave or die. Since then, the Tigers have kept attacking on several fronts, and continue to gain ground.

In the decades of fighting between the security forces and the LTTE, the battle for Jaffna, the heartland of the

Tamil people in the island-nation, has become something of a military high point; and the swing in the battlefield fortunes was symbolised by which of the two combatants had control over the town. The political and military stakes in Jaffna are high, for the town of over five lakh people remains the epicentre of the ethnic earthquake that has shaken Sri Lanka for decades.

When the Tigers were pushed out of Jaffna in a three-stage operation in 1995, international opinion swung overwhelmingly in favour of the Sri Lankan government. Ever since then, the retaking of Jaffna has been high on the LTTE's list of military imperatives. In a series of operations since December 1999, the LTTE built up its combat position around the Peninsula and slowly but steadily gained control of territory and towns that had high strategic value in its quest to reclaim Jaffna.

As the booming guns threatened to pound Jaffna, Sri Lanka appealed to "friendly countries" to help resolve what it had said for the past few years was an "internal issue". The first appeal was to India. However, India, which has paid a heavy price for its attempts in 1980s to help resolve the ethnic conflict, reiterated that it would continue to abide by its hands-off policy of recent years.

The Sri Lankan government then made a series of initiatives, directed internally and externally. A cabinet meeting decided to place the nation in war mode, suspended all nonessential developmental activities, and reinvoked the Public Security Ordinance that gives wide-ranging powers on security forces personnel.

On the external front, diplomatic ties with Israel, which had been severed since the 1970s, were resumed with immediate effect. Over the years, relations between the two countries have waxed and waned in tandem with the island-governments handling of the ethnic conflict. The Israeli link has, perhaps coincidentally, had its impact on the inter-ethnic dynamics. Nowadays, the Sri Lankan security forces have deployed the Israeli K-fir aircraft and Dvora Naval gunboats. In earlier decades, there was an Israeli connection to the resettlement schemes in the

Mahaweli dry zone. The unfolding events also pose serious challenges that will doubtless impact on Sri Lanka's identity as a nation-state.

The loss of territory in the north to the separatist LTTE may trigger chauvinistic responses in the south of the island. The immediate context in which these positions have been adopted is military rather than political. Public attention is focused on what the external players will do, rather than on the internal response. New Delhi and Tel Aviv, in that order, have for the moment eclipsed Oslo, which accepted the challenge of initiating direct talks between the LTTE and the government. Norway's initiative was made in February 2000 and although there were signs even then that the Tigers were making military advances, the overall mood in the Sri Lankan military establishment was one of optimism.

LTTE's "gesture of goodwill", the statement said, was intended to prevent further escalation of violence and to create a congenial environment for the soldiers to withdraw from the theatre of war with dignity and honour. It called upon the island government to consider our proposal seriously and respond positively. A positive response would create cordial conditions for a permanent ceasefire, peace talks and negotiated political settlement of the ethnic conflict. The statement warned that the Sri Lankan government would bear responsibility for the "disastrous consequences of heavy military casualties if it rejects our proposal... and continues the war effort."

The government promptly dismissed the offer and said that there would be no withdrawal of troops. Later that evening, President Chandrika Kumaratunga, in an address to the nation, said that there was no question of leaving over five lakh Tamils in the north to the "oppressive advances" of the Tigers. Terming the military situation as one of "temporary but serious setbacks", she vowed to "win the war as soon as possible".

There has nevertheless been a measure of speculation about Indian involvement. The belief in some quarters was that India would help in withdrawing the Sri Lankan troops from the battle-scarred Peninsula. Even though it may seem to be a non-military, mission, it would be loaded with perils. Given the intensity of the military conflict, particularly the use of heavy artillery by the LTTE, even a single hit on an Indian aircraft/vessel involved in the evacuation process would transform the situation dramatically.

All it needs to change India's role from that of assistance to involvement is one single, well-aimed bullet. The situation would be less complicated for India if the Tigers were not in a position to claim to be the sole representatives of the Tamil people on the island. The internal dynamics of Sri Lankan politics have, in their own way, complicated the plot.

The efforts to arrive at a power devolution arrangement for the north and the east went awry because there was no political consensus on this in the south. This has only served to strengthen suspicions among the Tamil people about the intentions of "Sinhala governments". And at a time when the Tiger's military fortunes are on the ascendant, popular Tamil sentiments tend to ride with them.

In the absence of a political leadership, the minorities are increasingly propelled to read the LTTE's victories as 'Tamil victories'. The Tamil United Liberation Front as well as erstwhile militant organisations such as the Eelam People's Democratic Party, the People's Liberation Organisation of Tamil Eelam, the Tamil Eelam Liberation Organisation and the Eelam People's Revolutionary Liberation Front are in a position where they have nothing to show to the Tamil people by way of political achievements.

An excessive dependence on the state, coupled with the fact that majoritarian organisations tend to expand their political base among Tamil voters at the cost of other parties, has thwarted any attempt by them to build up a Tamil political leadership. After elections to the local councils were held in Jaffna Peninsula, the councillors' demands for funds have not been met. The Tamil political leaders are therefore not able to tell their constituents that the political process has brought any benefits for the Tamil people.

Since the LTTE's claim to being the "sole representatives of the Tamils" goes unchallenged, any position that India takes would have to factor in the Chennai-New Delhi-Colombo-Jaffna linkage politics.

The Sinhala majority tends to see the battle against the Tigers as a do-or-die prospect: "the Tigers must be finished or else we are finished" is the view that prevails.

The minority Tamils, on the other hand, see the LTTE's advances as posing a challenge to the Sinhala policy. It is in this context that both Tamils and Sinhalese are eager to see how India's policy on Sri Lanka will unfold. The Sinhala expectation is that an Indian involvement, of whatever nature and degree, would help contain LTTE military advances; Tamils want to see how India, which "watched the Sri Lanka Army push the LTTE out of Jaffna in 1995", will respond to the LTTE's gains in the Peninsula. A section of the Sinhalese believe that since Tamil militancy gained strength in the 1980s with help from across the Palk Straits, India now has a 'moral responsibility' to step in to combat it. Additionally, there are some Tamils who believe that if India does not intervene militarily to check the LTTE's advance into Jaffna, the lives of those who do not support the LTTE will be in danger. Besides, if an external power were to fill the vacuum created by India's reluctance to take on a role in Sri Lanka, it might pose additional problems for India, particularly if the new player is not favourably disposed to India. Israeli assistance, if solicited, could take the form of supply of military hardware or the sharing of the expertise of Mossad, the Israeli secret service. With the LTTE increasingly resorting to long-range artillery fire, the Sri Lanka Army would look to acquiring adequate air support so as to get at LTTE gun positions.

The provision of effective air cover for the Sri Lankan troopers could change the current military setting. Israeli expertise in air surveillance and night-bombing could also prove crucial. The advantage with taking assistance from Israel would be that the present fleet of Sri Lanka Air Force aircraft comprise Israel-built K-firs, which Sri Lankan fighter pilots are familiar with. Additionally, there is speculation that Sri Lankan troopers could be given specialised training in combating the Tigers.

The revival of diplomatic relations with Israel could have one possible internal political fallout for the ruling People's Alliance (P.A.). The Sri Lanka Muslim Congress, which has a considerable presence in the Muslim-majority Amparai district in the east, has expressed its reservations about the decision. Until April 21, 2000 the Elephant Pass gateway garrison was considered the ultimate bastion against LTTE advances, and the sudden shift in the military balance has taken the people by surprise. And even before the loss of the Army complex could be fully absorbed came the realisation that over 25,000 troopers were trapped in the war-torn Peninsula.

After the Liberation Tigers of Tamil Eelam (LTTE) seized the vast military complex in the area around the Elephant Pass, the military balance in Sri Lanka's Tamil-dominated Northern Province has undergone a drastic transformation. The fall of Elephant Pass marked the first time in the history of the "Tamil Eelam war" that the area had come under the LTTE's control. The Dutch colonialists first built a small fortress in 1776, which was converted in modern times into a resthouse for tourists.

After Independence a permanent garrison was set up there to check illicit immigration, smuggling and unlawful transport of timber. As the intensity of the ethnic conflict escalated, the strategic importance of Elephant Pass also increased. The small camp gradually expanded into a sprawling complex. To celebrate the capture of Elephant Pass, the LTTE organised a flag-raising ceremony at 9 a.m. on Sunday, April 23, 2000. According to Tiger media outlets, hundreds of LTTE cadres and a large number of Tamil civilians who serve as members of an auxiliary force known as "Thunaippadai" watched as the crimson-and-gold LTTE flag was hoisted by 'Colonel' Bhanu. As Bhanu, 38, stepped back and saluted the flag, LTTE fighters fired ceremonially in the air, and seven artillery field guns fired three shells each. Thereafter, Bhanu addressed the gathering. In his speech Bhanu said this was only the first step in the war to liberate "our homeland" and there would be "many more battles". The valour and sacrifices of the LTTE fighters, he said, had made it possible to realise the "dream of annihilating Aanai Iravu". The camp, established by the Dutch over 200 years ago, had for long remained "a symbol of alien domination" and divided the Tamil people of the Peninsula from the mainland.

Paying tributes to the memory of "all our comrades who laid down their lives in this battle and the campaigns before," Bhanu said that the LTTE fighters had succeeded because of the "very intricate attack plan drawn by our national leader and commander-in-chief" (Velupillai Prabhakaran). The victory, he said, was a sign of "more things to come". What followed immediately afterwards was rich in symbolism, and marked a defining moment for the LTTE. Groups of hand-picked civilians and some Tiger cadres in uniform walked along the Elephant Pass causeway on the isthmus that links the Wanni area with the Peninsula. One group walked northwards from the mainland to the Peninsula, and another went southwards from the Peninsula to the mainland. The significance of this "walk" was that for the first time in living memory there were no barriers or men in khaki to stop the people crossing to and from the Peninsula.

Initially, the LTTE depended on artillery seized from the Army after successful raids; later the LTTE procured artillery equipment on the black market and transported them by sea to Wanni. The LTTE allegedly recruited foreign mercenaries on a contract basis to teach them the finer points of artillery deployment. Today, the LTTE's artillery unit is named after former Jaffna commander Kittu, and is still commanded by Bhanu. Pleased with Bhanu's work, Prabhakaran is believed to have directed him to establish an armoured unit.

Again, in the initial stages the LTTE could use only a few armoured cars and tanks seized from the armed forces. It is also rumoured that a renegade Sinhala army officer imparted some rudimentary training to the Tigers on the use of armoured vehicles. Later vehicles were purchased in the international arms market and shipped to Wanni. The armoured unit, named after former Mannar commander Victor and commanded by Bhanu, is still in a fledgling state. The artillery and armoured units played a crucial role in the fighting in the Wanni region. They were responsible for checking the advances of the armed forces.

In recent times the style of LTTE fighting in positional warfare situations has undergone a dramatic transformation. Owing to their artillery power and armoured vehicles, the Tigers can hold off the Army from afar with the minimum number of casualties. The nature of the war is increasingly becoming conventional, with heavy reliance on stand-off weapons. In the recent fighting around Elephant Pass, the LTTE's artillery and armoured units again played a big role and enabled the LTTE to seize control within a short period with relatively few losses.

The recent LTTE victory at Elephant Pass was the result of an elaborate but simple strategy drawn up by Prabhakaran. It is said that Prabhakaran analyses the LTTE's military defeats for mistakes and draws lessons from them for use in subsequent campaigns. In that respect, a failed attempt by the LTTE to capture the Elephant Pass camp in July-August 1991 must have yielded many lessons. That campaign was code named "Tharai, Kadal, Aahayam" (Land, Sea and Air) and lasted 53 days. The LTTE, by its own admission, lost 573 cadres; more than 1,500 others were injured. In terms of manpower and morale, these were crippling losses. The Sri Lankan armed forces were able to beat back the LTTE that time owing to two factors. The first was the tenacity of the besieged troops led by a talented officer Sarath Fonseka and the grit with which they held on despite the overwhelming odds. The second was Operation Balavegaya, led by the late Generals Denzil Kobbekaduwe and Vijaya Wimalaratne. They established a beach-head at Vettilaikerny on the east coast and then fought their way through to the army personnel trapped inside the Elephant Pass camp. Thereafter the camp was converted into a large base by absorbing almost all the buildings in the vicinity, including the salterns and the school.

After Operation SathJaya in 1996, Paranthan and Kilinochchi, to the south of Elephant Pass on the mainland, too were linked up with Elephant Pass. The Kilinochchi-Elephant Pass-Vettilaikerny base became a sprawling complex that housed an entire division and was considered impregnable.

The LTTE strategy was made easier by the second phase of Operation Oyatha Alaigal (Unceasing Waves) in September 1998, in which Kilinochchi was taken. Thereafter the LTTE began to creep in on Paranthan, to the south of Elephant Pass on the mainland. In a series of short, swift campaigns that went unreported in the Colombo media, the camps at Karadipokku, Paranthan junction, the Paranthan Chemical Corporation complex and finally at Umaialpuram, between Paranthan and Elephant Pass, were taken. Umaialpuram and Iyakachchi were the two points where the troops at Elephant Pass could get drinking water.

The first stage of the LTTE campaign to take control of the Peninsula was launched on December 11, 1999. The camps at Vettilaikerny and Kattaikadu on the east coast and Pullaveli to the north of Elephant Pass were taken in a land-sea joint campaign. An unsuccessful assault was conducted on the western flanks of Iyakachchi, but no direct attack was launched on the main base at Elephant Pass. The Iyakachchi camp, five km to the north-west of Elephant Pass, is situated along a bend on the A-9 Highway. With the fall of Vettilaikerny, Kattaikadu and Pullaveli, the land-sea supply routes to Elephant Pass were cut off, and the only way through was along the A-9 Highway from Chavakachcheri.

The LTTE conducted some limited operations that were aimed at stepping up the pressure on Iyakachchi without achieving any breakthrough. Meanwhile, the 53rd Division of the Sri Lanka Army was brought in to relieve the pressure on the 54th Division deployed in the Elephant Pass sector; it was stationed at the Pachilaippalli and Vadamaratchy East Pradeshiya division camps. The 53rd

Division was an elite force that had been trained by the United States and Pakistan.

The second stage of the LTTE campaign, a multi-pronged assault, unfolded on March 26, 2000. A joint operation led by Vasanthan of the Charles Anthony Infantry division and Veerendran of the Sea Tigers took control of the Chembiyanpattru Maruthankerny-Thalaiady complex that housed the 3rd operational headquarters on the Vadamaratchy east coast. These were on the land strip between the Bay of Bengal and the Jaffna Lagoon. The Army then vacated the camps at Maamunai and Amban; the soldiers relocated to positions to the west of the lagoon. There was, however, a circuitous route that helped maintain a road link. At Pallai, a road branched off westwards from the A-9 Highway towards Kilali via Puloppalai and then headed north towards Kachchai and Allippalai; from there it ran east towards Kodikamam, at which point vehicles could get back onto the Jaffna-Kandy road again. However, this route came under intense pressure from the LTTE which fired artillery barrages at Kilali from Pooneryn across the lagoon. Also on March 26, 2000, the LTTE's Kilinochchi commander Theepan led a team of men across the dried-up Chundikulam lagoon on the south-east of the Peninsula and established positions in the Mullian and Vannankulam region. But the team ran into the Forward Defence Lines and was prevented from advancing towards Elephant Pass in the Vathirayan area.

The third and decisive stage of the LTTE campaign was played out around noon on Tuesday, April 18, 2000. A Leopard commando raid saw the LTTE take control of the Maruthankerny causeway, which enabled it to proceed westwards on the Maruthankerny-Puthukadu junction road, which links the east coast and the A9 Highway.

The Puthukadu Junction is between Iyakachchi and Pallai. The LTTE proceeded along the southern areas of Muhavil, Soranpattru and Maasaar, after demolishing a 40-foot bund put up by the Army as a defence measure. The Tigers headed south on the A-9 Highway and reached the northern sector of the Iyakachchi camp. In effect, Elephant

Pass and Iyakachchi were marooned. Thereafter, the LTTE mounted a fierce attack on the Iyakachchi camp from Kovil Vayal and Sangathaar Vayal.

As the fighting intensified, the Tiger cadres to the south-east of Elephant Pass broke through and began assailing the camp.

The telecommunication tower in the Elephant Pass base was damaged; all telephone lines to the north were severed. At a critical juncture the bulk of LTTE cadres led by Balraj abandoned the A-9 Highway and joined the fighting around Iyakachchi after setting up two "cut out" posts to the north of Pallai and south of Eluthumattuvaal to prevent an Army advancement.

The LTTE advanced on Elephant Pass from the north, north-east and south-east. There was heavy exchange of fire all through that long night, and even as the fighting was on, the Army began to move out.

After the LTTE's stage-by-stage build-up against Elephant Pass, the abrupt capitulation by the security forces as an anti-climax. Curiously, however, the LTTE, which had until then put out news at each successful stage of the campaign, did not announce the fall of Iyakachchi on April 21; it announced that news along with news of the fall of the Elephant Pass camp. This perhaps implies that after taking control of Iyakachchi, the LTTE was supremely confident that Elephant Pass would fall soon or had advance knowledge that the troops there would withdraw within hours of the Iyakachchi debacle.

The security forces vacated Elephant Pass only after they received orders to that effect from the defence establishment. Army Commander Srilal Weerasooriya instructed Chief of Staff Lionel Balagalle to issue the order, which was sent by personal courier to Elephant Pass. Commanding Officer Brigadier Egodawela received it at 10 p.m. on April 21. The retreating troops initially started moving out to Pallai, 14 km away, along the A-9 Highway, but when the LTTE thwarted them, they took to a disused rail track and a sandtrack to its west. From Pallai, the soldiers headed west for the relative safety of Kilali. But when Tiger mortars pounded this route, the Army used another circuitous route—a dirt track going northwest from Elephant Pass to MIA through Kurinchatheevu, Oorvanikanpattru and Thanmankerny. On this longer route, however, many soldiers succumbed to heat and dehydration, apart from the unceasing LTTE shells.

Nevertheless a good number of the troops moved out from Elephant Pass, mostly on foot. Before leaving, they spiked some artillery pieces, but even so the LTTE seized some powerful guns, including 152-mm artillery guns, and a number of tanks and armoured cars, besides other arms and ammunition.

A preliminary list released by the LTTE reveals a mind-boggling armoury. Elephant Pass was in many ways a military debacle for Colombo. Although there were more than 15,000 troops in the Elephant Pass base and there are fewer than 5,000 LTTE cadres in the Peninsula, the Army was defeated because it was a demoralised force. Many factors had contributed to the lowering of troop morale. The frequent change of commanding officers was one factor, and the LTTE's repeated victories against the elite 53rd Division, the "Pride of the Army", were another. The haphazard manner in which the 53rd Division was plunged into combat caused many problems at the top.

The defence establishment's decision to move the troops out of the Elephant Pass base was, however, forced on it primarily by a shortage of drinking water. The camp was equipped with machinery for desalination of water, but it had broken down and not been repaired. The availability of potable water in Umaialpuram and Iyakachchi had perhaps lulled the forces into complacency. However, when Iyakachchi came under siege, the water crisis in the overcrowded base became unmanageable.

Ironically, the Elephant Base had ample quantities of canned food and dry rations; after taking over the camp, the LTTE distributed these to civilians in the Wanni area. Defence Ministry sources estimate that over 1,000 LTTE cadres were killed in the three phases of fighting from December 11, 1999.

The LTTE claims that only 303 of its cadres were killed, including 35 casualties in the battle for Elephant Pass. The Tigers further claim that over 1,000 soldiers were killed; the Army, however, says that only 80 of its men were killed and over 100 are missing in action.

Subsequently the Tigers returned through the Red Cross the bodies of 126 soldiers, of which 28 were identified. Among the top Army officers who were killed were Brig. Percy Fernando, Col. Bhatiya Jayatilleke, Col. Neil Akmeemana and Lt. Col. Hewage Hewawasam. On the Tigers' side, the women's brigade chief, Lt. Col Lakshiya, was reported killed. The Elephant Pass debacle shocked people across the country.

Sri Lankan Deputy Defence Minister Anuruddha Ratwatte, however, sought to put a brave face on the defeat. Addressing a ministerial function, he said that the "setback" at Elephant Pass ought to be seen as a "natural phenomenon in wars of this nature... We have to accept both victories and setbacks in the same manner."

After a brief lull following the LTTE's taking of Elephant Pass, fighting erupted again. The LTTE called on all civilians from Pallai to Kodikamam, including Eluthumattu-vaal and Mirusuvil, to relocate to safe areas. Thereafter, LTTE cadres moved along the A-9 Highway and seized the camps at Pallai and Soranpattru north, which the armed forces abandoned after a brief show of resistance.

The LTTE units then linked up on the A-9 Highway from the north of Pallai to the south of Eluthumattuvaal. The Tigers then launched a two-track assault on Kilali. One column proceeded on the 18.km dirt track from Elephant Pass to Mali along the coast. Another moved westwards from Pallai to Puloppalai and then on to Mali. Both columns reached the Kilali area, but as on May 5 they had not made further progress. A turnout, however, spread in Colombo, and a few newspapers carried reports, that Bhanu had been killed at Kilali. However, there has been no reliable confirmation of this.

The LTTE also opened another flank with an attack on Nagar Kovil on the Vadamaratchy east coast. The Tigers as well as the Army were engaged in heavy exchange of fire in the Kilali, Nagar Kovil and Pallai-Eluthumattuvaal areas. Meanwhile, the armed forces have begun constructing massive defences along a diagonal line from Kilali on the west through Eluthumattuvaal to Nagar Kovil in the east. Further, several small camps like those at Varany, Mathagal, Chankanai, Vaddukkoddail Mahiyapiddy, Navaly, Chulipuram and Kandarodai have been closed.

The anticipated progress of the LTTE has raised concerns about the future of around 35,000 troops in the Peninsula. The fear is that the Tigers, with their rapid mobility and artillery fire-power, could quickly take over the entire Peninsula including Jaffna and Palaly and besiege the Palaly-Kankesanthurai complex. If that happens, there may not be time enough to evacuate troops from the Peninsula.

The Sea Tigers and the LTTE's anti-aircraft unit, which possess missiles, could restrict the troops' sea and air movement. This would leave the troops marooned and defenceless. A "Dunkirklike evacuation" may then become necessary and the possibility of securing India's assistance for this purpose is being explored. Although the situation is quite bleak, the hysteria and panic about the necessity for a rescue operation are unfounded. Those who subscribe to this view believe that if troop morale is restored and adequate counter-measures are taken, the LTTE juggernaut can be halted, and eventually pushed back. In any event, the beliefs that there is no immediate cause for alarm about the fate of Palali.

Grim scenarios of Sinhala Tamil clashes were painted, but fortunately nothing of that sort has happened. Social scientists believe that much has changed since 1983: the riots of 1983 were characterised by a certain element of choreography, which the present government is emphatic to avoid; besides, there is a greater "public acceptance of, or desensitisation to battlefield realities" as a result of decades of fighting and violent disruption of public life. None the less, the government took no chances, and for the third time since 1971 the Public Security Ordinance was invoked as the island geared up to face what is perhaps the most serious challenge in the decades of Tamil separatist militantly. The Ordinance gives the security forces—the police and armed service personnel—wide-ranging powers to make arrests and effect seizures. Processions, strikes and demonstrations will remain banned, as will posters that incite hatred among communities.

The situation in Sri Lanka has, to a certain extent, been accentuated by the politics of oneupmanship practised by the two main formations—the PA and the UNP. At the popular level in Colombo, from high-society parties to street-corner tea shops, conversation invariably turns to what lies ahead in the immediate future.

Northern Sri Lanka is going through a painful phase, marked by an impasse, in both political and military terms. With the country set to face national and presidential elections in the year ahead, it is possible that positions will harden among both the separatist Liberation Tigers of Tamil Eelam (LTTE) and the government. The Opposition United National Party (UNP), whose endorsement of the policy decisions taken by the ruling People's Alliance (PA) is crucial to resolving the crisis, is also expected to adopt a tough stand.

Following a fierce battle between government troops and the separatists, Killinochchi and Mankulam changed hands. While Killinochchi came under the control of the LTTE, the government regained Mankulam. Since then nothing much has happened to alter the situation. But the security forces have scored a string of successes in the Wanni area, regaining chunks of territory from the Tigers. The crucial gain was the retaking of Madhu, a pilgrim centre in Mannar district. In the second week of September, the security forces started a fifth round of Rana Gosa (Battle Cry) operations in the Wanni area comprising four northern districts. The previous such operation had been conducted with remarkable ease. Going by reports coming from the north-eastern area, Rana Gosa has not made much gains as the LTTE has put up stiff resistance.

The Defence Ministry said that the troops "advanced from general areas north and east of Welimarandamadu

Tank and general areas east of Periyamadu tank". Indications are that the total number of casualties on both sides could well be above 150.

Heavy casualties have been reported from the northern Mannar district, where a fresh offensive was launched on September 12. The operation has strategic significance in that it seeks to cover areas which would, if successfully penetrated, lead to the opening of a much-needed main supply route to the northern Jaffna Peninsula.

The operation launched in September 1998 implied a rethinking on the part of the government with regard to its plans to open a main supply route to Jaffna through a series of offensives called Operation Jaya Sikuru (Sure Victory).

After Operation Jaya Sikuru was given up, the western offensive was launched, and it has been widely perceived as one aimed at opening a main supply route along the western coast. Operation Rana Gosa also marks a shift in military strategy after the Killinochchi operations in that an earlier approach to open a main supply route along the Kandy-Jaffna road, which runs through the Tiger heartland, was abandoned in favour of a more practical western route.

Bringing peace to the troubled north-eastern region would require more than a smart and successful military operation. While the military advance is crucial, equally important would be the progress made on a resolution of the political issues. Unfortunately, nothing has happened on this front as the goals of both the government and the LTTE have remained unachievable. For its part, the government is keen on a solution within a framework that envisages a united but non-unitary nation, while the Tigers remain committed to their separatist agenda. And so the attrition continues. So it is imperative for the government to address the ground realities in the north-eastern region, especially the situation faced by civilians living under the LTTE's sway.

Regulations on fishing, and movement between the government held and LTTE-held areas, lack of proper transportation facilities between Jaffna and the rest of the island and mounting pressures on the food delivery system are but early manifestations of more trouble ahead. The advantage now lies with the military, successive operations having eroded the territorial base of the LTTE. With the ongoing military thrust, the efficacy of the civil administration, already handicapped as a result of the government having to run basic affairs in an essentially enemy-held area, has been further affected. The prevailing no-win situation, according to Tamil politicians, could help the LTTE to try to prove that it has a presence all over the north-east. This could impel it to launch attacks on economic installations and security personnel.

By systematically dismembering the other militant groups, the LTTE is better placed to claim the status of the "sole representative of the Tamils". The assassination of Dr. Neelan Tiruchelvam, senior leader of the Tamil United Liberation Front (TULF), and those of Razeek of the Eelam People's Revolutionary Liberation Front and Manickathasan of the People's Liberation Organisation of Tamil Eelam are indicators of the LTTE's unwillingness to accommodate an alternative leadership for Tamils, either politically or militarily. However, the present delicate balance and uncertainty could change dramatically if the LTTE were to strike at an Army camp. Military strategists are in no doubt about the LTTE's capabilities. The question now is when and where it will strike.

Bibliography

Address of the Sri Lankan President at the inaugural session of the Eighth SAARC Summit, New Delhi, 2, May, 1995.

Arasaratnam, S., *Ceylon* (Englewood Cliffs, N. J., 1964)

Codrington, H. W., *A Short History of Ceylon* (London, 1947)

de Silva, K. M. 'Historical Survey' in K. M. de Silva, ed., *Sri Lanka: A Survey* (London, 1976).

Dixit, J. N., "IPKF in Sri Lanka," *United Service Institution Journal* (July-September 1989).

Economist Intelligence Unit (London), *Country Profile,* published each year, and *Country Report*, published each quarter, for India, Pakistan, Bangladesh, Sri Lanka and Nepal.

Godfrey Gunatilleke, *Cooperation, among Small Nations in Asia in the Context of Changing Political Economy*, Colombo, Marga Institute, September 1979.

Johnson B. L. C., and M. le M. Scrivenor, *Sri Lanka* (London, 1983).

Johnson B. L. C., and M. le M. Scrivenor, *Sri Lanka: Land, People and Economy* (London, 1981).

Malalgoda, K., *Buddhism in Sinhalese Society, 1750-1900* (Berkeley, 1976).

Mansingh, S., *India's Search for Power: Indira Gandhi's Foreign Policy, 1966-1982* (New Delhi, Beverley Hills and London, 198).

Moore, M. P., *The State and Peasant Politics in Sri Lanka* (Cambridge, 1985)

Oberst, R. C., *Legislators and Representations: The Decentralisation of Development Planning in Sri Lanka* (Boulder, Co., 1985)

Phadnis, U., Religion and Politics in Sri Lanka (London, 1976).

Sarvananthan Muttukrishna (1994), "Contraband Trade and Unofficial Capital Transfers Between Sri Lanka and India", *Economic and Political Weekly,* July 23, 1994.

Spate O. H. K., and Learmonth, A.T.A., *India and Pakistan: a general and regional geography;* with a chapter on Ceylon by B.H. Farmer, 3rd rev. edn (London, 1967).

Sumantra Bose: *States, Nations, Sovereignty: Sri Lanka, India and the Tamil Elam Movement* (Sage Publications: New Delhi, Thousand Oaks, London) (1994).

Tambiah, S. J., *Sri Lanka: Ethnic Fratricide and the Dismantling of Democracy* (Chicago, 1986)

Index